The
Second Dalai Lama

His Life and Teachings

The Second Dalai Lama

His Life and Teachings

Translated, edited, introduced,
and annotated by

Glenn H. Mullin

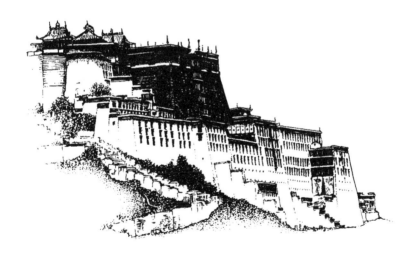

Snow Lion Publications
Ithaca, New York
Boulder, Colorado

Snow Lion Publications
P.O. Box 6483
Ithaca, NY 14851 USA
(607) 273-8519
www.snowlionpub.com

Printed in the USA on acid-free recycled paper.

ISBN 1-55939-233-9

The Library of Congress catalogued the previous edition of this book
as follows:

Dge-'dun-rgya-mtsho, Dalai Lama II, 1476–1542
    [Selections.   English.   1994]
    Mystical verses of a mad Dalai Lama / Glenn H. Mullin.
        p.   cm.
    ISBN 0-8356-0700-3
    1. Dge-lugs-pa (Sect)—Doctrines—Early works to 1800.
  2. Dge-'dun-rgya-mtsho, Dalai Lama II, 1476–1542.
  I. Mullin, Glenn H. II. Title.
  BQ7935.D493E5   1994
  294.3'923'092—dc20
    [B]   94-2560

Contents

PART THREE: *MYSTICAL VERSES OF THE SECOND DALAI LAMA:*
TRANSLATION AND COMMENTARY

Preface

I would like to begin by thanking His Holiness the present Dalai Lama, who loaned his personal copy of the Tibetan manuscript of this text for me to photocopy and translate. His kindness in giving his blessings to the project, as well as in providing the Foreword, was a great boon and honor. Since winning the Nobel Peace Prize in 1989, His Holiness has had increasing demands placed upon his time and energies; yet somehow he finds reserves to fulfill the needs of us all. Thus he continues to live up to the name by which Tibetans popularly know him, Yezhin Norbu, "the Wish-Fulfilling Jewel."

Next I would like to thank Gyatso Tsering, Director of the Library of Tibetan Works and Archives in Dharamsala, India, where the actual research and translation took place. Over the twenty years that I have been associated with the Library, first as a student and then as a research scholar, Gyatso-Ia has always encouraged and supported me in every way, both as a mentor and as a friend. Somehow the hundreds of Westerners who come to him every year with requests never seem to tax him but rather to instill him with a renewed energy and enthusiasm.

Finally, my special affections go to the three Tibetan lamas with whom I read the Second Dalai Lama's poems and who guided my understanding of them: Ven. Geshey Chomdzey Tashi Wangyal, Ven. Amchok Tulku, and Ven. Doboom Tulku. These three lamas are indeed perfect embodiments of the Buddhist Mahayana ideal, active within the world yet unstained by it. Their wisdom, patience, and humor will always remain as shining examples to me.

My treatment of this material is presented in three parts. In the first of these I provide a general background to the subjects of Tibet, the tradition of Dalai Lama incarnations, and the central concepts of Indo-Tibetan Buddhist thought. My aim is to facilitate an appreciation of the context of the Second Dalai Lama's songs and poems and a sensitivity to the language and structures that he uses.

In Part Two I present a biographical account of the Second Dalai Lama and attempt to project a sense of what Tibet was like for a lama of the late fifteenth and early sixteenth centuries. My purpose here is to create a portrait of the author as a man, Buddhist monk, and teacher, and of the world in which he lived and wrote.

Finally in Part Three are my translations of and commentary to the songs and poems that comprise his *namgur* (mystical verse works) collection. The commentary to each is in the form of a Translator's Preamble and introduces the reader to the content, context, and character of the individual entry.

Throughout the text I have transcribed the names of Tibetan people and places by informal phonetic transcription, much as they sound to my own ear and as I feel they will be most easily read by the nonspecialist. Tibetan spelling abounds in prefix, suffix, superscript, and subscript letters, most of which are silent but affect in subtle ways the pronunciation of the root letter of a syllable. For example, the Second Dalai Lama's name, Gendun Gyatso Palzangpo, is actually spelled *dGe- 'dun-brgya-mtsho-dpal-bzang-po*. To accommodate the specialist, I have affixed a Glossary with the formal spellings at the end of the book.

It has been an absolute delight for me to work on this volume. If it brings even a fraction of the reading pleasure to my audience, then the effort will have been worthwhile.

Glenn H. Mullin
Snow Lion Guest House
Chettrapati, Kathmandu
Nepal, Dee. 14, 1992

THE DALAI LAMA

Foreword

For me the Second Dalai Lama was the greatest of all the early Dalai Lamas. He possessed exceptional qualities and during his life became both a great Buddhist scholar and an accomplished practitioner. He himself admitted that he had achieved a profound realization of shunyata, or emptiness, the ultimate level of reality, as a result of meeting his guru Khedrup Norzang Gyatso.

The Second Dalai Lama typically signed most of his writings Trangnyon Gendun Gyatso, or "The Mad Beggar Gendun Gyatso." Sometimes he also used the name Yang chen Sheypai Dorje, "Melodious Laughing Vajra," and sometimes Namkhai Naljorpa, "The Yogi of Space."

He was ordained Gendun Gyatso. When he calls himself "Mad Beggar," he is referring not to his having no possessions, but to his not being attached to anything. When you have no attachment, like the beggar with no possessions, you are freed of all worldly concerns. This is an important theme in tantric teachings according to which a practitioner uses sensual objects without becoming attached to them.

The implication of "Mad" here is that when a person gains experience of emptiness, the ultimate mode of existence of all phenomena, his perception is as different from that of ordinary people as a madman's. Due to his or her realization of emptiness, a practitioner completely transcends the conventional way of viewing the world.

The name Yangchen Sheypai Dorje, "Melodious Laughing Vajra," refers to his sense of himself as a poet. He often refers to himself as "the Great Poet of the Land of Snows" or "the Great Himalayan Poet." The name Yang-chen, or Sarasvati in Sanskrit, is associated with music, song, and poetry. The third name that he liked to use, Nam-khai Nal-jor-pa, "the Yogi of Space," was used in those works that focus on emptiness.

The Second Dalai Lama was a prolific writer. His Collected Works contain a large number of works in which he elucidates the important doctrines of both Sutra and Tantra. Some of the most charming compositions are to be found in his collection of Nyam-gur, or mystical verse works, which are translated in this book.

The Tibetan term nyam-gur consists of two components: gur, which is an abbreviation of gur ma, a synonym of lu, meaning "song or poem," and nyam, an abbreviation of nyam-nyong, meaning "experience, knowledge, or realization."

As a result of achieving some kind of special spiritual experience or knowledge, people would spontaneously compose mystical songs of nyam-nyong gi gurma to express it. The Tibetan tradition of nyam-gur is rooted in the ancient Indian tradition of doha, a type of lyrical writing developed by the Buddhist mahasiddhas or tantric adepts. Many of the Indian dohas were translated into Tibetan and are preserved in the Tengyur or collection of translations of writings by the Indian masters.

Both the doha and nyam-gur traditions are more concerned with the expression of personal experience than the pedantic use of terminology. In this they differ from the literature of Buddhist metaphysics and philosophy, which uses language in a very precise way. Because it arises spontaneously from inner experience, the language of such verses is used quite differently from that of philosophical texts.

The Second Dalai Lama appears to have been a quite different personality from the First Dalai Lama. The First had been a quiet, introverted person, but the Second was assertive and outgoing. Where the First was humble and self-effacing in manner, the Second was outspoken, haughty, and loquacious.

Having been recognized, as a young child, as the reincarnation of the First Dalai Lama, he was brought to Tashi Lhunpo Monastery and seated on the teaching throne. During the ceremony, an old monk who had been a disciple of his predecessor noticed how different his behavior was from that of the previous Dalai Lama. He thought to himself, "This child is supposed to be the rebirth of my great guru, but his manner is very different. Surely he is not the real reincarnation."

The young Second Dalai Lama, who from birth had exhibited some kind of clairvoyance, looked at him intensely and whispered, "Due to the changing of bodies, the character must also undergo some kind of a change."

The Second Dalai Lama's nonsectarian approach to Buddhist tradition is a striking feature of his life, reflected both in his writings and in his spiritual activities. Many of the early Dalai Lamas followed a similarly nonsectarian approach, but they were generally not as broadminded as the Second. The Second Dalai Lama seems to have investigated different doctrines out of purely personal interest. During his own lifetime he was popularly referred to as Rimeypai Gyalwa Zhasermowa, "the Yellow Hat master with no sectarian bias." By monastic ordination he belonged to the Yellow Hat School, or Gelugpa tradition, but in his practice he studied and mastered the doctrines of many different traditions.

Here it is worth noting that to be sectarian in the sense of exclusively dedicating yourself to the study and practice of one particular school is not necessarily a negative thing. Most Tibetan lamas train in this way. It is better to understand one tradition well than to know bits and pieces of many without fully mastering any of them. This is positive sectarianism. Negative sectarianism is to follow one tradition exclusively while looking down on the other traditions.

The Second Dalai Lama transcended both positive and negative sectarianism. He had the capacity to study all without mixing or confusing them. In addition, he used his prestige to improve relations between the different sects of Tibetan Buddhism.

From infancy all signs indicated that Gendun Gyatso was the authentic reincarnation of the First Dalai Lama. However, there was no formal recognition, as became the custom later, because as a young boy the Second simply presented himself as the First's reincarnation and was accepted as such.

He made a number of prophecies concerning his own future incarnations. As a two- or three-year-old child still sleeping in his mother's bed, he sang that he would have to reincarnate at least five more times in order to complete his work. This was taken as a prophecy that the Dalai Lama lineage would continue up to at least the Seventh. Then, towards the end of his life, he remarked that he had dreamed of receiving four victory banners from the Nedong, or King of Lhasa. This was thought to indicate that the lineage would be stable until the Fifth Dalai Lama.

After his death, the Nechung Oracle became involved in the process of locating the Dalai Lama's reincarnation. The Second was the first of the Dalai Lamas to establish a special relationship with the Nechung Oracle, whom he recognized as authentic and reliable. This was linked to the relationship he had established with Drepung Monastery, where Pehar, the deity invoked as the Nechung Oracle, is the protective deity. The First Dalai Lama had visited and studied briefly in Drepung but had not become closely associated with it. The Second Dalai Lama became an important figure at Drepung and constructed the Ganden Potrang as his special residence there.

After Gendun Gyatso's passing away, his principal attendant, Lama Sung-rab-pa, approached the Nechung Oracle for advice on how to find the reincarnation. The answer he received was that the Second Dalai Lama had sent forth a hundred emanations into this world, but that out of these the reincarnation in the Tolung area was the main one. In due course, a child born in Tolung, who clearly expressed memories of his previous life as the Second Dalai Lama, came to be recognized as the Third Dalai Lama. From this time onward, the Nechung Oracle has always been consulted in the search for the Dalai Lama's reincarnation.

I look forward to seeing the Second Dalai Lama's songs and poems in English. Many of my friends have spoken highly of Glenn Mullin's writings on the lives and works of the early Dalai Lamas. They say that in capturing the meaning and spirit of the original Tibetan, his translations are a pleasure to read.

I would like to thank him for his work in this respect. On the one hand it contributes to the growing understanding of the Buddhadharma in the Western world, and on the other, by focusing on the Dalai Lamas, who have played such a prominent role in Tibetan history, he draws attention to the rich and unique cultural heritage of Tibet.

The Fourteenth Dalai Lama,
the Buddhist monk Tenzin Gyatso

July 21, 1993

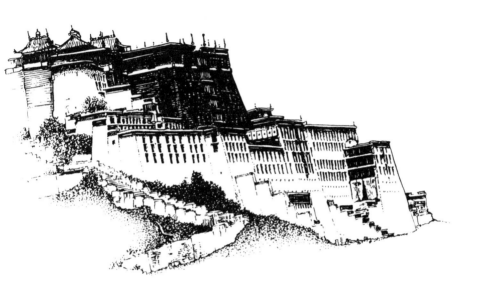

Introduction

Tibet's Buddhist Background

Tibet, located at the center of Asia, covers a territory of over two million square miles. A land of towering mountains and fertile valleys, the average altitude at which Tibet's people live is twelve thousand feet above sea level.

In ancient times Tibet served as both a crossroads to and a buffer state between Asia's superpowers: Persia to the west, India to the south, Mongolia to the north, and China to the east. Undoubtedly Tibet absorbed cultural influences from all four. However, in more recent times (since the mid-seventh century A.D.) Tibet has been principally a cultural satellite of India and a stronghold for the teachings of the Buddha.

His Holiness the present Dalai Lama once somewhat humorously summed up the situation for me in a private audience that I had with him in the mid–1980s. He commented, "We adopted our spiritual traditions from India, the mother of the greatest religions in the East; we took our culinary arts from China, the Eastern land with the best cooking; and we adopted the Mongolian style of dress, as the Mongolians had the most colorful sense in clothing."

The Buddha was born approximately 2,500 years ago in Lumbini, which is located on the Nepalese side of the present India-Nepal border. He is said to have visited and taught in the Kathmandu Valley of Nepal, which is a mere hundred miles from Tibet. Thus there must have been informal contacts with Buddhism and Tibet's indigenous religions from the earliest days. Little of this has been recorded, however, for in those ancient times, Tibet did not have a written script; or if it did, nothing of it has survived.

One of the first recorded contacts occurred in the fourth century, during the rule of King Lha Totori of Yarlung. At that time an

Indian monk is said to have visited the court and left a casket of Buddhist items, including a few scriptures and images. (As the legend puts it, these " . . . fell from the heavens.") The king felt that his country was not yet ready for the introduction of such a highly sophisticated spiritual tradition as Buddhism, and thus no effort was made to translate or study the texts. Nonetheless, he did recognize their worth and treated them with great reverence. He ordered that they be stored with care and prophesied that after several generations their significance would be appreciated by his people.

This prophecy was fulfilled in the mid-seventh century during the rule of King Songtsen Gampo. In order to consolidate his rule and establish stable relations with his neighbors, King Songtsen took five wives. Three of these were Tibetan, the fourth from Nepal, and the fifth from China.

Both the Nepalese and Chinese queens were Buddhists and deeply impressed him with their spiritual sensitivity. He decided to introduce Buddhism formally into his country in order to bring the benefits of this civilization to his people. Another account states that, as a condition of the Nepali queen agreeing to marry him, he consented to build her a hundred and eight Buddhist temples and monuments; the result was his own immersion in Buddhist practice.

However, he felt that the Tibetans did not possess a tradition of letters capable of expressing in translation the complex ideas embodied in the Indian Buddhist philosophical texts. Therefore he sent a group of twenty-five Tibetans to India for the purpose of developing a script and grammar suitable for this purpose. Under the leadership of Tonmi Sambhota, this team (or rather, those of them who survived the precarious journey to the Indian tropics) chose a Kashmiri version of the Gupta Sanskrit script as their working basis and formulated a grammar for Tibetan centered on the dialect of the Yarlung Valley, the residence of King Songtsen.[1]

In addition to creating a script and a well-articulated grammar, Tonmi Sambhota and his assistants translated numerous Indian works into Tibetan, including some of those that had been in storage from the time of King Songtsen's ancestor King Lha Totori.

Thus the foundations of Buddhism were established in Tibet and, over the centuries to follow, Buddhist knowledge flowed into the

Land of Snows in a steady stream, the movement perhaps suffering periodic setbacks during the reign of the occasional unenthusiastic king but generally building in momentum. By the twelfth century, when India fell to Turkic colonization and Buddhism disappeared from within the land of its birth, much of the most important literature that existed in Buddhist India had already been translated into Tibetan. Tibet then came to play an increasingly important role in the cultural and spiritual life of Asia. Today it is the form of Buddhism practiced from Siberia and Buriat of the eastern Russian republics to the Himalayan kingdoms to the north of India, such as Ladakh, Spitti, Nepal, Sikkim, Bhutan, and so forth. The Tibetan literary language developed by Tonmi Sambhota in the mid-seventh century is used in all these regions by the intelligentsia, much as Latin was adopted as the international language of intellectuals throughout Europe during the occident's classical period. Indeed, as Sarat Chandra Das wrote in the introduction to his *Dictionary of Tibetan* published in 1892, Tibetan became such an important literary language that as late as the end of the nineteenth century, a knowledge of it was considered a prerequisite of a learned person throughout Central Asia.

During the early period of its Buddhist experience, Tibet had absorbed transmissions from both India and China, as well as a number of smaller Buddhist neighbors. By the late eighth century, the Tibetan empire had consolidated its rule over much of Central Asia, including large tracts of northwest China (most significantly Tun-huang) and Turkestan (including Kotan), thus exposing itself to many different Buddhist influences.

However, Tibet's direction changed radically in 792 A.D., following a grand debate at Samyey Monastery between the followers of the Indian and Chinese schools. The Indians were victorious, and as a result, the Tibetan emperor Trisong Deutsen thereafter discouraged the use of the Chinese script in Tibet as well as editions of texts translated from Chinese and announced that henceforth all translations into Tibetan should be made directly from Sanskrit sources. Tibet had formally cemented its marriage to India and Indian Buddhism. This policy continued throughout the reigns of Trisong Deutsen's son Tri Senalek and grandson Tri Ralpachen.

In the early centuries of Buddhism in Tibet, most monasteries and practice hermitages were founded by a lama who had gone to India to study, carried particular lineages back with him, and then founded spiritual centers for the transmission of his doctrines. Others were founded by Indian masters who visited Tibet and passed their lineages on to various disciples, who in turn established training centers.

These days there is a tendency to speak of "schools" or "sects" of Tibetan Buddhism. When this is done, it is common to refer collectively to all lineages propagated in Tibet before the mid–eleventh century as the *Nyingma*, or "Ancient School." The distinguishing characteristic of the traditions classified as Nyingma is that they rely upon the language of the lexicons created during the seventh and eighth centuries and are based on scriptures translated during that period and using that approach to technical terminology.

Most of the Nyingma lineages today regard their most important forefather as Guru Padmasambhava, popularly known to Tibetans as Guru Rinpochey. This master from Oddiyana of northwest India (present-day Swat, Pakistan, which lies near Afghanistan), visited Tibet in the mid–eighth century and oversaw the construction of Samyey, Tibet's first monastery. He also formed a team of disciples who systematically translated many important tantric treatises from Sanskrit and updated the older translations made during King Songtsen Gampo's time. Guru Rinpochey's flamboyant tantric lifestyle continues to appeal to the Tibetan imagination.

The eleventh century saw a thorough revision of the translations made from Sanskrit as well as of the approach to Buddhist technical terminology. All lineages that emerged after this time and based on this revised linguistic formula are referred to as *Sarma*, or "New Schools."

Many "New Schools" were born in the eleventh and twelfth centuries, based on the new translations and using the new lexiconography. There is a tendency to speak of three principal ones: the Kadam, inspired by the visit of the Indian master Atisha Dipamkara Shrijnana (popularly known to the Tibetans as Jowo Atisha) to Tibet and formulated into a successful movement by his chief Tibetan disciple, a layman by the name of Lama Drom Tonpa; the Sakya, founded by Konchok Gyalpo from the lineages of the Indian mahasiddha Virupa and the translator Drokmi Lotsawa, and systemized by Kunga Nyingpo; and the Kargyu, founded by the

Tibetan layman Marpa Lotsawa and his yogi-poet disciple Milarepa and systemized by Milarepa's chief disciple Gampopa.

However, although the above three "New Schools" achieved predominance over the course of the centuries to follow, numerous other schools of significance also appeared during this renaissance period. Most of these lineages have since disappeared as independent entities and have been absorbed by the four super-schools mentioned above. Included in these are the Shangpa Kargyu, to which the Second Dalai Lama's father belonged, which had been founded by the Tibetan yogi Kyungpo Naljor largely from the lineages of the Indian female mystics Niguma and Sukhasiddhi; the Zhijey, founded by the Indian mahasiddha Padampa Sangyey and his female disciple, the mystical Machik Labdron, a lineage to which the Second Dalai Lama's grandmother was primarily devoted; the Rvaluk and also the Jonang, these latter two having been enthusiastically studied by both the First and Second Dalai Lamas.[2]

The next major development in Tibetan religious history came in the late fourteenth and early fifteenth centuries with the advent of Lama Tsongkhapa, whose ordination name was Lobzang Drakpa. Tsongkhapa studied in almost fifty Tibetan monasteries and collected together the most important New School lineages. Later he founded Ganden Monastery near Lhasa to preserve and transmit these under one roof. The school descending from him, which soon eclipsed all others and became the largest throughout central Asia, is known as the Gelug.

Essentially Tsongkhapa took the philosophical approach of the Kadam School that had been founded by the Indian master Jowo Atisha, and to it added various tantric lineages from the other traditions. Therefore the Gelug order is sometimes also referred to in Tibetan literature as the *Kadam Sarma*, or New Kadam.[3]

All Dalai Lamas have belonged to the New Kadam tradition by monastic ordination. (Even the Sixth, who refused to take higher monastic ordination, had nonetheless received his novice ordination from the New Kadam lineage.) For this reason the Second Dalai Lama opens many of his mystical songs and poems with a verse of homage to Atisha and/or Lama Tsongkhapa.

Most Dalai Lamas have also in their personal spiritual lives practiced a combination of the Nyingma and Gelug lineages. As His

Holiness the Dalai Lama mentions in his Foreword, this tradition was initiated by the First Dalai Lama and established as a tradition by the Second. It has continued to the present day, with only the Seventh and Eighth in the line deviating from it.[4]

The First Dalai Lama

The child destined to become known to history as the First Dalai Lama was born in Tsang Province, southwestern Tibet, in 1391, as the son of nomadic herdspeople. On the night of his birth, the tribe was attacked by bandits, and the adults fled into the hills. His mother, afraid that she would be captured, raped, and perhaps even killed, hid the newborn baby behind a rock before she ran away. When she returned in the morning, she beheld an extraordinary scene: a pack of wild dogs surrounded the child, hoping to make him their meal, but a large crow stood over him, protecting him from harm. Lamas later informed her that their divinations indicated the crow to be an emanation of Mahakala, the wrathful protective form of Avalokiteshvara, the Buddha of Compassion, and that Mahakala would watch over the boy throughout his life.

When the child was in his seventh year, his father passed away. The mother, unable to support her numerous children, thought to put some of them into monasteries, where they could receive free care and education. Divinations indicated that her son born on the night of the bandit attack would benefit most from such a training. Thus she put him in Nartang Monastery under the guardianship of his uncle, Geshey Choshey.[5]

It was not long before the Nartang abbot noticed that the child was a most promising student and took him under his wing. The relationship was a happy one, and by his twentieth birthday the First Dalai Lama had become Nartang's most accomplished scholar.

Shortly after receiving his full monastic ordination, he visited and began studies in central Tibet, where he met Lama Tsongkhapa four years before the latter's death. Tsongkhapa, too, instantly recognized the great destiny that lay before the youth, and on their first meeting he tore a piece of cloth from his robe, giving it to the young monk with the prophecy that he would become one of his most important disciples, particularly in the work of establishing the purity of Tibet's tradition of Sangha, or monastic community. During his life the First Dalai Lama studied with more than fifty gurus from many different schools of Tibetan Buddhism, but as the decades passed, he became ever more committed to the lineages he had received from Tsongkhapa and his principal disciples.

By the 1440s the First Dalai Lama had become one of Tibet's most revered saints, spending much of his time in caves and meditational hermitages and teaching to large gatherings of disciples. Students came to him from all over Central Asia.

In 1447 he established Tashi Lhunpo Monastery with the patronage of various kings and nomadic chieftains from southwestern and western Tibet, most notably the King of Gugey. Tashi Lhunpo soon became the greatest Gelugpa monastery outside of the Lhasa area and one of the four most prestigious monastic institutions in Central Asia (the other three being Ganden, Drepung, and Sera). He spent much of the remainder of his life teaching in Tashi Lhunpo and its nearby monasteries, such as Nenying, Nartang, and Sangpu, thus fulfilling the prophecy made by Lama Tsongkhapa many years earlier.

The First Dalai Lama was also regarded as an accomplished poet. His *Miscellaneous Works* (Tib., *gSung-'bum-thor-bu*) contains several dozen of his verse works. As we will see in Part Two, as a youth in Nartang Monastery the Second Dalai Lama received transmissions of all the First's writings and thus would have become familiar with his predecessor's songs and poems at that time. Consequently they would have influenced his own writing style.

However, the First's spiritual poems are not classified as *nyamgur*, or "songs of experience." He was too modest and retiring in character to write in that style. Only the Second, Fifth, and Seventh Dalai Lamas' collected writings contain *nyamgur*.

In the eleventh month of the Wood Horse Year (1474), the First Dalai Lama announced that he would soon pass away and summoned his most important disciples to gather around him for a final sermon. He was in his eighty-fourth year. On the eighth day of the twelfth month (the day associated with Arya Tara, his principal meditational deity), he called an assembly in the Tashi Lhunpo temple and delivered his final advice to his disciples. At the conclusion of the discourse, he sat in meditation, closed his eyes and, in the presence of the assembly, consciously dissolved the elements of his body. It was the half moon of the twelfth Tibetan month of the Wood Horse Year. (The year is usually given as 1474 by Western scholars, but is actually either late January or early February, 1475.)

It is said that for forty-nine days after his external death (after his heart and breath had stopped), he remained seated in *tukdam* (Tib., *thugs-dam*), a mystical state between life and death, wherein consciousness is withdrawn to the heart, and the body is preserved intact by the powers of meditation. Thus he made evident his accomplishment of enlightenment for all to see. His body took on the appearance of a sixteen-year-old boy and shone with a radiance that inspired joy in all who came near it.

Then on the forty-ninth day he projected his consciousness out of the body. Traditional biographies state that his head fell slightly to the side, and a drop of sperm was released from his sexual organ, as indications that the *tukdam* was complete.[6]

According to Yangpa Chojey's account of the Second Dalai Lama's life and deeds, after the First passed away he projected his consciousness to the Tushita Pure Land, where he came into the presence of Maitreya Buddha, Atisha, and Lama Tsongkhapa and asked them for advice on where he should go in the universe in order to work for the enlightenment of living beings. Tsongkhapa (as Jampel Nyingpo, his form in Tushita) took a white flower and tossed it down to earth, stating that he should reincarnate wherever the flower landed. It fell to earth in Tanak Dorjeden, in the Yolkar Hermitage of the yogi Kunga Gyaltsen. He then threw down two hailstones, one of which landed in central Tibet near Radeng Monastery and the other in Kham, southeastern Tibet.

Tibetan mystical writings take this legend to indicate that there were three reincarnations of the First Dalai Lama: one of body, one of speech, and one of mind. Of these three, it is the body emanation that is most suited to take up the work of the previous incarnation.

The flower that fell on the hermitage of the yogi Kunga Gyaltsen indicated the body emanation, and thus it is this child that eventually came to be recognized as the First's reincarnation. The other two presumably carried the First's work *incognito*, and nothing more is said of them in any of the Second's biographies.[7]

The Fourteen Dalai Lamas

Thus the First Dalai Lama achieved spiritual greatness during his lifetime. Although he studied in both southwestern and central Tibet, he mostly taught in the Tsang area of the southwest and inspired a lasting spiritual legacy there.

As we will see in Part Two, "Life of the Second Dalai Lama," a young child soon came forth and proclaimed himself to be the reincarnation of the First. He was recognized as such and was installed at Tashi Lhunpo. He continued the work begun by the First and extended the influence of the Dalai Lama's office to central and southern Tibet. The national prestige that he achieved exceeded even that of the First, and when he passed away in 1542, there was hardly a single important lama in Tibet who had not studied with or received a tantric initiation from him or one of his disciples. During his lifetime he changed his hereditary residence from Tashi Lhunpo of Tsang Province to Drepung Monastery near Lhasa.

Only the Second was a "self-proclaimed" Dalai Lama. Shortly after his death, a committee was set up to search for his reincarnation, and from that time on all Dalai Lama reincarnations would be identified by means of formal search committees. This was the case for the first time with the Third.

The Third Dalai Lama, Gyalwa Sonam Gyatso, also achieved national prominence. In the later part of his life he was requested by the Mongolian king Altan Khan to come to Mongolia and teach.

He arrived there in 1578 and, under his tutelage, Mongolia gave up the ways of war and converted to Buddhism. It has remained a spiritually devoted nation ever since (with the occasional regression to a minor war here and there). The Third also traveled and taught extensively throughout Kham and Amdo provinces of eastern Tibet, thus spreading the influence of the Dalai Lama's office to these areas.

The reincarnation of the Third Dalai Lama was recognized in the person of a young Mongolian boy. Thus the Fourth Dalai Lama was the first (and also so far the only) Dalai Lama to be born as a non-Tibetan. As a youth he exhibited great spiritual power and came to be known as *Tutob* Yonten Gyatso, or "Yonten Gyatso the Adept." His Mongolian heritage cemented the commitment of that nation to Buddhism and its allegiance to the Dalai Lama school.

The Fifth Dalai Lama, who generally is referred to by the Tibetans simply as Ngapa Chenpo, or "the Great Fifth," was the first to witness the politicalization of the Dalai Lama's office. This was not done as a conscious effort on his part but rather was a spontaneous outcome of a civil war that erupted in Tibet during his lifetime. Tibet at the time was comprised of numerous separate kingdoms, formed into three federations, these being the central, southwestern, and eastern provinces of what we think of as present-day Tibet. During the Great Fifth's life, the king of southwestern Tibet formed a pact with the king of Beri, eastern Tibet, to invade Lhasa and divide the spoils between them. Their plan backfired; their armies were defeated by Gushri Khan, a Mongolian ally of Lhasa, and thus in 1642 the three parts of Tibet were united under Lhasa's administration. Gushri Khan brokered an arrangement whereby the Great Fifth (and the subsequent Dalai Lama reincarnations) would serve as both spiritual and temporal leaders of Tibet, with Mongolia in the background as patron and protector.

Once in an interview I conducted with His Holiness the present Dalai Lama, he spoke of the interconnections between the lives of these first five Dalai Lamas, referring to a "masterplan" that they had lived out. According to His Holiness, the First developed a spiritual support base in Tsang, southwestern Tibet; the Second extended this to central and southern Tibet; the Third further extended it to the Kham and Amdo provinces of eastern Tibet, and also to Mongolia; while the Fourth cemented the Lhasa-Mongolia spiritual alliance, with the Dalai Lama's office at the heart of this bond. Thus when the Great Fifth appeared on the scene, all the pieces were in place, and the role of spiritual and temporal leadership of a united Tibet fell effortlessly into his hands.

Late in his life the Great Fifth began the construction of the Potala, which today still stands as Tibet's greatest architectural achievement. However, the project was not complete when the time came for him to pass away. He advised his prime minister, Desi Sangyey Gyatso, to keep his death a secret until the building work was finished. Consequently the search for and discovery of the Sixth Dalai Lama was kept secret for twelve years. Only after the Potala was complete was the Sixth brought forth.

At it turned out, the Sixth was the only one in the line of reincarnations not to accept the lifestyle of a monk. When the time came for his full monastic ordination, he instead returned his novice robes and declared that he would live as a layman. A reason commonly given for this is the unusual upbringing he had as a "secret Dalai Lama" during the early years of his life. It is possible that more mystical motives were behind the Sixth's behavior. At the interview mentioned above with His Holiness the present Dalai Lama, he spoke to me of a "masterplan" involving the Sixth. According to this theory, the Sixth felt that as the leader of the Tibetan people it would be inappropriate for him to remain as a "reincarnation," because between lifetimes there would always be a power vacuum of approximately twenty years from the time of the death of one Dalai Lama until the discovery, education, and growth to maturity of the successor.

Thus the Sixth refused to become a monk, feeling that it would be better to follow the spiritual model of the Sakya school of Tibetan Buddhism, in which the religious throne passes by blood lineage. Instead of composing religious treatises, he spent his time in the taverns and brothels of Lhasa, penning lyrics to love songs. Most Tibetans today still know many of these by heart. As well as having a charming romantic meaning, his verses are said to embody the quintessential message of the highest tantric teachings.

However, the Sixth's radical plan to revise the nature of the Dalai Lama institution did not work out. The Mongolians and Manchus, both of whose courts were patrons of the Dalai Lama school of Tibetan Buddhism, were extremely upset. The former invaded Lhasa and forcibly removed the Sixth. They wanted the Dalai Lama to be a monk, as his predecessors had been. The Sixth passed away shortly thereafter, under mysterious circumstances.[8]

All the subsequent Dalai Lamas lived and died as monks. When one would pass away, a search committee would be established to trace down the reincarnation, who would generally be a child born between nine and twelve months after the decease of the predecessor. The Seventh was probably the greatest of these and was, in my opinion, the most talented writer of all fourteen Dalai Lamas, with the possible exception of the Second.

The Eighth was profoundly spiritual but lived a quiet meditative life and did not teach or write to any significant extent; thus history books generally give him but a brief mention. The Ninth to Twelfth all died quite young, and histories therefore also largely do not mention them in any detail.

Thus the mantle of greatness was next picked up by the Thirteenth, who was born in 1876 and had the unenviable task of guiding Tibet through the period of European colonialism, when most of central Asia was being divided between the two superpowers, Russia and Britain. He in fact did an admirable job in this respect, preserving his people's political independence, cultural integrity, and spiritual dedication through two invasions by the British (1888 and 1904) as well as one by the Chinese (1909). For this reason he is referred to by Tibetans as "the Great Thirteenth."

The present Dalai Lama, His Holiness Tenzin Gyatso, was born in 1935 to a family of farmers in Amdo Province, eastern Tibet. As he once put it to me, "My task is the most difficult of all Dalai Lamas, for I must lead my people through the darkest period of our history." He was referring to the Chinese Communist invasion of Tibet in the 1950s and their mass destruction of Tibetan culture in the 1960s. Since then, all but thirteen of Tibet's 6,500 monasteries and temples have been totally destroyed, their artwork melted down for its precious metal, destroyed, or sold on the international art markets. Most of Tibet's ten thousand libraries were put to the torch, and more than a fifth of its population has been liquidated, with hundreds of thousands more put in concentration and slave-labor camps.

Thus the present Dalai Lama indeed has a most difficult task as the leader of the Tibetan people. He has spent more than half of his life as a refugee in India, from which he struggles to preserve the endangered Tibetan civilization and also to lobby internationally for the fate of Tibet. In 1989 he received the Nobel Peace Prize for the nonviolent effort that he leads in this regard.

In the same "masterplan" discussion mentioned above, the present Dalai Lama spoke to me of a third such phenomenon, one involving a link between himself and his predecessor, the Great Thirteenth. His Holiness commented that the Thirteenth had been prophesied to live until the age of seventy-nine or eighty. However, several times he publicly stated that the Tibetans had to take seriously his advice to modernize their country and in particular to tighten up the borders with China, or else the very existence of their civilization would be endangered. In 1932 he warned of the dangers of Communist invasion and spoke of his people being scattered like ants around the world and forced to live like beggars. Those who remained in Tibet, he said, would become like slaves in their own land and would see their days and nights pass with great suffering. He concluded by reminding them that the tragedy could still be avoided if they were to act quickly. He then warned them that he was almost fifty-eight and could soon pass away. He died not long afterwards.

His Holiness commented that the Great Thirteenth thus purposely shortened his life span because he realized that the Tibetans would not follow his advice. He perceived that the Chinese invasion was rapidly becoming inevitable and felt that the situation would be made hopeless if at the time of the invasion the Dalai Lama was an old man. Thus he mystically stepped aside and passed away, making way for the new reincarnation. As a consequence, when the Chinese Communists eventually invaded, they were forced to deal with a young energetic Dalai Lama, rather than with an old man.

His Holiness concluded by saying, "Thus these Dalai Lamas seem to have had three master plans: the first involving the First to Fifth Dalai Lamas; the second involving the Sixth, which failed; and then the third, which involves the Thirteenth Dalai Lama and myself. But the situation for me is under great pressure, and I don't have much room to move. Perhaps I will have to come up with some fourth masterplan."

I responded teasingly, "If you do so, then please take the opposite approach to that of the Thirteenth Dalai Lama. He used his powers of meditation to shorten his life and implemented his masterplan on that basis. If you devise a plan, please implement it by extending your lifespan by a few decades rather than the reverse."

I have been speaking here of fourteen Dalai Lamas. Indeed, the present Dalai Lama is always listed in Tibetan literature as the Fourteenth. But in fact the name *Dalai Lama* was first applied only to the Third. This occurred in 1578, when he visited Mongolia. His name was Gyalwa Sonam Gyatso, the last part of which (*Gyatso,* meaning "Ocean") translates into Mongolian as *Dalai* (or *T'alai*). Thus the Mongolians always spoke of him and all other incarnations in the line as "Dalai Lamas." The epithet was ascribed posthumously to Gyalwa Sonam Gyatso's two predecessors, and thus he became the Third Dalai Lama. Later the Chinese picked up the name from the Mongolians, and the British learned it from the Chinese. The rest of the world adopted it from the British.

Tibetans generally did not use the name. They have come to feel comfortable with it only in the second half of this century. Before that they always used (and even today still prefer) the traditional epithets. The most popular of these are Gyalwa Rinpoche, which means "Precious Jina" (or "Buddha Jewel"); Yezhin Norbu, which means "Wish-fulfilling Gem"; and Kundon, or "The Presence." Classical Tibetan literature usually refers to the Dalai Lama incarnations as Tongwa Donden, which translates as "He Meaningful to Behold." This is the name used in the eleventh-century books of prophecies and also today by Tibet's State Oracle when in trance. Biographies of the early Dalai Lamas mention them by the name Tamchey Khyenpa, or "Omniscient One," a nickname given to the First by his guru in the Jonangpa tradition, Bodong Chokley Namgyal. It stuck and was applied to both the Second and Third.

It may seem to the casual Western reader that all these epithets are somewhat flowery and flattering. In fact they are not any more so than most Tibetan Buddhist spiritual names, which are equally poetic. For example, I know quite ordinary people called Sangyey Samdrub ("He Who Fulfills the Aspirations of the Buddhas"); Tubten Kunkhyen ("All-Knowing One in the Enlightenment Doctrine"); Lobzang Dolma ("Liberating Savioress of Sublime Mind");

and Nyima Dorjey ("Sun-like Diamond"). Two of these people are more rogue than saint. My own Tibetan Buddhist name is Jampa Zopa, or "Patient Lover." In truth, I'm not particularly patient.

The Dalai Lamas and the Avalokiteshvara Myth

The standard biography of the Second Dalai Lama (begun by Yangpa Chojey in 1530 and completed by Konchok Kyab in 1560) begins with the legend of Avalokiteshvara, the Buddha of Compassion, of whom the Dalai Lamas are said to be emanations.

In the West we often see various statements on how and why this mythology arose around the Dalai Lamas. Most of what is said by Western scholars is wrong, simply because they did not take the time to examine the original Tibetan sources. Again, as with the common misunderstanding concerning the First Dalai Lama's genealogy, it seems that the error began with the late nineteenth-century Christian missionary and scholar L. Austine Waddell, who wrote that the legend was consciously created by the Fifth Dalai Lama after he assumed the leadership of Tibet in 1642. As Waddell would have it, the Great Fifth propagated the belief as a crafty political ploy in order to amplify the devotion of simple-minded Tibetans, for whom faith in the bodhisattva Avalokiteshvara was a centuries-old cult.[9]

A glance at any of the early Dalai Lama biographical literature immediately dispels Waddell's proposition. The Fifth Dalai Lama may have accepted the myth, but he certainly did not invent it. To the contrary, he inherited it. If anyone consciously created the legend, it was either Jowo Atisha or his chief disciple Lama Drom, both of whom lived in the eleventh century, three hundred years before the birth of the First Dalai Lama and more than five hundred years before the time of the Great Fifth.

As the story goes, Jowo Atisha and Lama Drom, together with another disciple, Ngok Lotsawa, spent a year in retreat at the caves of Yerpa Lhari Nyingpo (a site where the Second Dalai Lama penned many of his compositions centuries later). During the evenings they would pass a few hours in spiritual conversation, usually with Ngok asking questions and either Atisha or Lama Drom answering. On a number of occasions Ngok quoted a verse of scripture and requested Lama Drom to relate how he had internalized its meaning in a previous life. As the story goes, Lama Drom always modestly refused to comply to these requests, stating that there were many far more interesting topics that they could discuss. Undeterred, Ngok would pass the request to Atisha. Atisha would reply by stating, "Well, Ngok, as you know, Lama Drom is an incarnation of Avalokiteshvara, the Buddha of Compassion, so make a symbolic offering of the universe to him, and I will fulfill your request."

In this way the accounts of thirty-six "previous lives of Lama Drom" are told by Atisha, each beginning with the statement that ". . . as you know, Lama Drom is an incarnation of Avalokiteshvara." These thirty-six are embodied in chapter twenty-three of the Kadampa classic *Father Dharmas Son Dharmas* (Tib., *Pha-chos-bu-chos*), one of the most popular pieces of early Kadampa literature. This text was written down in the late eleventh century.

During his lifetime the First Dalai Lama was regarded as being the reincarnation of Lama Drom. Thus he inherited the mythology of being an emanation of Avalokiteshvara and came to be linked to all the "previous lives of Lama Drom" spoken of by Atisha. The myth consequently followed the Dalai Lama's office from that time onward.

The thirty-six "previous lives of Lama Drom" that Atisha relates to Ngok Lotsawa describe incarnations in India, usually as a young prince or Brahmin boy. And although this is all we find in chapter twenty-three of the *Pha-chos-bu-chos*, the stories do not end there. In other sections of the same text Atisha relates numerous other "previous lives" of Lama Drom, including ten as early kings of Tibet, such as King Nyatri Tsenpo, King Lha Totori, King Songtsen Gampo, King Trisong Deutsen, and King Tri Ralpachen (several of whom I have mentioned previously). Atisha also speaks of several of Lama Drom's previous lives as yogis in Nepal and as lamas in Tibet. Most of these are somewhat famous historical personages, regarded during their own lifetimes as being emanations of Avalokiteshvara. Thus the Fifth Dalai Lama did not have to invent the theory of being an emanation of Avalokiteshvara, as Waddell would have us believe. He had two choices: to disclaim it or to go along with it. He chose the latter.

To put the situation somewhat in context, it was not particularly unusual in Tibet to be regarded as being an incarnation or emanation of a particular Buddha or bodhisattva. Hundreds of lamas were associated with a mythology of this nature. For the Fifth Dalai Lama to disclaim the legendary association of Avalokiteshvara with himself would have been pointless; the myth had followed the Dalai Lama office for centuries, so everyone knew that it must be true. Moreover, a disclaimer would simply have been taken as a proclamation of modesty and would have had the effect of making people even more certain that indeed he must be Avalokiteshvara; for, as everyone knows, Avalokiteshvara is notoriously modest.

Thus Yangpa Chojey opens his account of the life of the Second Dalai Lama with a summary of the Avalokiteshvara legend: of how in ancient times Avalokiteshvara vowed to take care of Tibet; how he incarnated in the Yarlung Valley as a monkey and crossbred with an abominable snowlady in order to give birth to the first six human beings; then later, when human society had developed in Tibet, how he incarnated as various kings, such as Songtsen Gampo, Trisong Deutsen, and so forth, in order to bring the enlightenment teachings to the country.[10]

Yangpa Chojey then comments,

> . . . in order to establish the effective presence of the enlightenment tradition in Tibet, in the beginning he came to Tibet as King Trisong to assist Guru Padmasambhava; in the middle he came as Lama Drom to complete the work of Jowo Atisha; and finally as Gyalwa Gendun Drup (the First Dalai Lama) he made firm the doctrines of Lama Tsongkhapa.

In this way he manifested in Tibet as great spiritual masters during the early, middle, and later periods of Buddhism in Tibet, in order to establish the Dharma in the Land of Snows.

The Tibetan Tradition of Mystical Verse

One of the oldest, most enduring, and universal forms of spiritual and artistic expression is mystical song and poetry. Mystical songs have great antiquity, probably dating to long before societies achieved literacy.

Both as preliterate oral traditions and as literature, mystical songs and poetry have brought pleasure, inspiration, and guidance to countless people throughout history. Not limited to any particular civilization, time, or religious tradition, their sources are as diverse as the Psalms of the Bible, the inspirational works of great Sufi poets, Zen *haiku*, Indian *gita*, and native American "drum songs."

The Tibetans have been prolific in writings of this nature. No thorough study of their vast reservoir of verse literature has been made by Western Tibetologists to date, but it is clear that it has been around at least since the importation of Buddhism. Mystical songs probably existed before that time, in the context of Tibet's pre-Buddhist religions such as the Loba and the Bonpo, although these would have thrived only as oral traditions. A wealth of mystical verse can be found in Bonpo literature today, preserved in the medium of the script imported by Tonmi Sambhota.

As stated earlier, the Buddhism of Tibet is essentially an extension and development of Indian Buddhism, and Buddha's doctrine is of two main types: Sutrayana and Vajrayana. Consequently,

Tibetan Buddhist mystical writing, including its tradition of verse, has been strongly influenced by the Indian background; and it usually is expressed in two main types of language: that of the sutras and that of the tantras.

Verse composition was popular in the earliest days of Indian Buddhism. For example, many sayings of the Buddha himself are preserved in verse form. Dozens of these can be found in the Tibetan *Kangyur*, or collection of translations of discourses by the Buddha. Known as *gatha*, these traditional verses were not only attributed to the Buddha but also to many of his direct disciples.

One of the most popular Sutrayana works of this nature with the Tibetans was (and still is) the anthology known as *Collected Verses of the Buddha* (Skt., the *Udamvarga*; Tib., *Tsigsu Chepai Tshom*, spelled *Tshigs-su-byed-pai-tshoms*).[11] This verse compilation of Buddha's essential spiritual experiences and consequent advice to his disciples was translated into Tibetan in the early days of Buddhism in that country and served as a model in both spiritual verse writing and poetic technique. Much of the tantric literature attributed to the Buddha is also expressed in verse, known as *vajra gita*, or "diamond songs." The Tibetans are also very fond of these. Vajra gita of this category are generally found interspersed as passages in the original tantric texts.

Another Indian literary tradition that achieved a high level of popularity with the Tibetans was a style of Sanskrit *karika* (which means "verse") used by masters such as Nagarjuna, Aryadeva, Chandrakirti, Asanga, Vasubandhu, Shantideva, and so forth. Perhaps the most important of these figures is Nagarjuna, often referred to as "the father of the Mahayana," who was born in the first century A.D. The Tibetan *Tangyur*, or collection of translations of works by later Indian masters, contains over a hundred and fifty entries attributed to him. Many of these are verse works that combine elements of spiritual experience with advice to disciples. Nagarjuna's *Surrellika*, or "Letter to a Friend," is typical of the style. Several English translations of this text exist. His *Ratnavali*, or "String of Gems," is also fundamental reading.[12]

A third Indian tradition that exerted a major influence on Tibetan verse writing is that of the *doha*, a style of mystical song developed by the tantric yogins and yoginis of Buddhist India. In his Foreword, His Holiness mentions the importance of doha to the Tibetans.[13]

Another important Indian influence on Tibetan verse composition comes from the classical Indian approach to poetic technique. The most popular Indian writer on the subject is Dandi, whose treatise on poetic composition was translated into Tibetan in the early days of Tibet's adoption of Indian culture and has received continual attention in the Land of Snows over the centuries. Indeed, no Tibetan is considered well educated without having studied this work, in which the classical usages of similes, metaphors, meter, euphony, alliteration, and so forth are described and illustrated. Dozens of commentaries to this work have been written by Tibetans. The collected works of the Second, Fifth, Ninth, and Thirteenth Dalai Lamas contain works of this nature, as evidence of its continued popularity.[14] These various Indian influences reached Tibet in bits and pieces between the seventh and eleventh centuries.

A mention should also be made of the Indonesian connection to Buddhist verse. Buddhist Indonesia from the eighth to twelfth centuries was among the most developed civilizations in Asia, as evidenced by ruins such as the great temple and stupa complex at Borobodur. Tibet's major exchange with Indonesia came during the early eleventh century, with Jowo Atisha. Before visiting Tibet, Jowo Atisha had studied for twelve years in Indonesia under a master known to the Tibetans as Lama Serlingpa. Many of the lineages that he taught in Tibet were Indian traditions as redefined by the Indonesian sensitivity. In particular, Serlingpa claimed to have united two different Indian legacies within himself, namely, the wisdom tradition (the voidness teachings) rooted in Nagarjuna, and the method tradition (the bodhisattva trainings of the six perfections) rooted in Asanga. It was the unification of these two, as expressed through the Indonesian experience, that Jowo Atisha regarded as the most precious of all Buddhist lineages he had received from any of his fifty-five gurus.

Serlingpa "packaged" his lineages into various oral tradition forms. The two most important of these are those known to the Tibetans as *Lam Rim* (spelled *Lam-rim)* and *Lojong* (spelled *bLo-sbyong),* which respectively translate as "Stages on the Enlightenment Path" and "Transforming the Mind." These terms primarily refer to teaching traditions in which the complete path to enlightenment is presented within specifically designed frameworks.

However, they also refer to genres of literature, namely, the writings that embody these teachings.

Much of this teaching exists in verse form, as "Lam Rim Verses" (Tib., *Lam rim tshig chey*, spelled *Lam-rim-tshigs-byed*) and also as "Lojong Verses" (Tib., *Lolong tshig chey*, spelled *bLo-sbyong-tshigs-byed*), both being poetic structures that both express the experiences of meditators in these traditions and communicate advice of great masters to their disciples. Thousands of texts of this nature exist in the Tibetan language. Some take the form of simple songs of joy; others are verses of somewhat stern and serious advice; still others are prayers for the accomplishment of realization. The Second Dalai Lama was profoundly moved by this style of verse writing, and we can see strong elements of it in many of his songs and poems.[15]

It may be useful to look briefly at how songs and verses were experienced by the Tibetans and to review some of the principal personages whose writings remain as major landmarks on the terrain of Tibetan history.

As mentioned, in the mid–seventh century, King Songtsen Gampo and his emissary Tonmi Sambhota opened the window to Indian culture. In addition to translating numerous Sanskrit works into Tibetan, Tonmi Sambhota and his colleagues introduced a knowledge of Indian poetics, including a taste of many of the source texts mentioned earlier.

Tibet's intellectual and spiritual romance with India experienced a quantum leap forward a century later, when the illustrious Indian tantric master Padmasambhava was invited by King Trisong Deutsen to teach in the Land of Snows. Padmasambhava played a major role in furthering Tibet's tradition of mystical verse. Not only did he and his disciples translate numerous important verse works from Sanskrit, but many of his teachings, as well as voluminous collections of his prophecies, were recorded in verse form. Several of his biographies, as well as the biographies of his foremost disciples, were written as epic poems.[16]

Over the centuries to follow, the Land of Snows blossomed with mystical poets. A special mention should perhaps be made of the impact of Jowo Atisha in this regard and the literary renaissance that he inspired in the mid–eleventh century. I have discussed his religious activities earlier and mentioned his importation of Indonesian influences into Tibet's mystical culture. However, Atisha's impact was far more broad than this may suggest. In addition to this important activity, his work in inspiring the Tibetans to review Indian Buddhist literature as a whole, from the writings of Nagarjuna on down, should not be underestimated. An important collection containing several dozen of his own verse works, as well as many of his favorite Sanskrit gnomic poems in translation, is preserved in the Tibetan *Tengyur* under the title *Jowo Chochung Gyatsa (Jo-bo-chos-chung-brgya-rtsa),* or *The Hundred Little Favorites of Jowo Atisha.* The collection is well known to all Tibetans and undoubtedly influenced the Second Dalai Lama's writing style.[17]

The fact that Atisha was an inspired creator of mystical song and poetry is illustrated by the following anecdote associated with his arrival in Ngari, western Tibet. Lama Rinchen Zangpo of Ngari, one of Tibet's foremost translators and teachers, is said to have doubted the necessity of inviting Atisha. Nonetheless when the master arrived at Ngari, the elderly and revered translator politely accompanied him on a tour through the temple complex. Atisha paused for a moment in front of the paintings and statues in the temple and gave voice in Sanskrit to a mystical song associated with each image. Lama Rinchen Zangpo was overwhelmed by the beauty, profundity, and poetic excellence of the songs, none of which he had heard before, even though he was well versed in Indian literature. He asked Atisha their origin. "They are nothing special," Atisha replied, "I just composed them as we walked." Lama Rinchen Zangpo was humbled and became a devoted disciple of Jowo Atisha.

The discussion above looks mostly at the Tibetan tradition of spiritual and mystical verse from the perspective of external influences, in which India played the primary role. However, by this I do not wish to imply that the Tibetans merely imitated the Indians. Rather, they took their direction and inspiration from the Indians and developed their own style based on the Tibetan character.

As stated earlier, no doubt Tibet's "pre-Buddhists," such as the Loba and Bonpo, had their own traditions of mystical verse, even if these existed only orally. The ease and speed with which the Tibetans took to verse composition certainly indicates a long-standing indigenous tradition. Early Nyingma writers poured forth in verse from the first days of Tibetan Buddhism, suggesting a prior background in poetic expression.

Moreover, early Tibetan poets and songwriters who were barely literate had no difficulty in composition. The eleventh-century poet Milarepa, for example, had no (or at best minimal) training in literature and had certainly never studied classical composition. Yet the *Mila Gurbum*, or *Hundred Thousand Songs of Milarepa*,[18] remains one of the most popular collections of Tibetan mystical poetry throughout Central Asia. Milarepa had begun his spiritual career as a Bonpo (a follower of one of Tibet's religions from the pre-Songtsen Gampo period), briefly studied with the Nyingma school of Tibetan Buddhism, and then entered into yogic training under Marpa Lotsawa. Although he could read and write, his biography suggests that he was barely literate. In fact he did not write anything himself; his poems were sung orally and later transcribed by his students. The natural and free form of their composition suggests an indigenous background.

It is also important to note that there are tremendous differences between the Sanskrit and Tibetan languages, differences that make mere emulation impossible. Sanskrit, from the Indo-European language group, is constructed of mostly multisyllabic words and has an extremely sophisticated grammar. Quite to the contrary, Tibetan is from the Indo-Burmese language group (pre-Aryan and pre-Sanskrit); its words are mostly of one or two syllables in length, and it is sparse in its use of grammar. Tibet could look to India for ideas in content and approach to poetry, but the differences between the two languages would dictate that a direct transposition or imitation would be impossible.

Tibetan Verse in English Translation

Given the nature of the Tibetan language, it is obvious that no English translation of Tibetan verse can honor all elements of style. Tibetan verses are usually composed in four-line stanzas, with each line having six, seven, nine, or twelve syllables. As Tibetan words are mostly of one or two syllables, and as most English words are three, four, or five syllables, a translator has the choices of either dropping out many of the words, adding extra syllables or lines, or else simply ignoring formal meter and line-length altogether. Most translators opt for the last of these three courses. To leave out words seems too much like literary sacrilege, and to systematically add syllables or lines defeats the purpose of attempted metric emulation.

A saving grace for the translator is that Tibetan verse seems to play on a rhythm or pattern with the ideas contained within it, with each idea working quite as a line in itself. I, like many other translators, take this "rhythm of ideas" as the vein of gold to be followed in the work of translation and attempt to build around its movement. The end result is something like modern free-form verse, somewhat capturing the spirit and many of the techniques of the original, without losing any of the meanings nor creating an obviously forced and superimposed style. The art is in discerning the natural flow of the ideas in a given verse and then attempting to recreate this in free-form verse. The result seems to be far more readable and true to the original than what is created by attempting to stick to lines of six or seven syllables and by the rather crass tampering that must be done in order to effect this.

It is often said that poetry is the most difficult writing to translate. In a sense this is true, for it is like attempting to take the music of one culture and play it on the instruments and in the environment of another when the scales of the instruments do not precisely match. The two obviously will never sound quite the same. But it is not the job of the person undertaking the musical transposition to make the music identical in outer form. Those who want this sameness would be better off simply to study the original instruments on which the music was composed and to enjoy it within that medium. The art of the transposer of music is to capture the spirit, genius, and essential concept of the original, and to recreate it within his or her own culture, as played on the appropriate instruments. Bach played on a harpsichord will never sound like Bach played on an electric guitar, an Indian sitar, or an Andes flute. But this does not mean that Bach played on these different instruments is irrelevant, so long as his music brings listening pleasure to lovers of those instruments, and so long as the essential ideas in the original Bach composition are honored.

The same holds true with poetry. Shakespeare in translation will never sound like Shakespeare in English, yet he has nonetheless been translated into most major languages of the world. The secret of success in the mission of translating poetry is to avoid sticking to mere external poetic technique, and instead to look for the magical heartbeat of the original composition and then to find a milieu in the target language that resonates with the same clarity, humor, and joy.

Over the past two decades of working with Tibetan literature, I have developed a few simple rules of thumb. The first of these is that I never undertake to translate anything unless I have fallen in love with the original; that is, unless my reading of the original fills me with warmth, awe, and wonder. Secondly, when I approach the work of translation, I always attempt to keep those elements of the Tibetan text that originally inspired literary pleasure within me. Everything else I consider superfluous. My aim is simply to share that joy with an international audience, with people who do not have the ability to access the literature in its Tibetan form. When a confrontation arises between literal translation and the spirit of the message, as frequently does with a literature as non-Western as is Tibetan, I always give priority to the latter.

Of course there will be aspects of the original that I have failed to appreciate. These will therefore not be conveyed in the translation, other than by accident; for a translation is but one person's reading of a text and his or her attempt to recreate that reading as powerfully as possible in a different linguistic environment. I do not apologize for these shortcomings. To the contrary, I am quite comfortable with them. Art aspires to a different perfection, particularly the art of translation. My aim in this book is to transpose what I love about the Second Dalai Lama's songs and poems into English verse—nothing more and nothing less. Those who want more than that should make the effort to learn Tibetan so that they can read the originals for themselves. This book is not for them.

Technical Considerations

It is not possible to appreciate fully the Tibetan Buddhist tradition of mystical verse without having at least a basic understanding of either Indian or Tibetan Buddhism. Of course one does not need to be a Buddhist or a Buddhologist, but some understanding of the twenty or thirty most fundamental ideas and technical terms is essential. Hopefully most readers will have at least this degree of international cultural awareness; after all, Buddhism has been a large part of the lives of almost a third of the world's population for more than two thousand years.

It would be foolhardy to attempt to provide an extensive prep course for novice readers here. But it may be advisable to present a survey of some of the principal technical terms that the Second Dalai Lama uses in his poems.

Buddhism is essentially of two main branches: Hinayana and Mahayana, meaning "the Small Way" and "the Great Way." The former refers to the teachings of Buddha that were given openly; the latter refers to those delivered to more advanced students. The aim of the former is to achieve *nirvana*, which is the state of inner spiritual liberation from ignorance and its consequence of suffering. This is achieved through the three higher trainings of discipline (Skt., *shila*), meditative absorption (*Skt., samadhi*) and wisdom (Skt., *prajna*). All Buddhists cultivate these three.

The aim of the Great Way, or Mahayana, is the attainment of *samyaksambodhi,* the state of complete Buddhahood, which is characterized by perfect compassion, wisdom, and power. It also can be called *nirvana*, or spiritual liberation, although it is a more integrated level of that state.

The person who practices the Hinayana can be called a Hinayanist (Tib., *Theg-dman-pa*). When the goal of nirvana is achieved, he or she is known as an *arhat*, "one who has destroyed the inner enemies." Similarly, the person who practices the Mahayana can be called a Mahayanist (Tib., *Theg-chen-pa)*. He or she can also be called a *bodhisattva,* a Sanskrit word that roughly translates as "enlightenment warrior." The main difference between a Hinayanist and a Mahayanist is that the former aspires to *nirvana* in order to achieve individual liberation from the cycle of suffering, whereas the latter aspires to complete enlightenment in order to be of maximum benefit to all living beings. This extraordinary Mahayanist aspiration is known as *bodhichitta,* or "enlightenment mind," a term that I translate as "bodhimind" and sometimes as "enlightenment thought." The Second Dalai Lama uses it frequently in his songs and poems.

The Mahayanist cultivates this altruistic *bodhichitta* attitude and then applies himself or herself to the practice of the six transcendental perfections: generosity (Skt., *dana*), discipline (Skt., *shila*), patience (Skt., *ksanti*), enthusiastic endeavor (Skt., *virya),* meditation (Skt., *dhyana*), and wisdom (Skt., *prajna*).

The *bodhichitta,* or enlightenment thought, is also of two main types: aspirational, which refers to the stabilized aspiration for enlightenment as a means to benefit all living beings; and "engaged," which refers to this stabilized aspiration when engaged in the practice of the six perfections. Another twofold division of bodhichitta seen in Tibetan texts is into relative bodhichitta, which is the above two aspects of the enlightenment thought, and ultimate bodhichitta, which refers to the bodhisattva's meditative absorption focused on voidness, or ultimate reality. Again, the Second Dalai Lama uses the term *bodhichitta* in all these standard ways.

Bodhisattvas are also of two main types: ordinary, which refers to a Mahayanist on initial stages of the path, beginning from the moment that the altruistic and universal *bodhichitta* aspiration is made stable; and *arya,* which means "higher" and refers to those who in meditation have perceived the nature of voidness, the ultimate nature of phenomena, and thus have become saints. Arya bodhisattvas cross ten *bhumi,* or "stages," on their way to the state of Buddhahood, or complete enlightenment. Again, these terms frequently appear in the Second Dalai Lama's songs and poems.

The Mahayana state of complete enlightenment is characterized by the transformations known as the two, three, or four *kayas,* or "bodies of enlightenment." When two are spoken of, they are the *Dharmakaya* and *Rupakaya*, or "Truth Body" and "Form Body." The former refers to the consciousness of the practitioner transformed into the twenty-one wisdoms; this can only be known by the Buddha himself or herself, or by other Buddhas. The latter, or *Rupakaya*, refers to the practitioner's experience of form, that transforms into perfect expression and can be perceived by non-Buddhas.

These two—Dharmakaya and Rupakaya—become three when the Rupakaya is subdivided into two: *Samboghakaya* and *Nirmanakaya*, or "Beatific Body" and "Emanation Body"; the former of these is the level on which Buddhas can manifest to *aryas*, or saints, and the latter is the level of manifestation that can be perceived by ordinary beings.

The three then can become four when the Dharmakaya is also subdivided into two: *Svabhavakaya* and *Jnana Dharmakaya*, or "Essence Body" and "Wisdom Truth Body." The former is the natural voidness of a Buddha's mind as experienced in enlightenment; the latter is the active wisdom aspect of Buddha consciousness.

The Second Dalai Lama randomly speaks of two, three, and four kayas in his songs and poems. In that they all refer to the same enlightenment state, he does not seem to care much which usage he applies.

The various teachings of the Buddha were eventually recorded in two main types of scriptures, known as *sutras* and *tantras*. There are both Hinayana and Mahayana sutras, whereas all tantras belong to the Mahayana.

From this perspective the paths to enlightenment can also be spoken of as the *Sutrayana* and the *Vajrayana*. The former of these refers to all types of Buddhist practice that are inspired and guided by materials contained in the sutras (both Hinayana and Mahayana); the latter, or Vajrayana, refers to all forms of practice inspired and guided by materials contained in the tantras. These are also known as the exoteric and esoteric paths.

Thus the Sutrayana can be either Hinayana or Mahayana in nature, or a combination of the two. Tibetans always recommend the combination. The Vajrayana is exclusively the esoteric aspect of the Mahayana.

The Vajrayana is comprised of four categories of tantras: *Kriya, Charya, Yoga,* and *Maha Anuttarayoga*. These four translate as "Purification Tantra," "Action Tantra," "Union Tantra," and "Great Highest

Yoga Tantra." There are numerous tantric systems in each of these four categories, each of which represents a complete method of meditative training leading to enlightenment.

Each tantric system is symbolized by a deity, which represents three things: basis, path, and result. A tantric deity as "basis" is the aspect of our mind that can link to the path leading to enlightenment; as "path" it represents a system of meditation and yoga; and as "result" it represents the state of enlightenment to be attained.

Of the four categories of tantras, the first three are usually grouped together as "lower tantras" and the fourth kept by itself as "highest yoga tantra." The Second Dalai Lama most frequently refers to the latter.

All tantric systems have two stages of practice. In the lower tantras these are known as "the yoga with symbols" and "the yoga beyond symbols." In highest yoga tantra they are known as the "generation stage yogas" and "the completion stage yogas." In all tantric systems these two stages are also referred to as "the first stage" and "the second stage."

Generally the first stage in all tantric traditions refers to the process of *mandala* meditation. A mandala may be described as a cosmogram that houses a tantric deity or deities. In the process of mandala meditation (called *sadhana* in Sanskrit), one dissolves the ordinary appearance of oneself and the world into light and then recreates a sense of (i.e., visualizes) oneself as a tantric deity or tantric Buddha. All other living beings are also seen as tantric deities; all sound is taken as mantra and all thoughts as bliss and wisdom. After transforming the ordinary ego-sense in this way, one recites the various mantras associated with the mandala and its deities. This is common to both the three categories of lower tantras and highest yoga tantra. The second stage, however, differs considerably. (There are also differences in the first stage of practice, but I will not go into these here.)

The principal difference in the second stage of practice between lower and highest yoga tantra is that in the former the emphasis is placed upon a formless meditation focused upon *shamatha* (meditative serenity) and *vipashyana* (insight meditation) combined.

In highest yoga tantra this is not the case. Here the emphasis is on concentrating upon the energy centers (Skt., *chakras*), energy channels (Skt., *nadi*), subtle energies (Skt., *vayu*), and mystic drops (Skt., *bindhu*) of the body, as a means of inducing extraordinary physical states. In particular, one attempts to cut off all activity of the coarse level of physical energy, thus putting the body into a state of suspended animation. The subtle energies are withdrawn to the heart, and consciousness is forced to support itself solely on the basis of this subtle energy. The type of consciousness that subsequently arises is known as the "clear light"; it is said that one moment of meditation on the basis of subtle energy and clear light is equal to a hundred years of ordinary meditation.

The above is a brief sketch of the Tibetan Buddhist scheme of practice. It is a union of Hinayana and Mahayana, as well as of Sutrayana and Vajrayana.

The Buddhist world view is that as humans, we all are tremendously fortunate, because the human mind is wonderfully pliant due to its higher intelligence (Skt., *prajna).* Because of this we all have the capacity to achieve both nirvana and full enlightenment.

The ordinary world of cyclic existence, or *samsara,* is comprised of six realms: hell beings, ghosts, animals (including fish, insects, etc.), humans, demigods, and gods. The first three of these are "lower realms" or "states of misery"; the latter three are "higher realms" or "happy states." Yet all six are imperfect, and are prone to some degree of suffering. The lower the realm the more pervasive are the conditions of misery. The six are called "the wheel of life" because we revolve around in them endlessly, until nirvana or Buddhahood is achieved.

Another reason that humans have the greatest enlightenment potential of the six types of living beings is that we stand in the middle of the ladder. We are not oppressed by the constant suffering of the three lower realms, and thus we have the "leisure" (Tib., *dalba)* to cultivate wisdom; yet we experience a sufficiently healthy dose of pain in our lives so that we are able to appreciate the need for enlightenment. We do not have the excessive pleasures of the demigod and god realms, and thus we can more readily appreciate the importance of making the effort to achieve nirvana and enlightenment.

We move up and down on the wheel of life and experience pleasure and pain because of natural or "karmic" law. *Karma* in Buddhism means action or activity, both as the deed itself and also (and perhaps more importantly) as the "karmic instinct" (Tib., *las-gi-bag-chags*) that is placed on the mindstream of the perpetrator of the deed. This karmic seed is then carried within the mindstream until it "ripens" as an experience or is "purified" through spiritual exercise and understanding.

Action inspired by any of the three delusions (Skt., *klesha*) of ignorance, attachment, and aversion always sets up a pattern of negativity that sooner or later must be dealt with. Actions inspired by wisdom, compassion, tolerance and so forth set up positive karmic patterns. In turn, negative karmic seeds eventually ripen as suffering, and positive karmic seeds as happiness. However, neither are ultimately significant, because the misery or pleasure that arises eventually passes away. Nonetheless the latter is preferable, in that it can be more readily tapped as a condition conducive to spiritual transformation and growth.

Every phenomenon in the world around us is said to exist simultaneously on two levels. These are known as "the two levels of truth." The first of these is the "conventional" or "appearance" level—the aspect of phenomena that is perceived by untrained beings. The second is known as "the ultimate" or "final" level of truth, which refers to emptiness or the beyond appearance aspect of things—the voidness nature.

These two levels of truth are like two sides of a coin. On the one hand, nothing really exists in the mode of its appearance but has the ultimate nature of emptiness, voidness, non-true existence; nonetheless, on the conventional level all things seem to exist, including ourselves, and we are locked in the dream of cause and effect.

Thus Buddhist training aims at steadily cultivating and deepening our experience of the ultimate level of truth or voidness, while simultaneously encouraging us to live effectively with the conventional level of karmic cause and effect.

It is said that untrained beings experience only the conventional or appearance level of truth; they then mix this appearance with the innate tendency of grasping at things as being inherently existent or as having truly independent existence (as being truly separate from all other things). Based on this fundamental error untrained beings continually respond erroneously to the events around them. This is the *I*-grasping ignorance that is the root of all suffering. Based on this we experience attachment to the things that support this false sense of ego in ourselves and the things around us; and we experience aversion to the things that threaten this ego.

In Buddhism the purpose of spiritual training is to learn to live creatively within the framework of the two levels of truth and to integrate spiritual principles and attitudes into our everyday life by means of discipline, mindfulness, and introspection. In this way we pacify the gross activity of the *klesha*, or distorted emotions and delusions, and give rise to an inner environment of sensitivity and clarity. Based on this inner clarity, we can then cultivate higher meditation that focuses on emptiness, or the ultimate level of truth. The experience of this ultimate truth in turn totally releases the mind from the bonds of the self-imposed prison created by karma and delusion. The mind thus frees itself from the power that karmic instincts have held over it and arises in the sphere of wisdom, liberation, and radiant ecstasy. After that it emerges from the experience of ultimate truth and carries the experience back into the plane of the conventional.

Both Hinayanists and Mahayanists speak of five levels of the path to enlightenment. The Hinayanist does so from the viewpoint of conventional nonattachment linked with the experience of the wisdom of the ultimate; the Mahayanist does so from the perspective of great compassion as the conventional element, linked with the experience of the ultimate wisdom.

In the Mahayana, one enters the path when great compassion has been cultivated to the extent that it expresses itself as the aspiration to achieve enlightenment as the ultimately effective means of benefitting the world and in this sense cares for others as intensely as it does for oneself. This is the door to the first level of the path, known as "the path of accumulation."

This level of attainment is then amplified and also sublimated by techniques of investigation into the ultimate level of truth. When this ultimate level, or voidness, is glimpsed in meditation, one has reached the door to the second level, known as "the path of application."

One now intensifies both the *bodhichitta* aspect of great compassion and the meditational experience of voidness. When in meditation one gains a direct, nonconceptual experience of voidness, one has arrived at the third level, "the path of insight" and at the first of the ten *arya bhumi*, or "stages of an arya."

At this point the bodhisattva can experience the ultimate level of truth, or voidness directly when in single-pointed meditation; but when he or she arises from meditation, the conventional level of phenomena still appears with a hint of true existence. In other words, the two levels of truth—conventional and ultimate—cannot yet arise simultaneously within the mind.

The process of crossing the next nine *arya bhumi*, or "stages of an arya," is one of integrating the experience of the two levels of truth. Thus it is called "the path of integration" or "the path of meditation," the fourth stage on the way to enlightenment. Here each of the nine arya *bhumi* is crossed sequentially, and the bodhisattva gives birth to ever-increasing powers of spiritual realization, clairvoyance, and emanation.

Eventually he or she crosses the tenth *bhumi* and enters into Buddhahood itself, the fifth Mahayana stage, known as "the path of no more training." The two levels of truth can for the first time now be simultaneously experienced.

Here the practitioner first achieves the *Dharmakaya*, or Truth Body; and then from the Dharmakaya comes the *Rupakaya*, or Form Body, which emanates into the world to bring benefit to living beings: both as *Samboghakaya*, or Beatific Body, which works with arya bodhisattvas and as *Nirmanakaya*, or Emanation Body, which works with beings on more ordinary levels.

These same five stages of the path to enlightenment—accumulation, application, insight, integration, and no more training—are spoken of in both the sutra and tantra traditions. However, in highest yoga tantra the discussion of the two levels of truth is presented somewhat differently. Here the conventional level is represented by the "illusory body," or the most subtle level of physical energies, and the ultimate level of truth is represented by the "clear light" consciousness, the most subtle aspect of consciousness. One crosses the five stages and ten *bhumi* by generating an experience of them and by being able to integrate the simultaneous practice of illusory body and clear light yogas. This leads to the state of *yuganaddha*, or "great union," which is a tantric synonym for enlightenment.

A final term that is important in tantric literature is *mahamudra*, or "the great seal." This refers to the unique tantric practice of not dividing the world into good and bad, into positive and negative, into meditation and nonmeditation. The essence of tantric practice is to stamp all experience with "the great seal" of "the wisdom of great bliss born together with awareness of voidness." In this way all duality is immediately transcended, and the mundane ego-responses that we have toward events is undermined. The gap between samsara and nirvana is thus instantly bridged, and all activities can be taken as a condition for the experience of enlightenment.

The Buddhist path to enlightenment begins by reappraising our situation and realizing our imperfections together with our potential to improve. This involves the subject of the four noble truths, or, more accurately, the four truths perceived by the aryas: that unenlightened states are unsatisfactory and prone to frustration and suffering; that suffering and dissatisfaction arise from causes; that because all experience arises from causes, liberation from suffering and dissatisfaction is possible; and that through systematically working with the laws of cause and effect, one can follow a path by which enlightenment can be achieved.

The Buddhist then turns to the Three Jewels of Refuge—the Buddhas, the Dharma, and the Sangha—for guidance in the methods of traveling that path to liberation and enlightenment.

In his collection of mystical songs and verses, the Second Dalai Lama writes and sings from within the framework of the above spiritual and philosophical environment. The better we understand that environment the deeper we are able to flow into his creations. Nonetheless much of his vocabulary and message is universal, and I hope that even the casual reader will be comfortable with it.[19]

As His Holiness the Dalai Lama puts it in his Foreword, when we undergo philosophical training in the Buddhist doctrine, we deal with the above ideas and terms in a very precise manner, like preparing the ingredients of a meal. Then just as when we eat the meal we simply enjoy its flavors and textures without giving too much thought to the exact quantity of the various ingredients, so it is with mystical songs and poems; we simply take them at face value, for whatever pleasure and inspiration they can invoke within us through the reading.

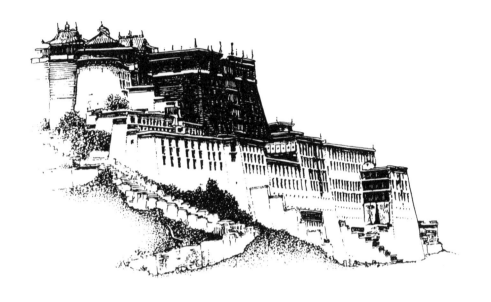

Life of
the Second
Dalai Lama

The Biographies of the
Second Dalai Lama

Although numerous texts on the life of the Second Dalai Lama existed in Tibet, most of these have been destroyed by the Chinese Communist invasion and the subsequent burning of Tibet's major libraries. However, two important works survive. The first of these, the Second's own *Autobiography* (Tib., *Je-nyi Ranggyi Dzepai Namtar*; spelled *rJe-nyid-rang-gi-mdzes-pai-rnam-rhar*) was written in the Earth Mouse Year (1528) when he was fifty-three years old and is an important sourcework for our knowledge of his physical movements and building activities. The sections in it of particular interest are his recollections of his grandparents and parents, the account of his early childhood, his discussion of the trauma of being expelled from Tashi Lhunpo Monastery when he was in his late teens, and, from a later period in his life, his description of the visions that occurred during the consecration and empowerment of Lhamo Latso, the Lake of Visions. He also speaks in some detail on the construction of Chokhor Gyal Monastery above the Lake of Visions. The remainder of the volume provides lists of teachings and initiations received or given in various years and a chronology of his travels.[1]

A second (and more readable) account of his life is entitled *The Wish-Fulfilling Tree* (Tib., *Paksam gyi Jonshing*; spelled *dPag-bsam-gyi-ljon-shing*). This book has two sections, called "Upper" and "Lower," each of which is written by a different author. (Although having two authors, the text is traditionally published as a single volume in sixteen chapters.)

The Upper Section is an account of the early part of Gyalwa Gendun Gyatso's life, as related by Yangpa Chojey (Tib., *gYang-pa-chos-rje*), a close disciple. It comprises the first thirteen chapters of the book and was written in the Iron Tiger Year (1530). Thus it was composed two years after the Second's *Autobiography* was completed and draws extensively from the latter. However, Yangpa Chojey became ill and had to put aside his writing project; he passed away soon thereafter.

The manuscript was completed thirty years later, when it fell into the able hands of the monk Konchok Kyab (spelled *dKon-cog-skyabs*). Konchok Kyab presumably edited Yangpa Chojey's text and then added "The Lower Section" to it, being an account (in three somewhat long chapters) of the remainder of the Second Dalai Lama's life, the period from 1530 to 1542. It also provides an account of his death and the ensuing funeral rites. Konchok Kyab was not a direct disciple of the Second Dalai Lama; he gleaned his information from various sources, mostly elder disciples who knew the master throughout that period of his life.

(Hereafter this two-part text is referred to simply as the *Biography*. Alternatively, when quoting it I sometimes mention the author's name rather than the textual title. Thus if I am quoting something in the first thirteen chapters, I refer to the author Yangpa Chojey; and if quoting something in chapters fourteen to sixteen, I give the source as Konchok Kyab.)

There are a number of shorter Tibetan biographies included in traditional compendiums of life stories. The most substantial is probably that found in Tsechok Ling Kachen Yeshey Gyaltsen's *Lives of the Teachers in the Lam Rim Transmission* (Tib., *Lam Rim Lagyu*; spelled *Lam-rim-bla-brgyud*), written in the late eighteenth century. As the tutor of the Eighth Dalai Lama, Tsechok Ling had access to the vast Potala libraries. He was also a brilliant author, and his *Lives of the Teachers* is a literary masterpiece in which he presents biographies of a couple of hundred Indian and Tibetan gurus (the latter being from the Kadampa and Gelugpa sects), namely, those who figure in the line of transmission of the *Lam Rim* teachings. The First, Second, Third, Fifth, and Seventh Dalai Lamas are included in these.

In none of the above three texts is the Second Dalai Lama referred to by the name "Dalai Lama"; as I mentioned earlier, he came to be known as such only posthumously. Both Yangpa Chojey and Konchok Kyab generally use the epithets Jenyi (spelled *rJe-nyid*) or Jey Lama (spelled *rJe-bla-ma*), which translate respectively as "the Venerable One" and "the Venerable Guru."

Although Konchok Kyab does not state the fact in the colophon to the Second's *Biography*, it would seem from numerous passages that he also drew from a biography of the Second Dalai Lama written by Chojey Sonam Drakpa, who in later histories is listed as one of the Second Dalai Lama's chief disciples.

Chojey Sonam Drakpa's biography of the Second does not seem to have survived. Although mentioned in his *Collected Works* both in the traditional Tibetan and recent Indian editions, it was never actually published in either of these. I do not know the year of its composition, but presumably it was before 1560 when Konchok Kyab completed Yangpa Chojey's manuscript. Chojey Sonam Drakpa was famous for his writings on philosophical matters, and several of his monastic textbooks (Tib., *Yig-cha*) are still studied today by both Drepung Loseling and Ganden Shartsey monasteries. However, he was a rather bland and unimaginative author, and no doubt this is the reason his account of the Second's life became buried in the shifting sands of literary history.[2]

The Ancestry and Parentage of the Second Dalai Lama

Earlier I mentioned the legend of how, after the First Dalai Lama passed away in early 1475, he traveled to Tushita Pure Land and came into the presence of Buddha Maitreya, Atisha, and Lama Tsongkhapa. He asked for advice on where he should go in order to work for the enlightenment of the world, whereupon Tsongkhapa threw a flower that fell to earth upon a hermitage in Yolkar of Tanak Dorjeden, Tsang Province, southwestern Tibet. This hermitage was the residence of a yogic family, one with an ancient legacy of spiritual practice and transmission. Yangpa Chojey's *Biography* goes into the subject in considerable detail.

The Second Dalai Lama's father, Kunga Gyaltsen, was a highly esteemed lama and lineage holder in the Shangpa Kargyu, Shijey, and Nyingma schools of Tibetan Buddhism, as well as a recipient of many teachings directly from the First Dalai Lama. His mother, also a disciple of the First Dalai Lama, was regarded as a reincarnation of the thirteenth-century yogini Drowai Zangmo, one of the renowned yogi Gyalwa Gotsang's principal disciples.

The *Biography* states that until the mid-eighth century his father's ancestors had been nomads in Kham, the southeast province of Tibet. They, along with members of several other nomadic tribes, were commissioned at that time by King Trisong Deutsen of Lhasa to come to central Tibet in order to help with the construction of Samyey, Tibet's first monastery. Here they met the illustrious Indian master Padmasambhava (Guru Rinpochey) and served under him in his numerous building projects. As well as Samyey Monastery, they assisted in the construction of Bata Horgyi Gomdra, an important meditation hermitage.

The *Biography* mentions that they also participated in the tantric rites when Guru Rinpochey invoked the Dharma protector Pehar and swore him to the guardianship of Tibet. This is an especially relevant connection, because eight hundred years later Pehar was to become the personal protective divinity of the Dalai Lama reincarnations and also the spirit invoked as the Nechung State Oracle after the Fifth Dalai Lama became the spiritual and secular leader of Tibet in 1642.

From this time onward (from approximately the mid–eighth century A.D.) the family remained strongly committed to Buddhist meditation. They settled in Yaru Shang and established a lineage of spiritual succession of father-to-son. This type of "family lineage" was quite common in ancient Tibet and had been the custom with pre-Buddhist clans.[3]

The *Biography* lists the names of the patriarchs in the family line who over the generations had received and passed on the spiritual lineages given to them by Guru Rinpochey. Not much is said about most of these figures, unless they became students of nationally famous historical teachers. For example, one of them became a disciple of the renowned yogi Lama Galo and achieved a high level of spiritual realization through the tantric practice of Heruka Chakrasamvara. Thus more detail is given on him. He later married and had several children, passing his lineages to one of his sons.

The Second's great-grandfather receives considerable attention. Kunga Zangpo by name, he became the first secretary to the king of Tsedong. However, worldly affairs quickly bored him, and he renounced his position in court for a life of meditation and yogic endeavor. He received Dvakpo and Shangpa Kargyu teachings from a number of prominent lamas of the day, including the fully accomplished tantric yogi and mahasiddha Gonpo Pel and " . . . achieved realization as vast as the sky."

Kunga Zangpo's son Donyo Gyaltsen, who was the Second Dalai Lama's grandfather, became the recipient of the family lineages. On top of the Dvakpo and Shangpa Kargyu lineages from his father, Donyo Gyaltsen collected various lineages from the Nyingma and Sakya schools. He also gathered the early, middle, and later lineages of the Shijey school, dedicating himself to the practice and dissemination of them with great enthusiasm. As the *Biography* puts it, he " . . . achieved clairvoyant powers able to discern everything in the past, present, and future." It seems to be from his time that the family became lineage holders of the Shijey traditions.

Concerning the great-grandfather and grandfather the *Biography* comments, "Thus father and son were great lamas who listened to and accomplished the lineages of both old and new schools. They received the scriptural transmissions, explanations, and oral instructions in their completeness, achieving both great learning and yogic realization."

The Second Dalai Lama's father was born as the son of Donyo Gyaltsen and received all the lineages from both his father and grandfather. In addition, he studied extensively with the First Dalai Lama (Gyalwa Gendun Drup) and also with the First Dalai Lama's guru Sherab Sengey, thus achieving spiritual adeptship.

Not much is said of his mother's ancestry in the *Biography*. However, several pages are given to a description of how intensely spiritual she was, how she was recognized by the community as being a reincarnation of the famed twelfth-century yogini Drowai Zangmo, and the many daily meditation sessions that she conducted. Of interest is the fact that her daily tantric *sadhanas* (mandala meditations and mantra recitations) focused on the tantric deities Guhyasamaja, Heruka Chakrasamvara, Yamantaka, and Kalachakra. All of these are central tantric practices in the Gelug school, and it seems that she had received initiation into them directly from the First Dalai Lama.

In his *Autobiography* the Second Dalai Lama speaks of her with warmth and affection,

> Then in order to perpetuate the family tradition, at the age of forty-five he (my father) married (my mother) Kunga Palmo, a recognized female reincarnate yogini who (centuries earlier) had studied under Gyalwa Gotsang and was renowned as the yogini Khadroma Drowai Zangmo.
>
> From childhood my mother could remember many of her previous incarnations. Then as a young woman she became profoundly accomplished in the three highest yoga tantras of Guhyasamaja, Heruka, and Yamantaka, as well as the Medicine Buddha and numerous other tantric systems. . . . In particular, she had profound realization of the Kalachakra doctrines.
>
> She was especially adept at meditation and had received many of the most profound Ganden oral transmissions directly from the First Dalai Lama.
>
> I had the great fortune to enter the womb of such an accomplished and dedicated spiritual practitioner. . . .

Thus both the father and mother had been direct disciples of the First Dalai Lama. The *Biography* suggests that it was this link that inspired the deceased First Dalai Lama to choose them as parents when he was seeking a place of rebirth.

The lifestyle of the family into which the Second Dalai Lama took birth is perhaps best described by a meeting he had with his paternal grandmother when he was six years old. The incident is related in Yangpa Chojey's *Biography* of him and also in his own *Autobiography*. I quote here from the latter of these two sources, this being the more personal of the two.

When I was in my seventh year my father's mother, Sangyey Gyalmo by name, became somewhat ill. She was eighty years old and had been living in solitary meditation for the previous forty-four years. I had been told that when she was thirty-six, she had bricked up the door of her meditation cave and made the vow never again to come down from the mountains.

At one time during her meditations she had become blind but cured herself solely by mystical means. Now in her old age, she was suffering from a severe build-up of bodily fluids, a disease referred to as "the Shijeypa affliction" because it seemed to befall so many meditators of the Shijey sect. She herself mainly practiced that lineage.

My father was her principal meditational advisor, and he would visit her from time to time in order to check on her progress. Generally he would take me along with him, and he did so on this occasion.

My grandmother seemed pleased to see me, and addressed me in the following manner. "O child of Tashi Lhunpo Monastery, you have mastered the powers of truth. Speak so as to inspire your aging grandmother to transcend attachment to this worldly body. Guide me to the Pure Land of Dakinis."

I replied with the following verses of song,

Machik Sangyey Gyalmo, victorious mother of all
    Buddhas,
You will indeed travel to the Pure Land of Dakinis.
The white lion of wisdom will serve as your mount,
The five types of dakinis will come to greet you
And you will traverse the white silken road of joy.

You will fill the skies with rainbows and light,
And the dakas and dakinis will surround you.
When you arrive in the Pure Land of Dakinis
You will sit on a great throne of knowledge
And will speak of Dharma with the mystical beings
    there.

O Sangyey Gyalmo, mother of the Buddhas, I salute you.

I composed this song spontaneously and sang it to her, which seemed to delight her.

Then, as a prayer for her well-being I sang the following verse to her, causing everyone in the room to break out in laughter,

Hara hu kyu na ra ra!
Grandmother afflicted by the demon of old age,
I sing these words to you now.
Droplets of snot fall from your nose
And the blood and pus have hardened within you.
Only lice and their eggs would cling to your body,
Which has become a vessel of every affliction.
Yet, woman of wonder, you have transcended all fear
    and suffering
And thus gained freedom from the demon of death.
I salute you, I salute you, I salute you.

She passed away not long after our visit and through her manner of dying manifested the signs of having achieved a high level of spiritual attainment.

The above passage reveals a number of important ideas surrounding the life of the young lama. First, the grandmother refers to him as a "child of Tashi Lhunpo Monastery." Tashi Lhunpo was the monastic university constructed by the First Dalai Lama in 1447 and thereafter served as the First's principal residence until his death a week after the new moon of January, 1475. Thus the grandmother is clearly referring to him as the reincarnation of the First Dalai Lama, Gyalwa Gendun Drubpa. Secondly, the incident illustrates the young Second Dalai Lama's propensity to speak and sing in spiritual verse, a characteristic of his referred to by the present Dalai Lama in the Foreword and which I deal with later in greater detail. Thirdly, it illustrates the intensely spiritual nature of the Second Dalai Lama's grandmother and father and of the intimate relationship in this regard that the boy shared with both of them.

Birth of the Second Dalai Lama

In the Tibetan biographical tradition, the account of the birth of a lama is usually prefaced by a description of the various dreams that the mother and father experienced immediately prior to the conception and during the nine months the child spent in the womb, as well as prophecies, visions, or dreams related by high lamas living in the area. Also, usually there is a list of auspicious omens that occurred at the time of birth.

Both the *Autobiography* and *Biography* honor this tradition. I will relate a few of the dreams and omens as given by Yangpa Chojey in his *Biography*. In my Introduction, I mentioned how Yangpa Chojey describes the First Dalai Lama's afterlife experience: his conscious journey to the Tushita Pure Land; his meeting with Maitreya Buddha, Atisha, and Lama Tsongkhapa, and the "flower prophecy" given to him by Tsongkhapa; and how the prophetic flower fell to earth in Tanak Dorjeden, in the Yolkar Hermitage of the yogi Kunga Gyaltsen.

At the time it is said that Kunga Gyaltsen was engaged in single-pointed meditation focused on the practice of dream yoga. A young boy came to him in his dreams and said, "The omniscient Gendun Drubpa (i.e., the First Dalai Lama) will soon come to Yolkar. You should receive him well." Kunga Gyaltsen then dreamed that he flew off into the air with the boy and traveled to a meditation cave of Gendun Drubpa. There he beheld the elderly lama, his body ablaze with light, his face white tinged with red. Gendun Drubpa looked at him and smiled.

A few days later he again dreamed of visiting Gendun Drubpa's cave. This time the lama said to him, "I have almost completed my retreat. You should go to my monastery, Tashi Lhunpo, and collect my robes and monk bowl for me."

Shortly after that the mother dreamed a small blue light the size of a sesame seed entered into her womb and shone with great radiance. The light utterly filled her and then flowed out through every pore of her body, filling the ten directions of the universe with its luminosity until all the darkness of the world had been dispelled.

After receiving these auspicious dreams, the father and mother decided to practice dream yoga together in order to invoke more definite signs and offered prayers to Gendun Drubpa for a prophecy.[4] Soon thereafter the father dreamed as before of visiting Gendun Drubpa in his meditation cave. The mother dreamed that Gendun Drubpa came to her, touched her stomach, and said, "A son will be born to you. You should call him Sang-gyey Pel, the Creator of Enlightened Beings, for this is the name by which the Buddhas of the ten directions and of the past, present, and future know him."

Over the weeks and months that followed, the mother repeatedly experienced auspicious dreams. On one occasion a Perfection of Wisdom Scripture (*Prajnaparamita Sutra*) appeared before her, transformed into light, and melted into her womb. On another, her husband appeared to her in her dream, constructed a Kalachakra mandala and offered it to her; it too dissolved into light and entered her womb. On a third occasion a thousand wisdom swords appeared to her and fell as droplets of light into her womb.

Gendun Drubpa himself appeared to her in her dreams on several occasions. On one of these he pronounced, "Your child bears the name Gendun Drubpa." On another he advised her, "This child of yours has the capacity to uphold the wisdom tradition of Nagarjuna and his disciples and also the vast bodhisattva activities tradition of Asanga and his disciples. Avoid carelessness during your pregnancy and always keep a pure mind. Soon every joy will be yours." She awoke immediately, feeling refreshed, light, joyous, and as though every physical discomfort had been lifted from her.

Yangpa Chojey also comments, "Throughout her pregnancy the mother continued her daily tantric practices of Guhyasamaja, Heruka Chakrasamvara, Yamantaka, and Kalachakra. Her meditations were characterized by an extraordinary clarity and spontaneity."

Shortly before the child's birth, the father dreamed of visiting a temple. When he arrived inside, he perceived Gendun Drubpa, sitting on a throne, reading the Kalachakra scripture entitled *The Stainless Light* (Skt., *Vimalaprabha*) and composing a commentary to it. "This suggests that the child will become especially renowned in the practice and teaching of the Kalachakra Tantra," he thought to himself. Gendun Drubpa turned to him and smiled.

The following night he again dreamed of Gendun Drubpa, sitting in meditation, holding a vajra and bell at his navel. Yangpa Chojey comments,

> Shortly after that the child took birth. It was the Fire Monkey Year (1475), the third day of the Month of Victory. The sky was clear and free from dust and mist. The sun was radiant, and a rainbow appeared over the house even though there were no clouds. The entire district was vibrant with an extraordinary light and brilliance. . . .Thus Avalokiteshvara took off his bodhisattva attire and descended into the ordinary world in order to fulfill the needs of living beings, leaving behind his exalted form as the Bodhisattva of Compassion and appearing as a conventional human being in accordance with the karmic tendencies and predispositions of those to be trained.

Yet the wonder child did not altogether leave behind his extraordinary form as a bodhisattva. As Yangpa Chojey points out, the new-born son carried all the signs of being a high incarnation: his eyes wide, clear and soft like those of an antelope; his hands visibly marked with auspicious lines, such as Dharma wheels and conch shells; and his fingers delicate, almost webbed in their beauty and subtlety. On his shoulders there were marks indicating extra sets of invisible arms with which he would work for the enlightenment of the world.

Yangpa Chojey concludes the chapter by saying,

> Immediately upon exiting from the womb the child looked around the room with clear eyes, acknowledging the presence of everyone there. He smiled, turned his radiant face in the direction of Tashi Lhunpo Monastery, placed his tiny hands together in prayer, and recited the mantra of Arya Tara, the mother of all the Buddhas.

In accordance with the dream prophecies that the parents had received they gave him the name Sanggyey Pel, Creator of Enlightened Beings. The father immediately performed numerous tantric rituals in order to stabilize the child's health and longevity and to facilitate the fulfillment of his potential destiny.

His Early Childhood

Not a lot is said in either the *Biography* or *Autobiography* about the child's first two years, other than that he showed none of the ordinary characteristics of an infant. As Yangpa Chojey puts it,

> He shunned ordinary childhood games and instead played at being a lama. He would sit on rocks shaped like teaching thrones and pretend to give discourses to imaginary multitudes and to give hand blessings to anyone who came into his presence. He would take clay and shape it into images of stupas and Buddhas or stack piles of pebbles into shapes of stupas and pretend to make offerings and prayers. This was before he even learned to speak. And when he did eventually speak, his first words were *om tare tuttare ture svaha*, the mantra of Arya Tara, the principal meditational deity of Gyalwa Gendun Drubpa (the First Dalai Lama).

Yangpa Chojey quotes the father as having once said to him,

> From his second or third year the boy frequently spoke to me of recollecting his previous lives and of his experiences in them. He showed no signs of an ordinary being, no matter if he was walking, sleeping, eating or whatever. . . . He never cried or misbehaved, and his body gave off only the sweetest of fragrances, even when he messed his pants. . . .

And he constantly recited the Tara mantra, even from his earliest days. . . . We always knew that we were in the presence of a great being and that we had a special responsibility to care for him well.

When the child was three years old he began to express the wish to return to Tashi Lhunpo. Generally he spoke in mystical verses, which were recorded by his mother. One such verse, sang when he was two, is as follows,

> This child cannot remain in this small house;
> Soon he must move to Tashi Lhunpo,
> For that is a more appropriate place for him.
> There he has a far sweeter tea to drink,
> And many monk disciples who await his return.
> Many images that he constructed sit in his temple
> And his dharma robes lie in storage for him.
> Take him there soon, that he may fulfill his destiny.

The father asked of him, "And who are you? What is your name?"

The boy replied in song,

> My name is Gendun Drubpa, the Sangha's great hope,
> Tara herself, mother of all Buddhas, witnessed my death,
> And from Tashi Lhunpo the monk Umdzey Sangtsulwa,
> An illustrious disciple of Gendun Drubpa,
> Will soon come to take me home.
>
> Tara advised me to incarnate in Dorjeden,
> And the protector spirit Mahakala accompanied me here.
> But now too much time has passed, and I must go
> To my monastery, Tashi Lhunpo, my destined home.

According to Yangpa Chojey's account in the *Biography*, it was the young Second Dalai Lama himself who described the death of the First Dalai Lama, his journey to Tushita in the afterlife, and the prophecy for him to take rebirth in Yolkar Dorjeden. He quotes the boy as having said to the parents when the latter was only two years old,

After my death I went to Tushita Pure Land. There I met with Maitreya, Nagarjuna, Asanga, Atisha, and Tsong-khapa. I asked them where I should reincarnate in order to continue my work. The Great Master took a flower and two hailstones, saying that I should take rebirth wherever they landed. One hailstone landed in Central Tibet and the other in Kham. The flower landed in Yolkar Dorjeden. Therefore I chose this place for my rebirth and you as my parents.

The *Biography* states that from the time the child could speak he constantly referred to Tashi Lhunpo. One day a group of monkeys came near the house. He called out to them, "Have you come from Tashi Lhunpo to take me home?" He would ask the same question of birds that came near to him.

Yangpa Chojey also points out that whenever the family went out to do rituals in nearby villages, the child would point at buildings and comment, "That looks like such-and-such a building in Tashi Lhunpo." Or he would say, "In Tashi Lhunpo there are many beautiful temples like that one." Often he would break out in song, describing the beauties of Tashi Lhunpo and the peace and quiet of his spiritual life there.

Once when the boy was three years old the family made a pilgrimage to some nearby temples. While the parents were making their devotions he wandered off and disappeared. They searched for him frantically, eventually discovering him sitting trance-like under a tree, his eyes gazing blankly at the sky. The area was as though bathed in rainbow light, and a small rainbow hovered above him. The parents sat quietly to the side, watching in wonder as the infant remained motionless. Eventually he rose from his trance and came over to them.

"What happened?" asked the father.

"Lama Tsongkhapa came and spoke to me," was the boy's reply.

"What is Tsongkhapa really like?" the father asked.

The boy described his vision, and then quoted a verse from *The Ornament of Mahayana Sutras* (Skt., *Mahayanasutra Alamkara*), even though he had never seen or heard the text before, which begins, "The spiritual master is at peace, gentle, quiet . . ."

One day when the family was visiting the temples at Shomolung, the child again went into a trance. When he emerged from it, he turned to his parents and said, "You know, I'm not really Sanggyey Pel. My actual name is Lama Drom. When I look into the sky I always see Avalokiteshvara, with Tara to his right and Sarasvati to his left. They talk to me continually and give me prophecies."

The father asked teasingly, "If that is the case, then how long will I live?"

"You will pass away in your seventy-second year," the boy replied.

Yangpa Chojey comments that indeed the prophecy came true. Kunga Gyaltsen lived and taught for many years to come, eventually passing away in his seventy-second year.

As stated by His Holiness in his Foreword, from childhood the Second Dalai Lama constantly and spontaneously composed mysti-cal songs and verses. Both the *Autobiography* and *Biography* mention many of them. Unfortunately most of these are referred to only by their opening syllables, which suggests that at one time there must have been a collection of them in print to which the reader could refer. This collection does not seem to have survived and is not included in his *Collected Works*.

A few of the verses, however, are quoted in their completeness. For example, one day when the boy was two years old he pretended to enact a mystical dance. In the middle of it he turned to his parents and sang,

This life is like a game that we play,
The objects of perception playthings in a dream.
Those who take them as real
Become lost in confusion.

The wise live in mindfulness of karma
They watch the white and black pebbles of action
And collect the white to build the foundations
Of their own happiness, freedom, and joy.

Even though the father is quoted earlier as saying that the child was a model of perfect behavior, it would appear that the mother did not always agree on this point and that several times in his young life he was disciplined by her. For example, the first poem in this collection of mystical songs and verses was composed after one such disciplinary action, when he was six years old. (This text is included in the main body of the present translation, and readers can refer to it there.)

Yangpa Chojey's *Biography* quotes several incidents of this nature. Thus it appears that the young lama in fact had something of a mischievous streak and that the role of disciplining him fell to his mother. On each occasion the boy responded with a song of indignation. One such incident took place when he was two years old. After his scolding (or spanking, the text does not say which), he came to his mother and sang,

> Mother, do not rebuke me, but instead pray to me.
> There are many beings who even now send me their
>   prayers.
> To rebuke me is but negative karma at play;
> To pray to me plants the seeds of liberation.

On another occasion when his mother disciplined him he sang,

> O mother, take heed how you treat me,
> For this child is not long at your side.
> Soon I will return to Tashi Lhunpo, my monastery,
> For there a house filled with joy awaits me
> And I have many joyous things to enjoy.

The second of these verses, also sung when he was two years old, is another reference to his being a reincarnation of the First Dalai Lama. It is often quoted in Tibetan historical literature to illustrate how from childhood he clearly remembered his previous life as Gyalwa Gendun Drubpa.

As the present Dalai Lama mentioned in his Foreword, a number of his childhood verses and songs were also of a prophetic nature, speaking of events to come in the lives of the later Dalai Lamas. One of these prophecies is found in the first entry in the present volume of mystical songs. In it he first admonishes his parents for punishing him for his actions and then delivers a prophecy concerning the Dalai Lama incarnations,

> The living beings, confused by their karmic instincts,
> Look down on and abuse the enlightened beings.
> Thus they fall into the lower realms of samsara.
> They (my parents) scold me with a seemingly good
>   intention,

But it only brings them negative karma of speech;
They would be better to see me as their crown jewel,
For then their wishes would be fulfilled like falling rain.

Acquiring (as a son) a holy being, like the Panchen
   (Gendun Drubpa)
Is as rare as finding a wish-fulfilling gem.
They should meditate (on me) as being Buddha Vajradhara.

Although he (the First Dalai Lama) completely flooded
This world with the sublime nectars of Dharma,
He did not complete all of his plans.
Therefore for seven incarnations he will come
To work for the living beings of this world
Before merging into the stainless *dharmadhatu*.
The fortunate beings who train under him
Will surely take rebirth in the Pure Land of Joy.

Yangpa Chojey quotes this song in full in his *Biography* and makes a number of interesting comments about it. According to him, the line "Therefore for seven incarnations he will come" is a reference to a passage in the early Kadampa classic *Father Dharmas Son Dharmas* (Tib., *Pha-chos-bu-chos*), in which the Dalai Lamas are prophesied. Readers may remember that I referred to this book in an earlier section in connection with its stories of the previous lives of Lama Drom Tonpa, a predecessor to the Dalai Lama incarnations.

In fact, as Yangpa Chojey points out, all of the first seven Dalai Lamas are prophesied in *Father Dharmas Son Dharmas*. He goes on to quote the verse in the *Father Dharmas Son Dharmas* related to the Second Dalai Lama's coming and explains how it is interpreted as prophecy,

Relying on various mystical means
He will come in successive incarnations
For as long as the doctrine does not decline,
And not allow a break in work begun long before.
From Rasa to Radeng he will go,
And spread a garland of magnificent lotuses.
He will be known as an emanation of Lama Drom Tonpa,
And will elucidate the meaning of the secret yogas.

The interpretation of this verse as given by Yangpa Chojey is that the spiritual being known as Tongwa Donden, "He Meaningful to Behold," will work for seven incarnations to ensure that the Kadampa doctrines brought to Tibet by Jowo Atisha will be firmly planted in the Tibetan spiritual world. The later incarnation (the Second Dalai Lama) will carry on the work of the former (the First Dalai Lama), and thus what was "begun long ago" by the First will not become broken; in other words, the legacy will be continued. Rasa refers to the temple at Lhasa, and Redeng refers to the Kadampa monastery near Lhasa where the Second Dalai Lama would spend considerable time and would experience numerous visions. The word "lotuses" refers to flowers and is a prophecy of the Second Dalai Lama's establishment of Chokhor Gyal Monastery at Metoktang, "The Flower Meadow," above the Lhamoi Lhatso, or Lake of Visions. All future incarnations would be connected with this monastery and would be found by relying on signs from the Lake of Visions.

Be all this as it may, it is clear from the *Biography* that the child regarded himself as one of great destiny, at least as far as his biographers are concerned. Throughout his childhood he continued to experience trances and visions, most frequently triggered by natural phenomenon. For example, one day during a thunderstorm he spontaneously entered a paranormal state. When he emerged some hours later he commented, "The sound of thunder is the closest thing to the voice of Lama Tsongkhapa that I have ever heard. Whenever I hear thunder it always carries me back to the time (in my previous life as Gendun Drubpa) that I sat at his feet and listened to his thunderous voice."

Although the young Second Dalai Lama seems to have been completely aware of his status and station as a reincarnation of the First Dalai Lama, he nonetheless developed a very strong guru-disciple relationship with his father, who was a great lama in his own right. Between the ages of four and eleven, he received numerous teachings and tantric initiations from him, including all of the traditional family lineages.

Almost from the time the boy could walk he accompanied his father everywhere, sitting through sessions of meditation and the performance of tantric rituals. He also sat through the numerous teaching and initiation sessions that his father delivered on various occasions to the general public and to private disciples.

Formally his education began with learning to read and write and with a study of the classic *A Guide to the Bodhisattva Ways* (Skt., *Bodhisattva-charya-avatara;* Tib., *Byang-chub-sems-dpa'-spyod-pa-la-'jug-pa*) by Acharya Shantideva, a sixth-century Indian master. (Interestingly enough, this work remains the favorite of the present Dalai Lama, who has taught it publicly as a preliminary to giving tantric initiations on more than a dozen occasions.) His father then gave him fundamental Gelugpa oral traditions such as the *Lam Rim* and *Lojong* systems of contemplative meditation and other lineages that he had received from the First Dalai Lama.

His father, however, was primarily a tantric master, and therefore, most of what he received from him was of a tantric nature. The initiations began with lower tantric traditions such as Avalokiteshvara, Tara, Amitayus, and so forth, together with the mantras associated with these and a basic instruction on the meditative techniques to be applied in mantra recitation. He would frequently join his father in short meditation retreats. The *Biography* informs us that during these initiation ceremonies the child experienced countless mystical visions.

Later, from the age of six or so, he was given various initiations into the highest yoga tantra systems, especially Vajravarahi (of the Heruka Chakrasamvara cycle), together with various Dharmapala empowerments, such as Mahakala. He was expected to memorize the ritual texts *(sadhanas)* associated with these tantric deities and to recite them daily. In particular, the father paid special attention to giving him the Shijey transmissions of *Chod* practice, based on the mandala of white Vajrayogini.

Also given with special care were the teachings and initiations of the traditions known as "The Six Yogas of Naropa" and "The Six Yogas of Niguma." Although the Second Dalai Lama received a symbolic transmission of these when only four years old, the actual study and practice of them did not begin until he was eight. The Six Yogas of Niguma had been in the family for generations and represented the heart of the family's involvement with the Shangpa Kargyu school. These yogas obviously agreed with the Second Dalai Lama's own predisposition, and later in his life he frequently taught them and also wrote two commentaries to them.

Other important lineages received from his father when the boy was nine years old were the Six Yogas of Sukhasiddhi, the Dvakpo and Shangpa Kargyu traditions of *mahamudra*, and the principal *Lamdrey* teachings of the Sakya school.

That the Second Dalai Lama both loved and highly respected his father is evident from the *Autobiography*. Many years later, when his father passed away, he composed a lengthy biographical poem of him to express this devotion. The father certainly also appreciated the son and gave him the secret tantric name Shepai Dorjey, or "Laughing Vajra." (It is this name that the Second Dalai Lama uses for himself in several of his poems, prefixing it with "Yangchen," the epithet of the deity of music, song, and poetry.)

In many ways the story of his visit to the meditation hut of his aged grandmother, which I quoted earlier from his *Autobiography*, quite typifies the relationship of father and son. Kunga Gyaltsen was a guru to him but in many respects always treated him more as an equal. Until the boy entered Tashi Lhunpo Monastery, the two were inseparable, and the father took him along wherever he went, whether it was to give a teaching or initiation, perform a tantric ritual for a patron's benefit, or visit a disciple in a meditation hut or cave.

As the Second states in his *Autobiography*,

> In the early part of my training my father served as my principal spiritual guide. In the middle of my training, this role was enacted by the abbot Jamyang Lekpa Chojor of Drepung Loseling. Then in the completion of my training the most important teacher to me was Khedrup Norzang Gyatso.

Recognition as the First
Dalai Lama's Reincarnation

As stated above, even before the Second Dalai Lama was conceived, his parents experienced prophetic dreams indicating that they would soon have a child who would be the reincarnation of Gendun Drubpa, the First Dalai Lama. Then during the pregnancy, they received many more dream visions indicating that the prophecies were about to be fulfilled.

Moreover, from the time the young child learned to speak, he frequently and clearly announced that he considered himself to be Gendun Drubpa's reincarnation, doing so in spontaneously composed songs and also by describing his memories, dreams, and visions to his parents.

Nevertheless no action was taken on the matter for some years, for a number of reasons. One of these seems to be that the topic of *tulkus*, or "officially recognized reincarnations," was somewhat controversial in the newly formed Gelugpa school of Lama Tsongkhapa. Although most of the older schools of Tibetan Buddhism had for some centuries maintained the tradition of official reincarnates, Tsongkhapa does not seem to have cared much for it. He did not speak out against it, but it also seems that he didn't encourage it. For example, he did not establish an official reincarnate office for himself nor did any of his four chief disciples: Gyaltsepjey, Khedrupjey, Sherab Sengey, and Jamyang Chojey Tashi Palden.

Thus it seems that in the Gelug school a famous lama such as the First Dalai Lama could informally be thought of as a reincarnation of Lama Drom, yet no special fuss would be made over him for it. The situation was strikingly different from that in some of the older schools, where anyone officially recognized as a reincarnation of a famous lama would actually inherit the houses, possessions, and so forth of the predecessor (or predecessors). In other words, the *Labrang*, or "estate" of the previous incarnation would pass to the child recognized as the reincarnation and not become the common property of the monastic community.

My feeling is that Tsongkhapa was not completely comfortable with bringing the tulku legacy into the Gelug school because in some ways the tradition contradicts the *vinaya*, or fundamental monastic code of discipline as outlined by the Buddha himself. According to the vinaya, monks are discouraged from owning personal property. At their death, their robes and other belongings are distributed among the community. In contrast to this, the incarnate lamas built up large estates from lifetime to lifetime; at the death of one in the line, a large portion of his or her accumulated property was kept in trust for the child to be recognized as the reincarnation.

Moreover, tulkus were a Tibetan creation, and Tsongkhapa seems to have wanted his school to follow the central guidelines of Buddhist India, modeling itself on monasteries such as Nalanda, Vikramashila, and Odantapuri. He also modeled the Gelugpa on the older Kadampa school that had been established by Jowo Atisha and Lama Drom Tonpa, and the Kadampa had not endorsed the tulku tradition within its monasteries. The Gelugpa essentially were "New Kadampas."

My reading of the situation is that the First Dalai Lama was aware of Tsongkhapa's discomfort with having Gelugpa tulkus but decided that the latter's decision was impractical in the Tibetan environment. Even given all the faults and complications of the system, Tibetans generally loved their tulkus more than they did the ordinary monks, even if some of those monks were great saints and scholars, and some of the tulkus were rascals. If the newly established Gelugpa school was to compete with the other sects on an equal footing, it would have to recognize and incorporate tulkus. Thus when the First Dalai Lama passed away, he determined to reincarnate as the Second and to claim his rightful position as the embodiment of the First.

Be this as it may, when the Second Dalai Lama was three years old, rumors of the unusual signs surrounding his birth and personage began to circulate to the extent that they could not be ignored. As the *Biography* comments,

At that time, when the boy was in his fourth year (i.e., when he was three years old), there was much talk that Omniscient Gendun Drubpa had taken birth in Tanak Dorjeden. This was intensified when the great master Chojor Palzang, a disciple of Gendun Drubpa, experienced a dream vision in which he was told, "Of all wonders in the world, the rebirth of omniscient Gendun Drubpa stands supreme. That great wonder, the reincarnation of Tongwa Donden, 'He Meaningful to Behold,' is among us now. . . ."

Chojor Palzang could not contain his curiosity and made the journey to Yolkar Dorjeden to see the child for himself. He was profoundly impressed by him, and asked many questions of the parents. . . .

That night he dreamed he heard a voice resonate from the sky, telling him, "Fulfill the wishes of the Buddhas." He was convinced that this was a sign admonishing him to report his meeting with the boy and the auspicious omens surrounding the birth to the authorities at Tashi Lhunpo.

As a consequence, Chojor Palzang soon returned to Dorjeden with a delegation from the monastery, including various disciples of the previous Dalai Lama. The child instantly recognized them, calling them by name and embracing them as old friends. They requested him to give them a symbolic transmission of the Dharma, which he did. The *Biography* comments, "The group was so moved by the child's words that throughout the entire event there was a continual stream of tears in the room."[5]

The following year he made an informal visit to Tashi Lhunpo. Here he instantly recognized all of his previous disciples, calling them by name without being introduced. He also recollected all the favorite places in the monastery frequented by his predecessor and made comments like, "In my previous life I would often come here for quiet meditation," and "It was on this throne that I gave such-and-such a teaching." The *Biography* states, "In this way he impressed the Tashi Lhunpo monks with his authenticity."

Nonetheless he did not enter the monastery at that time. The elders thought he was still too young and recommended that he remain in training under his father for some years.

He visited the monastery again in his eighth year. On this occasion he made the traditional tea offering and received the introductory ordination (Tib., *rab-'byung*).

News of the child spread like wildfire throughout southwestern Tibet, and Yolkar Dorjeden became a hub of activity as visitors came from far and wide to receive his blessings. One of the most prestigious of these visitors was Lobzang Rabten, the king of Gugey, western Tibet, who had been a close disciple and strong patron of the First Dalai Lama and had contributed much of the necessary funds for the construction of Tashi Lhunpo Monastery. When he arrived in the presence of the child, the two instantly recognized one another. The king broke out in tears and offered the following song to the child,

> In the lotus garden of the Buddhadharma
> The full moon of spring shone bright
> When Panchen Gendun Drubpa walked this earth;
> But then he left us for the western paradise.
>
> Yet it seems he could not bear to witness
> The withering of the lotus garden in Tibet;
> Thus a new moon is with us now,
> Radiant with the lights of compassion and knowledge.

The Second Dalai Lama responded with a song to the king, although unfortunately this was not recorded. He then gave him a symbolic teaching, and his father conferred the tantric empowerment of Mahakala. The *Biography* adds, "When the offerings to the Dharma Protectors were taken outside, they spontaneously flew off into the sky and disappeared. This and many other auspicious omens occurred."

That year the Tashi Lhunpo authorities began to press requests upon him to take up residence in the monastery. He agreed to come the following spring. Thus he arrived in the spring of the Fire Horse Year (1487), escorted with great regalia by high lamas and abbots of numerous monasteries, and was installed as the reincarnation of Tamchey Khyenpa Gendun Drubpa.

His Holiness the present Dalai Lama succinctly sums up the situation,

The tradition of "a Dalai Lama *tulku*," or "official Dalai Lama reincarnation office," seems to have spontaneously evolved from the Second's life and activities. For example, from his childhood all signs indicated that he was the authentic reincarnation of the First Dalai Lama. There was no formal search for the reincarnation of the First Dalai Lama, as became the case with subsequent Dalai Lamas. Rather, as a young boy the Second simply presented himself as the First's reincarnation and, because the signs were convincing, he came to be accepted as such.

A Young Monk in Tashi Lhunpo Monastery

The young Dalai Lama's new life in Tashi Lhunpo began with the taking of the prenovice ordination of a monk (Tib., *genyen;* spelled *dGe-bsnyen*). An auspicious day was chosen for the event: the fourth day of the sixth Tibetan month, being the annual day in commemoration of Buddha's first teaching in India almost twenty centuries earlier. This ordination was enacted in a grand ceremony, with the Tashi Lhunpo abbot, Panchen Lungrig Gyatso, leading the rites. As the *Autobiography* puts it,

> On this occasion my long hair was shaved from my head, and I put on the robes of a monk, the victory banners of the Buddhadharma.

With monastic ordination came a new name: Gendun Gyatso Palzangpo, which means "Sublimely Glorious Sangha Ocean," or "Sublimely Glorious Ocean (fulfilling the way) of Spiritual Aspirants." It is this name that was to remain with him throughout his life and with which he was to sign most of the books that he composed in later years.

Some months after this he took the ordination of a novice monk (Tib., *Getsul;* spelled *dGe-tshul*). The abbot of Nenying Monastery, who had been a close disciple of the First Dalai Lama, was invited to Tashi Lhunpo to preside over the ceremony. The Tashi Lhunpo abbot, Panchen Lung-rig Gyatso, assisted as *acharya;* Umdzey Sang-tsulwa participated as the timekeeper. This last name is significant. Readers will recognize it from a verse of prophecy quoted earlier, that the Second Dalai Lama had sung when he was three years old.

> My name is Gendun Drubpa, the Sangha's great hope,
> Tara herself, mother of all Buddhas, witnessed my death,
> And from Tashi Lhunpo the monk Umdzey Sangtsulwa,
> An illustrious disciple of Gendun Drubpa,
> Will soon come to take me home.

In fact Umdzey Sangtsulwa (an abbreviation of the name Umdzey Sanggyey Tsultrimpa, which translates as "Ceremonial Master Buddha Discipline") was among the party that had come to escort him from his home to Tashi Lhunpo when he entered into the monastery, thus fulfilling the child's prophecy. Here we see him assisting in the novice ordination of the young reincarnation. (*Umdzey*, by the way, is a title, meaning "chief chant master" or "master of ceremonies." In Gelugpa monasteries this position is second only to that of the abbot.)

In Tashi Lhunpo the young monk's life mostly revolved around studies, memorization of texts, debate, and participation in temple assemblies in which scriptures and prayers would be chanted. These activities were punctuated by the occasional brief meditational retreat, usually of a week or two in duration.

He seems to have followed much the same curriculum as his classmates, beginning with a study of Buddhist psychology (Tib., *bLo-rig*) and basic logic techniques (Tib., *rTags-rig*). After this was completed, he was allowed to go on successively to the first three of the five principal Indian Buddhist treatises: *The Ornament of Clear Understanding* (Skt., *Abhisamaya-alamkara*; Tib., *dNgon-rtogs-rgyan*) by Maitreya-Asanga; *A Guide to the Middle View* (Skt., *Madhayamaka-avatara*; Tib., *dBu-ma-la-'jug-pa*) by Chandrakiriti; and *Analysis of Valid Inquiry* (Skt., *Pramanavartikka*; Tib., *Tshad-ma-rnam-'grel*) by

Acharya Dharmakirti. (The remaining two Indian classics that make up the course of studies in the principal Gelugpa monasteries—*A Treasury of Knowledge* [Skt., *Abhidharmakosha*; Tib., *dNgon-par-mdzod*] and *The Treatise on Vinaya* [Skt., *Vinayashastra*; Tib., *'Dul-bai-bstan-bcos*], would have to wait until he was older.)

While resident at Tashi Lhunpo, he also continued his tantric studies. He often would travel to Nartang Monastery and spend intense periods there with the abbot. From this master he received the complete initiation into the system of the Kalachakra Tantra, as well as an extensive commentary to Tsongkhapa's *Ngakrim Chenmo* (spelled *sNags-rim-chen-mo*), or *Detailed Guide to the Buddhist Tantras*. He also received initiation into the Hevajra Tantra, together with the commentaries to the generation and completion stage yogas. In addition, the Nartang abbot gave him a complete oral transmission of the collected writings of the First Dalai Lama. The Second Dalai Lama also made numerous visits to the abbot of Nenying Monastery and received many transmissions and spiritual teachings from him.

When he was thirteen years of age a messenger arrived to inform him that his mother was critically ill. He rushed to Yolkar Dorjeden to be with her. What ensued was quite characteristic of the family in which he had been raised.

"There is no need to try and do anything for me," she calmly informed him. "Nothing will be of any avail. I have experienced repeated dreams of the complete mandalas of body, speech, and mind of the Kalachakra Tantra. In my dreams these mandalas dissolved from the outside into the center and then into me. The meaning is that I will pass away within fifteen days." Yangpa Chojey's *Biography* comments, "Indeed, she passed away thirteen days later, with many wondrous omens occurring as indications of her high state of spiritual accomplishment."

In accordance with tradition the family had her body cut into pieces and fed to the birds as a final act of generosity on her behalf. When the flesh was cleaned from the skull, they noticed that it was the color of pure pearl and that the inside of it bore a clear impression of Heruka Chakrasamvara. The young Dalai Lama kept this skull with him as a reminder of impermanence and of the great yogini that had been his mother. Years later, when he constructed Chokhor Gyal Monastery at Metoktang, he placed the skull there as a relic so that it would continue to be a source of spiritual inspiration to future generations.[6]

Not long after the Second Dalai Lama entered Tashi Lhunpo Monastery, the abbot Panchen Lungrik Gyatso retired and entered into solitary retreat in order to practice meditation. He was succeeded by Panchen Yeshey Tsemo. The Second Dalai Lama intensely admired the new abbot and received numerous teachings and initiations from him. Panchen Yeshey Tsemo had been a close disciple of the First Dalai Lama and showed great respect to the young reincarnation. In particular, Yeshey Tsemo gave him transmissions of all the fundamental scriptural traditions coming from Jowo Atisha together with the oral traditions; the principal lineages coming from the First Dalai Lama and his disciples; the commentaries of Heruka Chakrasamvara and Hevajra as transmitted by Tsongkhapa and his chief disciples; and many other lineages.

From Panchen Yeshey Tsemo he also received numerous Manjushri initiations and entered into retreat to complete the recitation of the mantras. The *Biography* states, "During this retreat he experienced numerous visions, and his karmic memories were stimulated to the point that he clearly recollected hundreds of his previous lives. . . . His memory became so enhanced that thereafter he was able to memorize a hundred lines of scripture in the time period of a single tea break." Yangpa Chojey's account thus hints that the young monk's insights at this time could be regarded as a mini-enlightenment experience.

He comes back to the subject later, in Chapter Seven of the *Biography.* Here he relates that in the Water Boar Year (1503), when the Second Dalai Lama was only twenty-eight, his guru Jamyang Lekpai Chojor and several other high lamas requested him to write a commentary to the *Manjushri-nama-samgiti,* or *Song of the Names of Manjushri,* that would bring together the central concepts of the tantric systems of Guhyasamaja and Kalachakra, both of which are extremely sophisticated highest yoga tantra systems. This commentary, they said, should reveal the differences between these two most subtle systems, as well as their points of convergence, while showing the different ways in which the two use technical terminology, especially fundamental tantric terms such as "the wisdom of bliss born together with voidness" and "the great unchanging bliss." Moreover, this monumental task should be accomplished within the framework of a commentary to the *Manjushri-nama-samgiti*.

Yangpa Chojey then asks, "How could a monk of such a tender age be expected to fulfill a request demanding such a high level of insight and understanding?" He answers the question himself,

> When he was only sixteen years of age he had made a meditation retreat focusing upon Manjushri, the Bodhisattva of Wisdom. One morning during this retreat his karmic memories were stimulated to the point that suddenly he remembered hundreds upon hundreds of his past lives.
>
> From that time onward he could comprehend the most subtle and profound teaching just by hearing it once.

If this was his great enlightenment, then the immediate years that followed were mere dramas enacted in order to project a semblance of conventionality.

Later that year he experienced a powerful dream vision that was to affect him strongly. A young naked girl came to him in his dream, holding a wisdom sword, a scripture, and a mirror. She invited him to look into the mirror, and when he did this he fell into vision upon vision and received hundreds of prophecies concerning his life's work. When he awoke he wrote numerous mystical songs and hymns, and from that time onward began to compose verse works, hymns, and prayers almost daily.

Expelled from Tashi Lhunpo

In the Water Mouse Year (1492), various invitations to teach began to come to him from nearby monasteries and hermitages where his predecessor the First Dalai Lama had frequently taught. He felt that perhaps it was time for him to begin serving the community in this way.

First he visited Nenying Monastery, where thousands of people had gathered from upper and lower Nyang to hear him speak. Both the abbot Nenying Yangpal Nyingpo and the great scholar-saint Jey Monlampal attended his teachings and initiations and later led an elaborate ceremony dedicated to his long life. At this ceremony they all, even the seniormost monks, offered many prostrations and hymns of praise to him.

After this he was invited to Palkhor Dechen Monastery, where he taught the monastic community; and to Drong Tsey, where he gave Guru Rinpochey initiations and a discourse on the Six Yogas of Niguma. Again, he was shown the greatest respect. Thus he traveled from one region to another for some weeks, teaching and giving initiations as he went.

Meanwhile back at Tashi Lhunpo a storm was brewing, and the stage was being set for his expulsion from the monastery. Yangpa Chojey in the *Biography* gives three quite different explanations—outer, inner, and secret—of how and why this occurred.

The outer interpretation is simply that the managers in the abbot's office became jealous of the increasing respect and honor that was being showered upon the Second Dalai Lama. They feared that the young reincarnate lama might soon displace the abbot as the Tashi Lhunpo head, which would have the effect of demoting them in status and stripping them of some of their privileges.

The inner interpretation is that Nenying Monastery was located in the vicinity of a malicious *gyalpo* spirit, and that the young Second Dalai Lama somehow invoked the spirit's wrath, thus bringing a hindrance upon himself. The events that followed were the result.

The secret interpretation is that the entire sequence of events was a mystical drama consciously enacted by the abbot Panchen Yeshey Tsemo, in order to push the young Dalai Lama out of his comfortable life in Tashi Lhunpo and help him fulfill a greater destiny.

In the *Biography* Yangpa Chojey presents each of these in turn. Concerning the first of them he states,

> At that time (when the Dalai Lama was on his teaching tour), the great benefits that the young bodhisattva was accomplishing caused the demon of bitter jealousy to enter into the hearts of several influential monks in the office of the Tashi Lhunpo abbot, Panchen Yeshey Tsemo. They became as though drunk with envy and paranoia and began

repeatedly to say many untrue and unpleasant things to the abbot about the master. In this way they managed to slowly cause the elderly abbot to seem displeased with him.

Concerning the second interpretation, which was that the Second Dalai Lama had incurred the wrath of the Nenying *gyalpo* spirit, Yangpa Chojey points out that the same problem had occurred for the First Dalai Lama when he had visited Nenying Monastery with his guru Jey Sherab Sengey, and that as a result the latter had become so ill that he almost died. Only the performance of numerous tantric rituals managed to turn away the *gyalpo's* curse. Now the Nenying *gyalpo* spirit was continuing his negative efforts by attacking the First's reincarnation.

The Second Dalai Lama in his *Autobiography* tells of dreams that he had experienced on the matter and comments that in some ways the problem was of his own making. He writes,

> Previously when I had been teaching in Nenying Monastery I had experienced a dream vision in which a mystical girl appeared to me and said, "In degenerate times it is easy for evil *gyalpo* spirits to make hindrances. At such a time you should rely upon the tantric practices of Hayagriva." I knew at the time that I should immediately enter into retreat and meditate in conjunction with recitation of the Hayagriva mantra, but unfortunately did not find time to do so. . . .
>
> In fact Panchen Yeshey Tsemo had earlier given me much the same advice himself.

The third interpretation is presented as follows by Yangpa Chojey,

> We can look at these events as having been produced by jealousy on the part of certain administrators in the abbot's office, perhaps with this negative energy having been aroused by a curse of the Nenying *gyalpo* spirit. But this is not the real story.
>
> In fact these events were all part of a mystical drama. What really happened is that the young reincarnate had a great destiny to fulfill for the peoples of Central and Eastern Tibet, and that he could not do so by remaining in Tashi Lhunpo.

Panchen Yeshey Tsemo understood this, and thus showed a wrathful countenance toward our master in order to push him toward the fulfillment of that destiny.

This is clearly indicated by something my guru Jetsun Chokyi Gyaltsen told me. He said that when the Panchen was residing at Nenying Monastery some months before all these events transpired, he remarked to certain of the elders there, "I have clearly seen in dream visions that the boy is without doubt the reincarnation of our guru Jey Tamchey Khyenpa, the omniscient Gendun Drubpa. Soon he must go to Central Tibet so that he can accomplish the higher works for which he is destined."

Thus it is clear that the great teachers function in mysterious ways for the benefit of living beings and on levels that cannot be fathomed by the conventional intellect.

In fact most clairvoyants say that Panchen Yeshey Tsemo was in no way an ordinary lama and that he was a reincarnation of the illustrious yogi Khuton Chenpo.[7]

Whatever were the motives and perceptions of the peoples involved, the young Dalai Lama arrived back at Tashi Lhunpo to be met by a strained atmosphere. He attempted to ignore it and to continue his studies as usual but met with little success. The monastic administrators hindered him wherever they could. [8] However, the *Autobiography* relates that the master appreciated the delicate nature of the situation. Panchen Yeshey Tsemo was one of his most important spiritual mentors, and thus he, as a disciple, was under a commitment to see his teacher's every action as a teaching,

Throughout these events I always from my side maintained the perception of the Panchen as an embodiment of the Buddhas and cultivated guruyoga toward him in both thought and action, for I had received many teachings and initiations from him. I meditated upon the manner in which the great practitioners of the past had dealt with their teachers, taking as my examples Milarepa's attitude toward his wrathful guru Marpa and Lama Drom Tonpa's relationship with the great guru Jowo Atisha, as described in the biographies of these masters.

Nonetheless, eventually the thought arose within me

that perhaps the time had come for me to leave Tashi Lhunpo for awhile.

Many of the monastic elders were caught in the middle of the conflict. They sympathized with the young reincarnate, but on the other hand, the power of monastic administration lay in the hands of the abbot's secretariat. They held council and advised the young monk that it may be wise for him to leave for awhile.

Coincidentally, just as all this was happening a letter arrived from the renowned lama Jamyang Lekpa Chojorpa, abbot of Drepung Loseling Monastery, Lhasa, requesting the Second Dalai Lama to come to central Tibet. In fact the invitation harmonized with his own ambitions; for some time he had harbored the wish to move to the great monastic universities of central Tibet in order to complete his education. He writes in his *Autobiography*, "Previously the great master Jey Monlampal of Nenying Monastery had invited me to travel with him to Lhasa, but at that time the Tashi Lhunpo elders would not grant me permission to accompany him. Now they were pushing me in that direction. It was a somewhat confusing situation."

However, he did not wish to leave Tashi Lhunpo under negative circumstances. Thus he remained throughout the autumn and winter, attempting to smooth matters with the abbot's office. The new year came and went, with no improvement in the state of affairs. Consequently in the second month of the Wood Tiger Year (late spring, 1494) he went to the abbot and offered parting prostrations.

Yangpa Chojey concludes the chapter in the *Biography* with several rather touching songs that the Second Dalai Lama's students and devotees sang to him, requesting him not to leave them and the songs that he sang back in response. One of the most touching of these is voiced by Solpon Dolma, an old monk who had been a disciple of the First Dalai Lama and had been in charge of the Second's welfare since the entrance of the latter into Tashi Lhunpo almost a decade earlier. Here are a few verses from the Second Dalai Lama's song of parting advice to them,

> Friends and students, there is no need for tears,
> For I go only a short distance away,
> To Drepung Monastery, to fulfill my destiny

By studying with the great lama Jamyang Lekpa Chojor,
A spiritual son of Buddha Maitreya himself,
And a master with whom I have ancient karmic links. . . .

Whatever comes together one day must part;
At the end of every sowing comes the harvest
And then the process of recycling.
This is the law of nature. . . .

Remember that life is unstable and quickly changes,
Like the weather in the midst of a lightning storm.
Therefore make firm the powers of your mind,
The only friend that always accompanies you,
By enriching it with the jewels
Of a generous spirit and inner self-discipline. . . .

Remember that the traces of one's every action
Follow the mind like the shadow the body.
Thus always avoid the ways of negativity
And cultivate the spirit of creative goodness;
Keep your eyes fixed on things that benefit forever. . . .

This, my friends, is my parting advice.
Follow it as a reminder of me,
And soon we will meet again.

A Student in Drepung Monastery

Thus in the second month of the
Tiger Year (1494) the Second Dalai Lama left Tashi Lhunpo for
central Tibet. Jampal Drakpa asked to travel with him as attendant;
Rabjampa Darma requested to come as escort and guide. The three

made their way to Langbu, where the Langbu chieftain Nangso Luwangpa, the Second Dalai Lama's principal sponsor, outfitted them with the horses, mules, and supplies required for the journey, and they immediately set off for Lhasa.

That night in Lhasa, Lama Jamyang Lekpai Chojor of Drepung Loseling Monastery dreamed that a sunball arose from the west, filled his room and from there flooded throughout the Land of Snows, until all darkness was dispelled. "Soon my greatest disciple will come to me," he said. Shortly thereafter the Second Dalai Lama arrived in Lhasa and presented himself to Jamyang Lekpai Chojor with the request to be accepted as a student. As the *Biography* puts it, "He then embarked upon an intense course of traditional studies, in order to set an example for future generations." Over the next three years he systematically reviewed everything he had studied in Tashi Lhunpo and completed his higher philosophic training under Jamyang Lekpai Chojor.

Some of the materials included in the list of classical Indian philosophical texts that he read with this great master are as follows: Acharya Nagarjuna's *Fundamental Treatise on Wisdom* (Skt., *Mula-prajna-madhyamaka-karika-shastra*; Tib., *rTsa-bai-shes-rab*); Acharya Chandrakirti's *A Guide to the Middle View* (Skt., *Mad-hyamaka-avatara*; Tib., *dBu-ma-la-'jug-pa*); Acharya Dharmakirti's *Analysis of Valid Inquiry* (Skt., *Pramana-varttika*; Tib., *Tshed-ma-rnam-'grel*); Acharya Vasubandhu's *Treasury of Abhidharma* (Skt., *Abhi-dharmakosha*; Tib., *dNon-par-mdzod*); Gunaprabha's *Treatise on Discipline* (Skt., *Vinaya-shastra*; Tib., *'Dul-bai-bstan-bcos*); Maitreya/ Asanga's *Ornament of Mahayana Sutras* (Skt., *Mahayana-sutra-alamkara*; Tib., *mDo-sde-rgyen*); Maitreya/Asanga's *The Peerless Stream* (Skt., *Uttaratantra*; Tib., *rGyud-bla-ma*); and Maitreya/ Asanga's two texts known as *The Differentiatings* (Skt., *Vibangha*; Tib., *'Byed-rnam*). These he read together with both Indian and Tibetan commentaries, thus getting at the heart of their meanings. He also read numerous standard Tibetan philosophical texts, such as Lama Tsongkhapa's *Figurative and Direct Philosophical Presentations: The Essence of Sublime Teachings* (Tib., *Drang-nges-legs-bshad-snying-po*), and his *A Detailed Guide to the Stages on the Tantric Path* (Tib., *sNgags-rim-chen-mo*).

From Jamyang Lekpai Chojor he received initiation into the two principal mainstream highest yoga tantra systems, Guhyasamaja and Heruka Chakrasamvara, together with all the standard Indian and Tibetan tantric commentaries to the philosophy and yogas of these traditions. In addition, under this illustrious master he reviewed the principal commentaries to the Kalachakra tantric system, as well as those to the Six Yogas of Naropa. In this way in three years he accomplished the studies that ordinary monks of the monastery would be expected to take twenty to complete.

In the Wood Hare Year (1495), the Nenying abbot was invited to Drepung to preside over his *bikkshu* ordination ceremony. He was in his twenty-first year, this being the minimum age at which this level of ordination can be given. His Drepung Loseling guru, Jamyang Lekpai Chojor, acted as the ordaining *acharya*. It was the eighth day of the second month, the annual day in commemoration of Buddha's performance of fifteen days of miracles in India almost two thousand years earlier.

As an auspicious connection, immediately after his full ordination he read the Indian master Acharya Shantideva's two great practice classics with Jamyang Lekpai Chojor: *A Guide to the Bodhisattva Ways* (Skt., *Bodhisattva-charya-avatara*; Tib., *Byang-chub-sems-dpa'i-spyod-pa-la-'jug-pa*); and *A Compendium of Bodhisattva Trainings* (Skt., *Shiksha-samuccha*; Tib., *bsLab-bsdus*). He also received initiation into and teachings on the practice of all the tantric systems classified as kriya, charya, and yoga. Yangpa Chojey comments, "In brief, whatever lineages Jamyang Lekpai Chojor held, all of these without exception were transmitted to the young disciple, like pouring nectar from one vessel into another."

His studies were now quite complete, and the young Dalai Lama turned his mind to making pilgrimage to the major holy places of central Tibet in order to practice the essence of meditation in them.

A Young Lama on the Road

During his three-year study in Drepung, the Second Dalai Lama had visited the major temples and monasteries in the Lhasa area, such as the Jokang, Tibet's oldest and holiest temple. Other than this, however, he stayed almost constantly in the monastery, absorbed in his studies and meditations.

In the Wood Hare Year (1445), he and his teacher Jamyang Lekpai Chojor made pilgrimage to Radeng Monastery, a site made holy by Atisha and Lama Drom. The *Biography* informs us that on the night before his arrival, the Radeng lama Pakpa Kunga Gyaltsen experienced a dream vision in which a young girl appeared to him and said, "Tomorrow Lama Drom Tonpa himself will visit."[9] The lama placed two hundred flower cuttings in a vase and made the prayer, "If this really is the reincarnation of Lama Drom Tonpa, may these flowers multiply and increase in number during the period of his pilgrimage here."[10] The next day the Second Dalai Lama arrived. First he paid homage in the main temple and then gave a short discourse to the monks and people of the area. During the discourse, the *Biography* states, all the flowers blossomed and greatly multiplied in number. They remained in full bloom throughout his stay at Radeng.

Meanwhile a monk who had been a close disciple of the First Dalai Lama, Panchen Choklha Odzerwa, was teaching in Riwo Dechen.[11] Here he dreamed that a young girl in exquisite ornaments appeared to him, gave him a golden vajra, and said, "Place this on top of your banner and the wishes of all sentient beings will be fulfilled." He awoke and thought to himself, "This must refer to the reincarnation of Tamchey Khyenpa (the First Dalai Lama)." Sometime later he dreamed that a black woman with an eagle-like face appeared to him and said, "Soon I will send Gendun Drubpa to you." Thus Panchen Choklha Odzerwa knew that the time had come for him to serve his guru's reincarnation. He sent a messenger to Jamyang Lekpai Chojor of Drepung with the request to allow him to arrange a pilgrimage, meditation, and teaching tour for his disciple (the Second Dalai Lama).

Jamyang Lekpai Chojor was delighted, and immediately gave his blessings. He commented,

> When I was recently at Radeng (with the Second Dalai Lama) I had a dream vision, in which a black woman appeared to me and said that the activities of this disciple would be like the tracings of her hand in the sky. . . . She then pointed her finger into each of the four directions and began to draw pictures, until all of space was filled. At that time I knew that he would soon embark upon his mission, and that it would be of great benefit to living beings.

Shortly thereafter Panchen Choklha Odzerwa approached Chogyal Dorjey Tsetenpa, the king of Chonggyey, with the request to patronize the Second Dalai Lama on a large pilgrimage and teaching tour. The king agreed and in fact for the remainder of his life remained one of the Second Dalai Lama's most loyal disciples and patrons.

The section of the *Biography* covering the next twenty years of the Second Dalai Lama's life could quite easily be used as a textbook study of Tibetan spiritual life in the early fifteenth century. It could also be used as a geographical guide to all the important holy places of central, southern, and southwestern Tibet, which he visited repeatedly in order to practice meditation and also to teach to increasingly large gatherings. Moreover, it serves as an important reference to who's who in these areas at the time: kings, queens, tribal chieftains, lamas and yogis eagerly rushed forward, vying with one another to have the Second visit and teach in their areas. Every monastery, temple, and hermitage wanted the blessing and prestige of having received him.

As Yangpa Chojey puts it,

> His attentions were not demanded merely by lamas of one particular sect or region; all schools without exception invited him to teach, and he gave equal care and attention

to them all. . . . Dvakpo Kargyu schools, Shangpa Kar-
gyupas, Sakyapas, Kadampas, Shijeypas, Jonangpas, and
Gelugpas all received him with equal respect and honor;
and for each of them he poured forth the nectar-like teachings of Dharma. Indeed, there was not a place in central,
southern, or southwestern Tibet where he did not leave
his footprints, and where the people did not hear, see, and
meet with him. . . .

Thus he placed limitless masses of living beings on the
path leading to higher being, liberation, and enlightenment.

His energy seemed boundless. Request upon request poured in,
all of which he accepted and satisfied with equal humility and
dedication. This first pilgrimage and teaching tour began with a
visit to the Jokhang Temple of Lhasa, where he led a large ritual
and prayer ceremony, with King Ngawang Namgyal of Neudzong
(Lhasa) acting as principal benefactor. He then left for the Yarlung
Valley, home of Tibet's early civilization. On the way he stopped
and taught at various monasteries and hermitages, including Sang
Ngak Kar and also Samyey, Tibet's first monastery. His *Autobiography* comments that prior to visiting Samyey, he had dreamed of
the temple there and when he arrived found it to be exactly as in
his dream.

He then continued to Tsetang Monastery, where he encountered
several old disciples of the previous Dalai Lama, and then to Riwo
Dechen Monastery, where Panchen Choklha Odzer met up with
him for the first time. The *Biography* comments on how impressed
the Panchen was with the reincarnation of his guru and waxes
eloquent on the impression that the Second Dalai Lama made:

(The master) sat cross-legged, with his right foot slightly
extended, just as had the First Dalai Lama whenever he
taught. His robes flowed around his body like clouds
around a crystal mountain.

He taught to hundreds of listeners, his body radiant like
a full moon in the midst of a sky of stars. Although still very
young, he was fearless in the presence of the many sages
who had gathered to listen to him, like a lion in the midst of
humbler animals. His presence exuded utter strength and

poise, like Mount Meru at the center of the universe. His smile was soft and radiant, immediately disarming those who sat before him and clearing away any doubts they may have had.

And his voice! What music! It was strong, rich, and vibrant, an absolute delight to listen to and clearly audible to all in the room, both near and far. He used it like a celestial instrument as he spoke, causing the body hair on everyone there to tremble with joy and anticipation. . . .

That night the Panchen had a dream vision, in which he saw a victory banner of truth being firmly planted at the peak of Riwo Dechen.

At the new year the master made pilgrimage to Tiger's Peak, Chonggyey. Here he gave numerous initiations to King Chogyal Dorjey Tsetenpa and his family, and many teachings and initiations to the general people. Also, at the invitation of chieftain Zhangkharwa, he visited and taught in Chenyey and Zhangkhar.[12] The Chenyey abbot requested him to teach at Tsetang Monastery. Here he taught extensively and ordained more than twenty monks. After this the Chonggyey king sponsored him to lead a large prayer service in the temple at Dradruk.[13] Dradruk was Tibet's oldest palace, having been constructed in the second century B.C. Here in the Fire Snake Year (1497), he had a vision of Lama Tsongkhapa and wrote a song of the experience. (This song is included in the present collection.) The teaching pilgrimage continued through all the holy places of the region, with the Chonggyey king acting as his principal sponsor.

In the spring of the Earth Sheep Year (1498) he left on pilgrimage to the holy places of the Olkha mountains. Lama Tsongkhapa himself had spent many years there in meditation, and he wanted to practice in the places blessed by that great guru. In addition, he had heard stories of a wonderful and quite eccentric yogi, Khedrup Norzang Gyatso, who had been living in the caves at Odey Gungyal of Olkha.[14] This great yogi had been a direct disciple of the First Dalai Lama, had spent more than fourteen years in solitary meditation at Olkha upon the yogic tradition of the Kalachakra Tantra, and allegedly had achieved full enlightenment. The Second Dalai Lama was determined to meet him.

The night before the Dalai Lama arrived, the old yogi experienced numerous dream visions indicating that the reincarnation of his great guru was about to come to him. When they met, the yogi came out of his cave and bowed. The young Dalai Lama placed his hands on the yogi's shoulders and restrained him, saying, "Now it is your turn to serve as my guru." He then prostrated to the yogi and requested to be accepted as his disciple. In particular, he asked the old yogi to transmit his experiences of the Kalachakra tantric yogas to him. The yogi agreed, and the two spent the following months traveling and practicing meditation together in the holy places of Olkha. From this time on the two remained like father and son. In fact most historians state that it was under this great master that the Second Dalai Lama accomplished his enlightenment.

In the Water Boar Year (1503) a strong urge arose within him to make a pilgrimage to his birthplace and spend some time with his father, Chojey Kunga Gyaltsen. Thus he left for Tsang, teaching at the monasteries and temples as he went. In Yolkar Dorjeden he met with his father and reviewed all the family lineages he had received from him as a child. The two practiced meditation together in the family temple and had long conversations that went on deep into the night. He also gave numerous discourses and initiations to the local people.While in the area, he applied to the office of the Tashi Lhunpo abbot for an audience. "The time is still not ripe," came the reply. Thus he spent the summer with his father and then quietly returned to central Tibet and to retreat at Radeng Monastery.

Just before the new year, a messenger arrived to inform him that his father was seriously ill. He rushed back to Yolkar Dorjeden, but by the time he arrived the old yogi had already passed away. Yangpa Chojey's *Biography* goes into considerable detail on the many auspicious signs that accompanied this passing, indicating his high state of mystical accomplishment. After his heartbeat and breath had stopped, Kunga Gyaltsen sat in the state of *tukdam* for fifteen days, his body showing no ordinary signs of *post mortem* decomposition. The Second Dalai Lama himself led the cremation ceremony and later commissioned an elaborate golden stupa to encase the ashes. In honor of his father, he composed a biography of him in the form of a mystic song. (Unfortunately this is not included in *Mystic Verses of a Mad Dalai Lama*, and I have not been able to locate a copy of it.) True to the prophecy that the Dalai Lama had given to his father when the former was only three years of age, the old man had passed away in his seventy-second year.

Over the decade to follow, the Second Dalai Lama spent most of his winters in the Lhasa area and his springs, summers, and winters on pilgrimage, meditating in holy places and teaching as he went. He had also begun to compose major textual commentaries, sometimes in order to use these as a basis for his discourses and also in response to the requests that came to him. Thus his name as a teacher and author was growing. It was not unusual now for his audiences to include two or three thousand monks and nuns, as well as tens of thousands of lay people. He was also increasingly being asked to lead ordination ceremonies for new monks and nuns, and the recipients of these ceremonies would often number in the hundreds. The list of the texts that he taught and tantric initiations that he gave during these years reads like a catalog of the complete body of Indo-Tibetan Buddhism. We will see the accounts of some of his travels later in the translations of his songs and in my preambles to them.

Fulfilling a Prophecy

Throughout these many travels the Second Dalai Lama repeatedly experienced dreams and visions of a mystic lake and a monastery that he would construct near it. His work in building Chokhor Gyal Monastery near the Lhamoi Latso, or "Lake of the Goddess" (which I generally refer to as "the Lake of Visions" due to its quality of inducing visions), and his work of empowering the lake is said to have been prophesied by many great masters of the past.

Yangpa Chojey's *Biography* of the Second Dalai Lama gives a half-dozen pages of prophecies concerning these activities, mainly drawing from a mid–eighth century text by Guru Padmasambhava entitled *A Guide to the Holy Sites of Yolma* (Tib., *Yolmai Neyik*; spelled *Yol-mai-gnas-yig*); and also a mid–eleventh century text by Jowo Atisha, entitled *The Book of the Kadam* (Tib., *Kadam Lekbam*; spelled *bKa'-gdams-gleng-'bum*).

Quoting the second of these two sources Yangpa Chojey writes,

> The *dakini* spoke as follows:
> In the land of the north, blessed by the presence of seven
>   great kings (*gyalpo*)
> Is a mandala-like plateau, blue like lapis,
> Adorned with walls of a thousand pearls,
> A place blessed by a thousand Buddhas (*gyalwa*).
>
> It is adorned by a (mountain shaped like)
> A stainless turquoise *stupa*
> And is the playground of a hundred thousand *dakinis,*
> A place most conducive to one-pointed meditation. . . .
> There a victorious one (*gyalwa*) will make his residence
> And perform secret activities to benefit the world.
> This will come to pass before very long. . . .
>
> Blessed by all the Buddhas (*gyalwa*) of the ten directions,
> It has a plateau smooth as lapis lazuli
> And is surrounded by a ring of majestic mountains. . . .
> It is adorned by numerous mystical signs
> And is beautified by a net of radiant flowers (*metok*).
> It can be known from the mystical number thirteen;
> Even now Buddha Amitabha resides there.

Here the repetition of the syllables *gyalwa* as an epithet of the Buddhas, *gyalpo* for kings, and *gyalwa* as a word meaning "victorious one" is said to suggest the region of Gyal, where the lake was located. The mention of flowers (Tib., *metok*; spelled *me-tog*) refers to Metoktang, near where the Second Dalai Lama was to build his meditation hermitage, Chokhor Gyal of Metoktang.

Yangpa Chojey then quotes Guru Padmasambhava's *A Guide to the Holy Sites of Yolma* as stating,

> To the east of the Yolma region
> Is a place like a mound of jewels,

> A secret site of great virtue. . . .
> King Songtsen Gampo and his retinue went there
> And constructed a small hermitage. . . .
> When one looks out from it to the west,
> One sees a small plateau
> Which indeed is delightful to behold
> And has meadows, forests, and water. . . .
> When one looks to the southeast, one sees
> A meadow, a plateau, and a valley,
> And a place sacred to Mahakala.
> When one looks to the northeast. . .
> (And so forth, until . . .)
> There I have buried 108 secret treasures.

Thus Guru Padmasambhava described the qualities of the site where the Second Dalai Lama would construct Chokhor Gyal Monastery. Elsewhere in the same text, he speaks of the person (the Second Dalai Lama) who would empower the area,

> When the time comes to open the door to this holy place
> An emanation of Avalokiteshvara will appear,
> A youth who carries the blessings of Vajrasattva,
> Whom to see, listen to or remember inspires faith.

Elsewhere (in the same text), Guru Padmasambhava speaks of the qualities of the site as follows,

> Eh ma! This place that inspires joy
> Is more radiant than any other.
> It is a residence of Vajrasattva,
> And a place blessed by Avalokiteshvara.
> The dakas and dakinis gather
> And samadhi is accomplished without effort.
> Those who practice meditation here transcend sorrow.

Thus the Second Dalai Lama and his work at Chokhor Gyal of Metoktang was prophesied long ago.

As a condition to the fulfillment of the prophecies, in the Wood Mouse Year (1504) the Second Dalai Lama was approached by King Nangso Lhagyari Dzongpa[15] to teach in Ehchok and from there went to Dvakpo Monastery. This monastery now had become part of his annual teaching circuit, for he had earlier been given a complete department in it in which to train and house his Olkha disciples. This department, called Dvakpo Tsennyi Dratsang, or The Dvakpo Academy of Philosophy, was more like a submonastery within the Dvakpo complex than a mere department as such. It received his care and guidance throughout his life.

At that time several of the local chieftains began to pressure him to build a meditation hermitage and summer residence in the Gyal region. The Second Dalai Lama puts it like this in his *Autobiography*,

> At that time numerous people approached me with forceful requests to build a monastery at Gyal Metoktang. I did not have time to do so then due to my traveling schedule, but this was an auspicious omen (for when I would later do so). . . . Nonetheless I led a purification ritual at Gyal in order to affirm my karmic connections with the place.

The actual work of creating Chokhor Gyal Monastery began in the Wood Snake Year (1509). First he erected a small residence and then slowly added the fundamental buildings that constitute a monastic dwelling. As the Second Dalai Lama puts it in his *Autobiography*, his role in the construction of the monastery was a passive one, and the project seemed to come together and proceed toward completion almost by itself. He writes,

> The monastery seemed to rise up by itself. The construction materials, such as stones, wood, and clay, came forth quite magically. . . . It was as though we humans would build a bit during the day, and after we went to sleep at night the spirits of goodness would slip in quietly and work all night. . . . The auspicious signs that appeared were amazing. Every day flowers fell from the skies, and rainbows hovered above us. At night we could hardly sleep for all the auspicious dreams that occurred. . . . The entire summer passed in that way.

Building work continued through the summers of the Iron Horse (1510) and Iron Sheep Years (1511). Because of the altitude at which the monastery stood (approximately fifteen thousand feet above sea level), this was the only season during which any amount of construction could be undertaken. King Lhagyaripa supplied seventy workers during this period, and several hundred local disciples came on a voluntary basis, many of them from the nearby Dvakpo Monastery. The Second Dalai Lama would give teachings and initiations during breaks in the construction work, and in this way, the project moved steadily toward completion.

Traditionally the size of a Tibetan building is spoken of in terms of the number of pillars required to support it, with approximately six feet between each pillar. Thus the *Biography* describes the size of the main assembly hall by stating that it was seventy pillars in size, with the side chambers and entrances bringing it to eighty-eight pillars. This was the main building, and around it stood the residences for the monks, the communal kitchen, and a variety of smaller temples for restricted gatherings and rituals.

However, the monastery was essentially conceived as a practice hermitage. Therefore, in addition to the monastic residences, numerous meditation huts were constructed on the mountain above. The Second Dalai Lama's idea was continually to have seventy monks in solitary retreat, with the remainder of Chokhor Gyal's inhabitants engaged in study, temple rituals, and the everyday running of the monastery.

The task of creating the statues and paintings for the main and auxiliary temples was not to begin until a couple of summers later. Yangpa Chojey's *Biography* here gives a detailed account of the master artists involved in the work. During much of it the Second Dalai Lama would visit the artists every day in order to supervise the development of the various images, several of which were made from pure gold. He was in fact a highly talented painter himself, and the artwork in Chokhor Gyal Monastery certainly benefitted from his critical eye.

During the summer of the Iron Sheep Year (1511) three hundred accomplished lamas gathered at Gyal and joined the Second Dalai Lama in a ten-day prayer vigilance. Shortly thereafter he dreamed of Lhamoi Latso Lake and was told of its mystical potential as a source of visionary experiences. In his dream a woman appeared to him and said,

> In negative times there are waves of suffering
> And many hindrances to the ways of truth.

Visions inspired by this lake can offer guidance,
For it has the power to offer prophetic images.

Moreover, the extraordinary qualities and powers of the Lake of Visions had been prophesied by both Guru Padmasambhava and Jowo Atisha in the texts quoted earlier. Yangpa Chojey lists several of these prophecies in the *Biography.*

Over the weeks to follow, the Second Dalai Lama repeatedly dreamed of the lake and of his responsibility to unlock its powers. Several of these involved the protective spirit Palden Lhamo, the wrathful tantric deity and *Dharmapala* that the First Dalai Lama had frequently propitiated and that consequently the Second had relied upon from his early childhood. The lake, he now understood, was one of the principal residences of this powerful spiritual force.

Yangpa Chojey's *Biography* here mentions two elements: the lake itself and the key to the lake. This latter item refers to a sacred sword made of meteorite metal that had been unearthed during the construction of Chokhor Gyal Monastery. Meteorite metal, or *namchak* (spelled *nam-lcags*) as the Tibetans call it, is a sacred substance to central Asians, and the discovery of the object the previous summer had created something of a sensation.

There is a very exciting story related to this sword told by the Second Dalai Lama in his *Autobiography*: a black magician attempted to steal it, and efforts were made to get it back. The outcome of the adventure was that the Second Dalai Lama had a replica of the sword made for ritual purposes and together with ten yogic assistants went to the shores of the lake. Here they performed an extensive invocation and empowerment ceremony and tossed the replica into the lake's waters. The *Biography* states that the sword sank to the bottom and then suddenly, as though by divine coincidence or conspiracy, an extraordinary transformation took place before their very eyes. The Second Dalai Lama tells of the experience in his *Autobiography,*

> When we arrived at the lake, a great clamor of sound arose from the skies, like that of a severe hailstorm. I had come with some ten ritual masters to open the gates of this sacred site. We performed a rite of offering to the guardian spirits. . . .

Then we went to the shores of the lake, performed a ritual invocation of Palden Lhamo, and threw the effigy into the waters.

Suddenly the color of the lake began to transform before our eyes, becoming all colors of the rainbow one after the other. Numerous images began to appear in it, such as mandala shapes and so forth. Then it went as clear as the sky, and from within the clarity countless images appeared, such as geometric patterns. . . . All sorts of dramatic scenes appeared.

Finally the lake seemed to bubble and boil and to turn the color of milk. Not a drop of it appeared as mere water. During the entire period, the things seen in it were perceived by us all simultaneously.

From that time onward, hundreds upon hundreds of people have visited the lake in order to receive a vision from it. . . . For those of pure mind and conviction, this mystical place of power seems to inspire these experiences in an unbroken stream.

Thus the master fulfilled two important prophecies concerning his life: the construction of Chokhor Gyal Monastery and the empowerment of the Lake of Visions. This lake has continued to be used over the centuries by central Asians, most of whom aspire to visit its waters at least once in their lifetime in order to receive a vision from it that will help to unravel the mystery of their life. In particular, it came to play an important role in the discovery of reincarnate lamas, especially the Dalai Lamas. In the search for a lama's reincarnation, the signs and indications gleaned from the Lake of Visions are considered to be among the most compelling and authoritative. This tradition has continued well into modern times. For example, after the Thirteenth Dalai Lama passed away in 1933 and the search began for the child that was his reincarnation, the Regent Radeng Rinpoche went to the lake and meditated beside its waters. Soon various images and signs began to appear to him, including a house and its surrounding areas and various letters of the alphabet. These later became instrumental in identifying the child who became the present Dalai Lama.

This power of the Lake of Visions had been prophesied by Guru

Padmasambhava in his mid–eighth century text *A Guide to the Holy Sites of Yolma*, wherein it is said,

> This holy place will give prophecies of seven incarnations of Avalokiteshvara. The first reincarnation (the Second Dalai Lama) will empower the great holy lake, which in turn will empower a hundred and eight minor holy lakes.

This vision-inducing power of the Lhamoi Latso Lake thus became one of the most enduring gifts of the Second Dalai Lama to the peoples of Tibet. Some time after empowering it, he wrote a song in praise of the Lhamoi Latso Lake and its mystical qualities. A passage from it reads,

> For those who maintain the tantric precepts well,
> Visions of empty appearances and events
> Appear in its waters most miraculously.
> There is nothing that cannot be seen in it. . . .
>
> For those wishing enlightenment in one lifetime,
> It is a supreme place of practice;
> All phenomena appear in it as void,
> And their conventional nature is made obvious.
> This mystical lake thus points a yogi's mind
> To this sublime union of both the ultimate
> And the conventional levels of truth.

Resolving the Tashi Lhunpo Conflict

The Second Dalai Lama was now only thirty-six years of age, yet already he had come to be regarded as one of the greatest saints and Buddhist scholars in Tibet. However, there was still one issue that clouded his life. This had to do with Tashi Lhunpo, the monastery that had been built by the First Dalai Lama and therefore was his hereditary residence. As a youth he had lived in Tashi Lhunpo between the ages of ten and nineteen; but then, because of difficulties with certain administrators in the office of the abbot Panchen Yeshey Tsemo, he had been forced to leave. Over the years he had applied several times to be given an audience with the Panchen; each of these requests had been refused. However, the situation was about to change.

In the Iron Sheep Year (1511), just after completing the main buildings at Chokhor Gyal, a letter arrived from the Panchen. It began, "It seems as though my guru the omniscient Panchen Gendun Drubpa (the First Dalai Lama) has indeed taken rebirth as . . ."; and it concluded with the humble and self-effacing signature, "The little disciple Yeshey Tsemo." The gist of the letter was a request for the Second Dalai Lama to return to Tashi Lhunpo and take his rightful seat at the monastery.

In his *Autobiography* the Second Dalai Lama writes,

> Previously no matter how many times I had requested an audience with the Panchen I was refused. Now here before me was a letter from him asking me to come and take over the throne of the monastery.
>
> I felt that it was the natural outcome of the test in *guruyoga* that he had put me through and was an indication that somehow I had passed the ordeal.
>
> Actually, even in the most challenging moments, I had never stopped regarding him as one of my principal gurus nor allowed myself to think that his actions had any motivation other than to teach and mature me. The letter in my hands was the result.
>
> Generally, if we point a searching finger inside of ourselves, then no matter how we look at it, the benefits of always holding the traditional attitudes toward the guru are clearly effective. The whole thing seemed to me like a perfect proof of how important it is in these degenerate days to take every action of the guru as a teaching.

The Second Dalai Lama now found himself in a dilemma, as it would not be easy for him to leave Chokhor Gyal Monastery for any length of time due to the energy and dedication that so many people had put into its construction. Moreover, much of the project still remained to be completed. In particular the interior had to be finished, with the many sacred statues, paintings, and other images still to be created and installed.

Nonetheless, he thought, it would not be appropriate for him to ignore the invitation from Tashi Lhunpo. As he puts it in his *Autobiography,* "People would think that I was refusing the request in order to spite the abbot, and as a consequence they would unnecessarily collect great negative karma by losing respect for the Sangha." Thus he accepted to come as soon as possible. He left almost a year later, in the autumn of the Water Monkey Year (1512), teaching in the principal temples and monasteries on the way.[16]

At Tashi Lhunpo a grand reception had been organized for him. The Panchen came out to greet him and began to offer prostrations. The Second Dalai Lama stopped him. As he puts it in his *Autobiography,* "I discretely requested him not to do so in public, for he had been my guru, and I would prefer to keep it that way. Instead I bowed to him and requested his blessings." Nonetheless the Panchen did vacate the First Dalai Lama's residence in Tashi Lhunpo and hand it over to the Second.

He remained in Tashi Lhunpo throughout the autumn, winter, and spring, teaching numerous classical Indian Buddhist scriptures. Included in his discourses were Acharya Dharmakirti's *An Analysis of Valid Inquiry;* Acharya Vasubandhu's *A Treasury of Abhidharma;* Acharya Chandrakirti's *A Guide to the Middle View;* Maitreya/ Asanga's *Ornament of Clear Understanding;* and Gunaprabha's *A Treatise on Monastic Discipline.*[17] In addition, to those with high tantric initiation he taught Chandrakirti's commentary to the Guhyasamaja tantric system, *The Clear Lamp,* and to the general people of the area he taught *The Book of the Kadam.*

At that time Tashi Lhunpo Monastery had approximately five hundred monks involved in the program of philosophical studies and another four hundred who lived at the monastery for purposes of meditation, performance of rituals, running the day-to-day activities of the community, and so forth. Thus the total population was about nine hundred. But one night the Second Dalai Lama dreamed that a woman appeared to him and told him, "After Panchen Yeshey Tsemo you should take care of Tashi Lhunpo. If you do so, the number of monks will increase to nineteen hundred during your lifetime, and the mountains around Tashi Lhunpo will become decorated with many smaller monasteries, hermitages, and temples."

While residing at Tashi Lhunpo, the Second Dalai Lama made frequent visits to other holy places and monasteries in the area, teaching and giving initiations in them. Included in the list of these are Lhunpo Tsey, Sengey Tsey Chodey, Nartang, Nenying, Zhalu, Palkhor Dechen, Bodong Eh, Sinpori, Tanakpu, and Riwo Gepel.

To make clear to one and all his respect and admiration for Panchen Yeshey Tsemo, he composed a biography of him in the form of an epic poem (unfortunately I have not been able to locate a copy of it). Also, while in Tashi Lhunpo, he requested the elderly Panchen for a number of teachings and initiations that he had planned to acquire from him years earlier as a teenager but had not been able to at that time due to the problems he had had with the Panchen's administrators. In brief, the Dalai Lama seems to have picked up with his guru near the point at which he had been cut off two decades earlier, almost as though there had never been a rift in their relationship. The *Biography* comments that throughout his stay at Tashi Lhunpo, he gave six or seven teaching sessions a day, generally speaking to the monks during the mornings and afternoons and to the lay people in the evenings.

Meanwhile the people back in the Olkha region, who had worked hard and invested great sums of energy and money to build Chokhor Gyal Monastery for him, were becoming restless with his absence. A letter signed by four hundred senior monks and patrons arrived toward the end of the spring session at Tashi Lhunpo, firmly requesting him to return soon and hinting that if he were not to do so then the progress of work on Chokhor Gyal might slow down drastically. Therefore in the summer of the Water Bird Year (1513), he set off back toward Gyal.

Over the following years he was to return frequently to Tashi Lhunpo and thus continued to supervise its training program and state of development. In fact the prophecy that his efforts in this regard would cause the Tashi Lhunpo community to increase in number to nineteen hundred monks and that numerous other temples and hermitages would appear in the area quickly came to be fulfilled.

A Lama's Meditations

Chapter Ten of the Second Dalai Lama's *Biography* gives a lengthy description of the daily meditations that the master practiced during his travels and teaching schedules, as well as of the monthly and annual tantric meditational rituals that he led. The list is long, as he certainly packed his days with activities of this nature.

Most of these practices are *sadhanas*, or tantric liturgical texts that are chanted as the basis of a meditation session. This type of meditation involves the generation of the visualization of the mandalas of specific deities, including the visualization of oneself as the tantric deity or (deities) and/or the visualization of the deity in the space before oneself. It also involves the recitation of large numbers of mantras associated with the mandala deities and meditation upon the symbolic meaning of the process. On a higher level, this type of tantric practice also entails absorbing the mandala and deities into one's own body and then using the powers of mantra to bring the subtle bodily processes under control in order to be enabled to rest awareness in its own primordial nature, the clear light consciousness.

The *Biography* explains that from the age of seven or eight the Second chanted and meditated daily upon the mandalas of the Thirteen Vajravarahis, or female Heruka Buddhas, as well as the Dharmapala invocations of Mahakala and Palden Lhamo (this latter being the goddess of the Lake of Visions). He had received these lineages from his father. The *Biography* adds that from the time the master left Tsang for Central Tibet at the age of seventeen, he included a thousand recitations of the Palden Lhamo mantra in his daily practice.

By the time he left Drepung Monastery, he had also adopted daily meditation upon the sadhana practices of the highest yoga tantra systems of the Guhyasamaja mandala, the Heruka Chakra-samvara "body mandala" in the lineage of Gandhapada, the Vajra-bhairava mandala, the Kalachakra mandala, and the Dharmapala practices of Dharmaraja and Vaishravana. He had received most of these lineages from his father, although it appears that he did not adopt most of them as daily practices until later. As we saw above, he received more comprehensive transmissions of these practices later in his life: first in Tsang, from the abbots of Nartang and Tashi Lhunpo monasteries, and then in Drepung, from the guru Jamyang Lekpai Chojor. He received the Kalachakra again in even greater depth several years later from the yogi Khedrub Norzang Gyatso.

The *Biography* comments that his day generally began with *Sitatara* (White Tara) mantra practice; then he made the traditional prayers to the various lineage gurus in the past line of transmission. He would then incorporate the above list of sadhana-based meditations throughout the day. In all, his formal daily meditations demanded more than five hours of his time. In addition to this, on days of the lunar cycle especially associated with particular Dharmapala practices and ritual meditations, he would dedicate the entire day to the ritual invocation. These usually included the eighth, tenth, twelfth, fifteenth, nineteenth, twenty-fifth, and thirtieth days of the month.[18]

The fourth and fifth months of each year were also given particular attention by him. Yangpa Chojey states, "During these two months he would divide his time between meditating, teaching, writing, leading ordination ceremonies for new monks and nuns, giving blessings to patrons and crowds of people, and so forth. His body, speech, and mind would be actively involved in Dharma in an unbroken stream, and he would not rest for even a moment."

Concerning the Second Dalai Lama's attitude toward the many offerings that came to him as a result of his activities, Yangpa Chojey writes,

> No matter what material offerings or wealth came to him, he never ever kept anything for himself. Offerings and gifts fell daily in great rainfalls, but he gave all of this away to various spiritual purposes, like building or supporting temples and monasteries, the support of solitary meditators

and elderly lineage holders, and to the poor. I have heard this said repeatedly by everyone who knew him.

He himself often stated that his only personal possessions were his monk robes and bowl and his ritual implements of vajra, bell, and hand drum. Everything else that came to him he regarded as merely being entrusted to him for higher use, as having been given to him in order for him to disperse it in the most appropriate manner.

Drepung Monastery's New Abbot

On his way from Tashi Lhunpo back to Gyal, the Second Dalai Lama accepted invitations to visit the Khongpo region and teach there. In addition, the kings Tashi Rabten, Lodro Wangpo, and Palden Lodro had sponsored the building of a statue of Maitreya Buddha that was of solid gold and over a story in height; they strongly requested him to lead the consecration rite. He did this, and during the ceremony, countless auspicious signs occurred. The *Biography* comments that " . . . the skies became filled with mystical sounds." He also taught at Ganden and Khar Demo on the way and at Kongpo Nyima Drakdrub, Nyangpo, Rato, and many such places.

From the time he finished his studies in Drepung Loseling Monastery at the age of twenty-one until he completed Chokhor Gyal Monastery when thirty-six years of age, the Second Dalai Lama had generally given only a month or two each year to Drepung and the Lhasa area, with the remainder largely being spent on the road as he traveled from place to place, meditating in holy sites and teaching as he went. His lifestyle would soon begin to change, and he would develop a pattern wherein his summers would be spent in Chokhor Gyal and winters in Drepung, with only spring and autumn being given to pilgrimage and teaching tours.

In the Fire Bull Year (1517) he was requested to accept the abbotship of Drepung, the largest monastery in Tibet, where he himself had completed his higher philosophical studies after leaving Tashi Lhunpo as a youth. He was installed on the half-moon day of the fourth Tibetan month, which is the date annually commemorated as the celebration of Buddha's birth, enlightenment, and passing away. It was also in this year that he composed his commentary to the tantric system known as the Six Yogas of Niguma.

As the abbot of Drepung, Tibet's largest monastery, he now made links with all of central Asia; for the monastic community at Drepung was comprised not only of the peoples of the Lhasa area but of the most promising students and scholars from hundreds of smaller monasteries throughout the land.

Restoring the Great Prayer Festival

Throughout the Second Dalai Lama's life, the Gelugpa school to which he primarily belonged was under considerable oppression from a number of the older schools, especially the Karma Kargyu. In particular, the Monlam Chenmo, or Great Prayer Festival, that had been established by Lama Tsongkhapa, had been taken from them, and Gelugpa monks were banned from attending it in the Lhasa area. Instead, the festival was led by either the Sharmapa or the Sangpupa lamas.[19]

Because it was created as a Gelugpa festival, the Second Dalai Lama felt somewhat responsible for getting the Great Prayer Festival back. One of his first acts after assuming the abbotship of Drepung was to visit the *Gongma* (king) of Lhasa and discuss the matter with him. The Gongma conceded the point, and from the following year, the festival was returned to its rightful owners. In fact it has remained as such from then until today.

To the casual reader this may seem like a small matter. However, it is considered by Tibetans as one of the great accomplishments (or, as they would put it, one of the "great kindnesses") of the Second Dalai Lama's life. The reason for this is that the festival is considered to be a symbol of extraordinary spiritual transformation. It represents the active presence of the enlightenment tradition in the world, and the meritorious energy created by the festival is said to be a major factor in sustaining world peace and prosperity, not just for Tibet but on a planetary level. When Tsongkhapa created the festival in 1409, he is thought to have gently pushed the world toward an age of enlightenment. Indeed, the invention of the festival, which lasts for between two and three weeks at the beginning of every new year, is said to have been one of his "four great deeds."

In this respect the Tibetans regard themselves as merit-makers and peacekeepers for the human community, much like the Hopi natives of New Mexico. Their spiritual rites, although performed in a traditional setting, are seen as contributions to universal well-being. Thus when the festival was tampered with for sectarian and political reasons, the matter was considered very serious indeed.

I have not looked into the actual history of the conflict over this festival in detail. Essentially the problem seems to have derived from the intrigues of the Fourth Sharmapa Tulku, Chokyi Drakpa by name, who from 1499 to 1523 masterminded a number of sectarian rivalries with the aim of furthering his own position with the Tibetan aristocracy. Not only did his plotting adversely affect the Gelugpa, it also nearly split his own school, the Karma Kargyu, into two branches, one under him and the other under the Eighth Karmapa Tulku, Karmapa Mikyu Dorjey. The Second Dalai Lama, as well as the Gelugpa school in general, had good relationships with the latter lama; the problem was with the Sharmapa.

The Second Dalai Lama's *Autobiography* only comments as follows on the Great Prayer Festival controversy,

> Previously Lama Tsongkhapa had established the Great
> Prayer Festival, and throughout its early years it had been

led by the lamas of Drepung Monastery. Then the Rin-pung of Lhasa interfered with it and took it away (from Drepung). For nineteen years it was presided over intermittently by Karma Kargyupa lamas and the Sangpupa lamas. This continued until the Bull Year (1517).

In the middle of that year I approached the Gongma with the request that, in accordance with the original tradition, it should be placed in the hands of Drepung Monastery. The Gongma thought my application was reasonable, and therefore in the Tiger Year (1518) the Great Prayer Festival was conducted by 2,500 monks from Drepung and 300 from Sera monastery. We made extensive prayers in the Jokhang Temple of Lhasa for the benefit of living beings and the stability and increase of the enlightenment tradition in the world.

As Lama Tsongkhapa had done, at each session of the festival I read from the Buddha Jatakas. From then until now (the time of writing, which is 1528) I have continued to lead this festival every year.

Yangpa Chojey gives a bit more information, although he uses a distinctly less polite language for the monks who had usurped the festival from the Gelugpa. He writes,

This festival was established in the Earth Bull Year (1409) with sponsorship from the king Gongma Chenpo Drakpa Gyaltsen and the Neu Dzong king, Namkha Zang-popa by name. It continued unbroken for ninety-one years. . . .

Then the power-brokers of Kyisho disrupted it and had other lamas take it over.

Suddenly for nineteen years this source of boundless enlightenment energy that Tsongkhapa had created was made to decline in quality. It was now performed by monks of impure ways, and its light became like that of the sun after sunset. By their wrong understanding of it, the monastic community performing it had broken the continuity of its meritorious energy. It was now a mere empty name of the festival. . . .

Then the Bodhisattva Avalokiteshvara came in the form of a monk in order to save it. He went to the Gongma and explained the many reasons for the inappropriate state of affairs. The good man listened, and he answered well.

Yangpa Chojey comments that the Second Dalai Lama's work in this regard had been prophesied long ago. He quotes Guru Padmasambhava's *The Hundred Thousand Kingly Instructions* (Tib., *rGyal-po-bka'-'bum*),

A bodhisattva monk will be born in the south,
A supreme being holding many tantric lineages.
This supreme being will perceive the essence;
He will transform appearances and then make worship.
That monk is indeed an arya bodhisattva.

Yangpa Chojey points out that in this verse, the statement "... will transform appearances..." refers to the Great Prayer Festival, the high point of which occurs when Tibet's two holiest Buddha statues are made the focal point of activities and five-pointed crowns are offered to them. This symbolizes the transformation of their appearance from that of the formless *Dharmakaya* to the aspect of *Samboghakaya*, which is associated with form and the manifestation of the spirit of enlightenment on more conventional planes. In other words, it represents transforming enlightenment energy into a dimension that can operate within the world of form. The words "...and then make worship..." refer to the Second Dalai Lama's act of leading the Great Prayer Festival. "A bodhisattva monk will be born in the south" is said to clearly indicate the Second Dalai Lama, who as an emanation of Avalokiteshvara is an arya bodhisattva. His birthplace, Yolkar Dorjeden, is located in the southwest of Tibet, and from a young age he lived as a monk.

Thus from the Earth Tiger Year (1518), the Second Dalai Lama took over as head lama in charge of the Great Prayer Festival of Lhasa. He continued to fulfill this role until his death twenty-four years later.

The Gongma was obviously deeply impressed by the Second Dalai Lama and his performance at the Great Prayer Festival. Later that year he offered him the Ganden Podrang as his residence in Drepung Monastery.[20] The Ganden Podrang was to act as the

Second Dalai Lama's principal residence in the Lhasa area from that time on. In fact, it became the principal home of the subsequent Dalai Lamas, until the Great Fifth became spiritual and temporal leader of a unified Tibet in 1642 and shortly thereafter made the Potala his home.

The Second Dalai Lama was now forty-two years of age. As the abbot of Drepung he had numerous responsibilities in the Lhasa area and generally would base himself there during winters and springs, teaching not only at Drepung but at all the monasteries and hermitages in the region. Similarly, he would base himself at Chokhor Gyal Monastery during summers and autumns, making various teaching tours from there into the outlying areas. Meanwhile, he still continued to visit Tashi Lhunpo from time to time and to oversee its well-being. Disciples came to him from all across central Asia, later returning to their homelands with the lineages he had imparted to them. The *Biography* comments, "Thus from Kashmir on the west to China on the east, there was not a place in Tibet that was not touched by his teachings."

At the conclusion of Chapter Eleven of the *Biography*, Yangpa Chojey makes another brief reference to a sectarian skirmish in Tibet,

> In the Fire Dog Year (1526), when the Red and Yellow Hat schools fought . . . eighteen Kadampa monasteries were forcibly converted into traditions of other schools. . . . The master performed many prayers for peace and harmony; the conflict was brought to an end, and the Kadampa banner was raised on high (that is, was returned to its rightful owners). . . .
>
> He accomplished this through ritual invocation and mantra recitation of the Dharmapalas, mostly the protector Dharmaraja. Thus his fame as a *mahasiddha* spread throughout U-Tsang.

The Creation of a Maitreya Statue

Chapter Twelve of the *Biography* by Yangpa Chojey mostly deals with the many wonderful images that the Second Dalai Lama commissioned for Chokhor Gyal Monastery. These included hundreds of statues and paintings, as well as various altar decorations and so forth. The work continued for almost a decade, with the Second Dalai Lama closely overseeing the artistic developments. Accounts of activity such as this are to be found in almost all Tibetan biographies of great lamas and are of tremendous value to the art historian. For example, here Yangpa Chojey provides us with the names and backgrounds of the master artists who worked on the project, as well as details of the types of images made and the mediums used.

I remember reading the First Dalai Lama's biography some years ago and marvelling at the wealth of information given concerning the artworks he commissioned for Tashi Lhunpo Monastery in the 1450s. Yangpa Chojey here provides us with some of the same kind of reading pleasure in his account of the Second's activities at Chokhor Gyal. Unfortunately much of what he says is outside the scope of this book and is probably somewhat too specialized for the general reader.

There is one particular image I would like to mention, however: a human-sized statue of Buddha Maitreya made of pure gold. Various disciples wandered for several years (between 1519 and 1522) throughout Tibet in order to gather the gold for the project. Several kings contributed to it, and every disciple from Kham on the east to Gugey on the west made a small offering. In all, more than three thousand *zho* of gold was collected for the purpose.

The First Dalai Lama had made a similar gold statue of Buddha Maitreya in Tashi Lhunpo Monastery approximately half a century earlier. The one now constructed by the Second Dalai Lama was completed and consecrated in the Wood Monkey Year (1524).

Yangpa Chojey states that Panchen Yeshey Tsemo, who had witnessed the consecrations of both the First and Second Dalai Lama's gold Maitreya statues, commented, "During the consecration of the First Dalai Lama's Maitreya image, the skies were constantly filled with rainbows, flowers fell from empty space, and the earth shook several times. I thought I would never again witness anything so overwhelmingly miraculous. However, the magical signs that occurred during the consecration of the gold image at Chokhor Gyal were even more amazing and fabulous."

As the *Biography* points out, the gold Maitreya statues created by the First and Second Dalai Lamas were not intended as mere temple decorations but had a far more profound spiritual purpose. Both these Dalai Lamas had insisted that the statues not be made under the patronage of a single person but that they should contain a small contribution from every disciple. Thus the statues would forge a spiritual bond between the disciples and make them into one great family. In addition, they would create a link between the disciples, Buddha Maitreya, and Maitreya's Pure Land of Tushita. Tibetans regard sacred images such as this as "power vessels" having the ability to transform the energy and karma of living beings, not only of a specific area or people, but as merit-generators for the planet in general.

Yangpa Chojey, who was present during the construction of the Second Dalai Lama's image, offers as evidence of this purpose a dream he had one night during the period of the consecration ceremony. In his dream the gold statue attracted the attention of Buddha Maitreya and caused him to emanate hundreds of thousands of beams of light into the world. Each of these acted as a rope by which countless sentient beings could climb up to the Tushita Pure Land. The lightbeams served not only one generation of disciples but continued to shine and provide the opportunity of liberation for many generations to come throughout the world.

The *Biography* also quotes a verse by the eleventh-century master Jowo Atisha as recorded in *The Book of the Kadam* that Yangpa Chojey feels is a prophecy of these two golden Maitreya statues (by the First and Second Dalai Lamas) and of their power,

> O Lama Drom Tonpa, in the future certain of your
> reincarnations
> Will create images forging links with Tushita

By which wise trainees who follow pure ways
Will easily find the way to Tushita Pure Land.

Yangpa Chojey then goes on to say that Lama Drom Tonpa's "reincarnations" here refers to Avalokiteshvara appearing in the form of a monk, as the First and then as the Second Dalai Lamas, and that the " . . . images forming links with Tushita" refers to the two gold Maitreya statues. These, he continues, will act as powerhouses by which the prayers of Buddha Maitreya may be fulfilled in the world.

Other buildings, as well as the images and paintings required for them, were slowly added to Chokhor Gyal Monastery as the years passed. For example, in the summer of the Fire Boar Year (1527) the chieftain Sonam Lhundrub sponsored the fresco paintings of the Jetsun Shalrekang Temple, with images of Guru Padmasambhava, Jowo Atisha and disciples, Lama Tsongkhapa and disciples, several of the previous incarnations of the Second Dalai Lama himself, Buddha and the sixteen arhats, the eight Medicine Buddhas, and various tantric deities and dharma protectors.

Also, in the Earth Bull Year (1529), a second assembly hall, forty-eight pillars in size, was added, with a residential building of sixty pillars. King Amoghavajra Namgyal Palzangpo acted as the principal sponsor.

In this way Chokhor Gyal Monastery gradually evolved, with the gold Maitreya statue acting as its spiritual heartbeat.

The Later Years

In the Fire Bird Year (1525) the Second Dalai Lama was strongly requested by the elders of Sera Monastery as well as by the various patrons of the Lhasa region to accept the responsibility of the Sera abbotship. Thus from this time on he served as head lama of both Drepung and Sera. Meanwhile he continued to oversee both Chokhor Gyal and Tashi Lhunpo monasteries.

He had previously visited and taught in Sera on several occasions. This monastery is located near Lhasa, a short distance from Drepung and, although smaller than Drepung, was nonetheless considered to be one of the most important Gelugpa institutions. When he visited Sera to teach the following year, he experienced a dream vision in which he was told, "From the time Sera was built until now its numbers have remained quite small." Thus he decided to dedicate greater energy to it and to increase its numbers and had a special Buddha statue constructed for Sera in order to bring it prosperity. Over the years to follow, he ordained many more monks into the community there.

As I mentioned earlier, Yangpa Chojey passed away in the Iron Tiger Year (1530), when the Second Dalai Lama was fifty-five. Thus the *Biography* from that time onward was written by another monk, Konchok Kyab. In fact this did not occur until the Iron Monkey Year (1560), eighteen years after the Second Dalai Lama died. Konchok Kyab was not a direct disciple of the Second Dalai Lama but rather a disciple of numerous of the Second's disciples. As a result, his section of the *Biography* is not graced by the historical precision present in the part composed by Yangpa Chojey.

A character that appears in Konchok Kyab's account with increasing frequency is Queen Sanggyey Paldzomma, the wife of *Gongma* (King) Tashi Drakpa Gyaltsen Palzangpo of Kyormo Lung. By the mid–1530s, the Second Dalai Lama seems to have come to regard her as his greatest patron and lay disciple. Certainly she was both extremely wealthy and intensely dedicated to Buddhism. The bond between her and the Second Dalai Lama seems to have been cemented in the Wood Monkey Year (1524), when she invited him to teach at Namsey Lhatsey. After that she and her husband acted as major patrons of his activities in the Lhasa and Tolung areas. As the *Biography* puts it, "Every year (from that time on) they made central Tibet shine with a spiritual light equal to that of central India during the time of the Buddha."

It seems that shortly after Chokhor Gyal Monastery was established, the Second Dalai Lama appointed one of his disciples, a senior monk by the name of Lopon Losel Sheynyen, as principal administrator and acting abbot. Later on, presumably after Losel

Sheynyen became too old, the position was given to another disciple, Lobpon Sherab Pelwa. This latter monk became one of the Second Dalai Lama's principal confidantes, caring for Chokhor Gyal in the Dalai Lama's absence and overseeing its development. He also supervised the seventy monks who lived in meditational retreat and was responsible for the feeding of the entire community.

The Second Dalai Lama now had a number of responsibilities revolving around an annual schedule. These included leading the Maitreya Festival in Lhasa toward the end of the year and also the various new year ceremonies, such as the *torgya* rite for exorcizing all negativities of the old year (performed on the last day of the year). Also as part of the new year rituals, there were religious ceremonies for opening the year auspiciously and thus encouraging prosperity and harmony in the months to come. After this came the Great Prayer Festival, celebrated by thousands of monks in the Jokhang Temple of Lhasa. He presided over this for two or three weeks in the first month of the year. He would then generally teach in Sera for a couple of weeks and also in either Drepung or Ganden. Thus his schedule from the late autumn to the first month of spring generally kept him in the Lhasa area. Following this he would often make teaching pilgrimages to various regions accessible from Lhasa, such as Tashi Lhunpo of Tsang or the Tolung area. Most years he returned to Chokhor Gyal in late spring and remained in retreat there during the summer. Again from here he would make several teaching pilgrimages each year to the outlying areas, such as Kongpo and southern Olkha.

His life was not without obstacles, however. For example, in the autumn of the Fire Bird Year (1537), hostile armies threatened to attack and destroy his monastery at Gyal. As Konchok Kyab puts it, "Evil demons had caused jealousy of the master's great works to arise within the hearts of certain sectarian people. Numerous armies began to move toward Gyal from the east. . . . Many negative signs appeared in the Lake of Visions."

The Second Dalai Lama responded with yogic means. He retreated to the Lake of Visions and performed invocations of and prayers to the Dharmapala goddess Palden Lhamo, requesting her to release her spiritual force and restore peace and harmony. A great storm erupted, and the skies were filled with terrible sounds. Palden Lhamo had given them a sign; all would be well. The

Biography continues by stating that, as an external condition to fulfilling Palden Lhamo's magical works, King Nangso Donyopa of Droda suddenly swept down from nowhere upon the invading armies and routed them. Konchok Kyab concludes his account of the incident by saying, "As for the routed soldiers, many of them died in flight. Others died in battle on the way.... Moreover, those of them who reached home carried many contagious diseases with them, thus disseminating their community's population.... Since that time, no one has dared to attack Gyal."

In the above account Konchok Kyab is very careful to avoid giving the actual identities of the "invading armies" and the leaders behind them. This is quite typical of Tibetan biographical writings, in which it is thought that the best approach to malicious and violent people is to relegate them to historical obscurity in this way, rather than giving them immortality by listing their names. The incident is only included in the *Biography* in order to illustrate the Second Dalai Lama's use of tantric ritual to pacify the forces of evil. Thus the names of the pacification rituals that he performed are given in great detail, yet not a mention is made of the names of the peoples at whom the "pacification" was directed.

In the Earth Dog Year (1538), there seems to have been something of a hot philosophical debate going on between some of the lama *intelligentsia*. The Kargyupa lama Karmapa Mikyo Dorjey (the Eighth Karmapa) had written a commentary to the *Prajnaparamita Sutra* that the senior monks of Sera monastery considered to be an utter misrepresentation and misinterpretation of the meaning of the *Perfection of Wisdom* scriptures. They approached the Second Dalai Lama with the request that he write a refutation to it.[21] He accepted, but composed only a single verse,

> The Buddhas teach in various ways;
> Sometimes what they say is literally true,
> And sometimes they teach in metaphors
> When this is more appropriate to the minds of listeners.
> They speak indirectly when to do so directly
> Would impair the understanding of those to be trained.

Thus he made it known that he himself greatly enjoyed the Karmapa's philosophical text and was amused by the passionate controversy it had aroused in the Sera community.

Preparing His Disciples for His Passing

In the Earth Boar Year (1539)
King Nangso Donyopa of Droda, the hero who had saved Gyal from invasion and pillage two years earlier, invited the Second to Zhekar Dzong to teach. The chieftain had completed the construction of a new monastery there, and he requested the Second Dalai Lama to name it and also to accept responsibility of guiding it spiritually. He gave it the name Kadam Lhunpo.

At the end of his discourse there, the Second Dalai Lama sang a verse to his disciples,

> O hark. All of us who are friends
> Are held together by fragile links,
> Like clouds in a windy sky.
> Impermanent things know no stability,
> And are like an illusory mirage.
> Rely therefore on spiritual practice,
> The only stable force in a world of change.
> This is my advice to you; you should
> Try always to live by it.

When he had completed this song, the room turned very quiet. He sat in silence, color drained from his face, and his eyes closed. His head fell to one side, and he released a long sigh. Sung-rabpa, his principal attendant, became concerned that the master was perhaps suffering from a severe illness, such as a stroke or a heart attack. He touched him gently on the arm to inquire of the situation.

"Be quiet," the lama said to him. "The real question is not how my health is, but whether or not the minds of you disciples have been established on the spiritual path. . . . Those of you who call yourselves my disciples, your thoughts should not be about me, but about your own practice of Dharma. It was only for this reason that many years ago I began to come to this region to teach."

After speaking in this extraordinary way he left for the Tiger's Peak at Olkha.

The Iron Bull Year (1541) began as usual with the Dalai Lama leading the festivities. Again, he presided over the Great Prayer Festival at Lhasa. Many of those present during his Jataka discourses were strongly moved by his intensity and feared that he may be signalling them that he was preparing to pass away.

He stayed in Drepung during the spring and gave a large number of discourses on Indian classical treatises and also a complete reading of everything that he himself had written. At the beginning of this discourse he said, "Those of you who are my disciples should listen closely, for this may be the last time that I am able to give you such extensive teachings." He had never spoken to them like this before, and it filled them with apprehension. During the teaching there were several earth tremors, the wind in the mountains made a sound as though weeping, and an eclipse occurred. Many high lamas had repeated nightmares at night.

Konchok Kyab writes in the *Biography* that all the head lamas held council to decide what course of action to take. The master seemed to have no illness of any kind, yet he continued to make references to his own passing. They decided to have all the principal monasteries in central Tibet perform elaborate long life prayers for him. In addition, they all approached him with the request to use his meditational powers to extend his life.

A contingent of lamas from Tashi Lhunpo rushed to Lhasa to request him to stay in the world and teach. The Gandenpa king Sonam Gyalpo and his queen also came with the same request, as did Queen Butri Gyalmo of Gongkar. In this way disciples rushed in from every direction to express concern with his well-being.

Konchok Kyab implies that certainly the master would have passed away that summer had all this fuss not been made over him. He writes, "In this way the disciples gained the meritorious energy for the master to live in their midst one more year."

During the summer the Second Dalai Lama made an extensive teaching tour throughout all the regions where he had large numbers of disciples. First he went to Ganden Tsey and then to Chennga and Chushul Lhunpo Tsey. At each of these places he gave lengthy public discourses. After this he continued on to Samyey Monastery, where he led an extensive invocation of all the Dharmapalas bound by Guru Padmasambhava. Next he went to Taktsey, Pudrukda, and Mondrong. Thus he circled through the various areas and eventually arrived back at Chokhor Gyal.

Here he embarked upon an extensive teaching schedule. During the discourse he seemed as though a young man again; but, as on previous occasions, he concluded his talk with ominous words. Konchok Kyab quotes him as saying,

> My friends, listen well. You have all met me personally and heard me many times speak on spiritual ways with you. What is important is that you take the essence of what I have said to heart and guard the practice of it as carefully as you guard the pupils of your eyes.
>
> If you do not put into practice the quintessential message that I have spent so much time discussing with you, it renders our time together meaningless. It then is as though we had never met, and you had never listened to me speak. Should that be the case, you will not achieve even the slightest benefit through our meeting.
>
> I request you: Make effort to keep the reins of your practice firmly in your hands. Keep to the essence. Then we will have really met, and you will have really listened. In this way you will achieve the benefits of your own spiritual liberation.
>
> For example, if a sick person goes to a doctor and receives the medicines appropriate to his cure, yet neither eats the medicines nor heeds the advice given by the doctor, there is no benefit from the visit. Merely meeting a doctor and receiving medicines and advice is not enough.
>
> Therefore I request you: Make every effort to apply yourself to the actual practice.

He spoke like that at length, giving the monks there the impression that it could be their last summer session with him.

In the autumn, the King of Gugey, Jigten Wangchuk Pedkardey, together with his prime minister Ngawang Namgyal, sent him a letter requesting him to create a monastery in Gugey like that he had built at Gyal. He sent the master Jey Tenpa Darzangpa in his place, who constructed Ngari Dratsang.

After completing his teachings at Chokhor Gyal he went to Dvakpo Dratsang and taught his disciples there. One night he dreamed of his guru Khedrub Norzang Gyatso, who said to him, "You have built Gyal very well. Very well indeed." He took this as a sign that his guru now regarded his life's work as complete. The next day an earth tremor occurred, and a strong wind arose. "We must return to Gyal immediately," he announced.

Back at Chokhor Gyal Monastery he led a prayer ceremony for peace and harmony and then said to his disciples, "My friends, soon I must go in order to work with the peoples of the north. When I am gone, absorb yourself in the essence of practice. If you can do that, then I will return to you before long."

The next day he left for the Tiger's Peak at Olkha. King Amoghavajra Namgyal Palzangpo of the east sponsored a large ceremony and teaching. At its conclusion, the master again said, "My friends, all who meet must one day part. Soon I must go to help the peoples of the north." To the king he said, "You should continue to support the Dharma and to care for your subjects as though they were your own children. Do this, and soon we will meet again."

Konchok Kyab comments, "Afterwards he left in the direction of the Lhasa valley, showing his old body to all his disciples in the various places as he went, giving them final teachings and advice."

At Samyey Monastery he again made prayers in front of the image of Guru Padmasambhava and the religious kings of old. Konchok Kyab writes, "The sky turned awesome, and a sweet fragrance pervaded the area. Rainbows appeared in the sky above the temple, and there was a rainfall of flowers."

Eventually he arrived at Drepung Monastery. Here he taught *The Lamp on the Five Tantric Stages* (Tib., *Rim-lnga-gsal-sgron*) and also the chapter on mindfulness from Acharya Shantideva's *A Guide to the Bodhisattva Ways* (Skt., *Bodhisattva-charya-avatara*; Tib., *Byang-chub-sems-dpa'-spyod-pa-la-'jug-pa*). He then led the Maitreya Festival and the ceremonies to close out the old year.

On the first day of the Water Tiger Year (1542), he led the annual *torma* ritual. At the end of the rite he said to his disciples, "Now my life is complete. . . . There is no need for me to stay any longer." Nonetheless he led the Great Prayer Festival as usual, teaching in the mornings to the vast crowds and leading the chanting sessions in the afternoons.

Konchok Kyab states that one day he said to the people,

> Lama Tsongkhapa put a great deal of thought into two essential questions: in general how to benefit the six types of living beings and uplift the Buddhadharma; and in particular how to bring spiritual benefits to the peoples of the Land of Snow.
>
> His answer was to create the Great Prayer Festival, wherein a spiritual gathering of tens of thousands of monks and lay people celebrate in the presence of the two Jowo images.
>
> This is a source of great spiritual energy for the world, and we must continue it in accordance with the tradition. . . . It is an extraordinary way to bring ourselves into a special destiny.

In this way once more he gave parting advice to his disciples, and prepared their minds to accept the fact that his life was drawing to a close.

Preparing for His Future Incarnation

The next day a messenger arrived from Kyormo Lung carrying a letter from Queen Sangyey Paldzom, wife of Gongma Ngawang Tashi Drakpa Gyaltsen. The letter requested him to come to their palace at Kyormo Lung. His attendants requested him to postpone the trip, as he seemed somewhat exhausted from the many new year ceremonies and the activities of the Great Prayer Festival.

He refused to hear of it. "I have no illness," he replied. "There is no other patron of the Buddhadharma equal to Queen Sangyey Paldzom. The meeting with her is very important. I would like to go immediately, as I do not know if I will have the strength to do so later."

Konchok Kyab states in the *Biography* that the reason he was insistent upon this trip was because he planned for his future reincarnation to take birth in the Tolung area, of which Kyormo Lung was a principal hub, and he wished to perform various rituals there to create an auspicious atmosphere and also to clear any possible obstacles.

He arrived on the twenty-sixth and for much of his visit spent his time engaged in the performance of tantric rituals. On the last day of the month he led a large *gu-tor* ritual, and at the end of the ceremony commented to the king and queen, "Soon I must leave this old body. But do not be sad. We will meet again before long." In all he remained in the Kyormo Lung area between nine and ten days. This symbolized that his reincarnation would be reborn in the area within nine or ten months after he passed away.

After leaving Kyormo Lung, he received an invitation from King Namgyal Drakpa and Queen Paldzom Butri to visit them at Kangsar Gong of Tolungda. They came to meet him beside the banks of the Tolung River. "These days my body is not very strong," he said to them. "But do not be sad. I will come to you soon." Thus he hinted that he would take birth in the area.

As the group passed through the Tolung Valley, they came near an old stupa called Kyerwa. Here the master's horse stumbled and hurt its leg, and they had to pause for some time while a fresh horse was summoned. He told Sung-rabpa, "Take note of this."

Konchok Kyab concludes this section of the *Biography* by commenting, "Thus the bodhisattva Avalokiteshvara, manifest as an ordinary human being in the robes of a Buddhist monk, paved the way for his future life and left clear signs that would help in discovering his reincarnation."

It is important to keep in mind, however, that all of this is being written by Konchok Kyab in retrospect, as he did not compose his section of the *Biography* until 1560, eighteen years after the Second Dalai Lama had passed away. By that time the Third Dalai Lama had already been discovered and, in fact, was almost seventeen years of age. Nonetheless, it is certain that the comments made by the Second Dalai Lama during his trip to Kyormo Lung and Khangsar Gong of Tolungda were instrumental in pointing the team in charge of locating the reincarnation to the Tolung area.

The Death of a Lama

The Second Dalai Lama arrived safely back at Drepung and took up residence in the Ganden Podrang. Although he was not suffering from any specific illness, he looked rather thin and weak. His attendant Sung-rabpa called doctors to examine him, but the master shrugged off the issue. "What need is there of a doctor or of medicines?" he laughed. "I have no illness." On another occasion when his disciples seemed concerned about him, he called to them and said, "All phenomena composed of aggregates are impermanent. Perhaps you disciples are not aware of this truth, and need a lesson in it."

The state oracle was also called to do a reading of the situation. The master received him well, and the two spent much time together; but again he insisted that he had no physical problems. The oracle merely recommended to the disciples that they pray to the master to remain with them.

One day his attendant Sung-rabpa seemed distraught by the master's weakened condition. The master laughed at him and said, "Tell me, which is best: to take care of an old lama like me, or to take care of a young reincarnation?" He spoke like this every day to his disciples, thus teaching them and preparing their minds for his passing. Some days he would seem old and tired; on others he would seem young and brimming with energy.

On the eighteenth of the month, he summoned his chief disciples and asked them to prepare an altar for prayer and meditation. He said to them, "Today I had a vision. Jowo Atisha and his disciples, Lama Tsongkhapa and disciples, and countless Buddhas and bodhisattvas appeared in the sky. They then dissolved into my three places (crown chakra, throat chakra, and heart chakra). Many youthful male and female tantric deities appeared and requested me to go with them. Please do not be sad when I go. I will care for you in future lives."

The disciples begged him a hundred times not to pass away. He laughed and said to them, "I can extend my life by a few days or even weeks but not beyond that time." In this way, the *Biography* states, he continued to play with them, using his own death as a means to impress upon their minds the nature of impermanence.

During this time he also sang numerous tantric songs to them and spoke prophecies concerning his future lives. Two such prophecies are as follows. One day he said to Sung-rabpa, "Last night I dreamed I heard four conch shells resound with the melody of Dharma. Make a note of this dream." On another occasion he said, "At dawn I dreamed of four golden victory banners. These came to me from the Neudong Tsey (the place upon which the Fifth Dalai Lama later was to build the Potala) and were fixed firmly above my residence in Drepung." Both of these dream prophecies indicated that from him to the Fifth Dalai Lama, his incarnations would make their residence in the Ganden Podrang of Drepung Monastery and would work for the Buddhadharma and living beings from Drepung. The second dream indicated that the Fifth Dalai Lama would move his residence to the Potala.

He continued like this, receiving his disciples in his room and teaching them every day in informal ways, throughout the second month of the year. One day he offered a tea ceremony in the main temple. At the end of it he said to his disciples, "This old body of mine has just about reached the limits of being of benefit to the world. Do not be sad when I pass away. I will watch over you in many future lives." He then sang them numerous tantric songs as a means of leaving them with spiritual advice. One of them went,

> Listen to a song by a happy man!
> Soon this illusory illness
> That has created such a drama in my life
> Shall fade away of itself;
> No regrets. Together we accomplished much, and
> Only a few small efforts remain to be made.
> There will be no need to fuss over my corpse. . . .
> The best funeral rite you can perform for me
> Is, through listening, contemplation, and meditation,
> To fulfill the essence of what I have taught.

On the third day of the third month he again called his chief disciples to him. "It would be auspicious for us to meditate together," he said to them. They all sat in communal meditation. This continued without break for the next four days. The master never slept during this time. Sung-rabpa became concerned that perhaps he was overextending himself and requested him to take a rest. "Why should I sleep?" the master exclaimed. "Instead of sleep I absorb my mind in *mahamudra,* the ultimate nature of things. I have no need for meditation as such any more. I have no sleep, no dreams, no illnesses. I am free from such conventions."

At the end of the fourth day the sky became filled with rainbows, and a rainfall of flowers fell from the heavens. The master looked up from his meditations and said,

> In general, separation is the final result of coming together. In particular, the Buddhas of the three times, as well as Jowo Atisha and Lama Tsongkhapa, continue to work for the world in countless mysterious ways. . . .
>
> This old body of mine has completed its work for those to be trained by me in this life. Therefore I will now abandon it. But I will not abandon you. Soon a young reincarnation will come to take my place and continue my work. . . .
>
> Until then, rely upon your spiritual practice, and on meditation upon the tantric deities. Regard them as my regents. Do not be half-hearted in your spiritual efforts. When you need to rest, rest your mind in meditation. . . .

Having spoken in this way he then sat in the half-vajra posture, with his right foot slightly extended, his two hands in his lap in the meditation posture, and his eyes in the meditation gaze. It was the sixth day of the third month. At dusk that evening he began the tantric meditation known as the vajra recitation, slowly withdrawing the subtle energies from his body and directing them to the heart. This continued throughout the night.

At dawn of the following day he completed the energy absorptions and brought his breath and heartbeat to a state of stillness. He then absorbed his sense of form into the clear light of *dharmadhatu,* causing the appearance of all phenomena to become of one taste with voidness. Konchok Kyab concludes the account of his passing by stating,

Thus he absorbed into the *Dharmakaya*, and from there arose on that other plane in the *Samboghakaya* form as the tantric Buddha Heruka Chakrasamvara, sending out millions of *Nirmanakaya* emanations in order to benefit the world while himself abiding in the enlightenment state of great union characterized by the wisdom born together with bliss. . . . Thus he made evident to all his disciples his attainment of the state of complete and perfect enlightenment.

He was cremated shortly after that. When the cremation pyre was opened it revealed numerous relic pills and other auspicious signs. In particular, the heart had not been consumed by the flames. Instead, it had crystallized into the shape of a Buddha in the form of the tantric deity Heruka Chakrasamvara.

His reliquary was constructed at Kyormo Lung. Made from silver and gold and studded with countless precious gems, it was made in the shape of a Victory Stupa and stood thirteen *tou* (Tib., *mTho*) in height.

Konchok Kyab concludes his account by saying,

> Thus our guru Tamchey Khyenpa ("The Omniscient One"), who in actual fact had accomplished his enlightenment long ago, here played out a drama of life, enlightenment, and death for us. His deeds could only be comprehended by another fully enlightened being; even a tenth stage bodhisattva could not fully understand the multitude of levels on which he worked. . . .
>
> However, for the benefit of future generations, I have herein tried to relate a few of his most obvious physical activities. But what I can write down in words is about as much of what he really did as is a drop of water on the tip of a blade of grass compared to the amount of water in the ocean.

As His Holiness states in his Foreword to the present volume, the Second Dalai Lama was in many ways the greatest of all the Dalai Lama incarnations. Certainly he paved the way for the enthusiasm with which all future incarnations would be received by the Tibetans. It could even be said that the success of the future incarnations can in many ways be traced to the foundations that he laid. In fact, without the many traditions that he instituted, it is doubtful that the Dalai Lama office would have arisen at all. He not only took the legacy of the First Dalai Lama and continued it but carried it to a height beyond all expectations and set a clear agenda for the incarnations that were to follow.

As Yangpa Chojey puts it in his section of the *Biography,* by the end of the Second Dalai Lama's life, there was not a single person of consequence in central Asia—either monk or householder, chieftain or simple nomad—who did not connect with him either directly by means of receiving teachings or initiations from him or indirectly through studying with some of his close disciples.

As promised, not long after he passed away, a child was born who demonstrated all the signs of being a high reincarnation. This child, who eventually was traced in the Tolung area by means of the signs left by the aged Second Dalai Lama on his final visit to Kyormo Lung, was installed in the Ganden Podrang as the Second's reincarnation. He proved to be a brilliant student and quickly fulfilled expectations by easily completing his spiritual education.

Several times in his final years the Second Dalai Lama had commented, "I must soon go to work with the peoples of the north." This promise was fulfilled when his reincarnation the Third Dalai Lama traveled to Mongolia in 1578 and tamed the violent Mongolian peoples, thus ushering in an era of peace and harmony. This era of peace affected not only Central Asia but in fact much of the known world, for Mongolia at the time was one of the most aggressively violent and militarily powerful nations on earth.

Thus his kindness in this respect extended not only to Asians but also to the peoples of Europe. Had there been an international peace prize at the time, he certainly deserved it for this act alone. When the present Dalai Lama received the Nobel Peace Prize in 1989, it may be also regarded as being in part a posthumous award for that great deed of the Third Dalai Lama, which the Second several times had indicated that he planned to accomplish in his future incarnation.

A Concluding Note

As I stated in the opening section of my account of the Second Dalai Lama's life, I have drawn exten-sively from his own *Autobiography* for my interpretation of the first years of his life, particularly his relationships with his parents and grandparents, and for details of his early travels. However, in accordance with tradition, he writes somewhat modestly about himself, and therefore the *Biography* by Yangpa Chojey and Konchok Kyab makes for a more colorful read. Moreover, it presents him in the light of how the general public perceived him and thus tells a different side of the story. Consequently, I have drawn more extensively from it for my account of his adult years. Thirdly, the eighteenth-century text by Tsechokling Kachen Yeshey Gyaltsen in *Lives of the Teachers* offers a more succinct and well-tempered sketch, so I have also used it as a source. For the account of the fourteen Dalai Lamas, I have mostly followed the picture drawn by Purchokpa Rinpoche in his *Summary of the Lives of the Dalai Lamas* (Tib., *rGyal-bai-sku-'phreng-rnam-thar-dor-bsdus*) as found in his preface to the Potala edition of the *Kangyur*, published in the 1930s.

I have not attempted to provide a critical analysis of the events of the Second Dalai Lama's life but simply to tell the story in the way it is perceived within the tradition. My purpose is to convey a sense of the character and lifestyle of the author of the songs and poems that comprise this collection of mystical verses and also to shed light upon the nature of life in Tibet at the time of the composition of the collection, the late fifteenth and first half of the sixteenth centuries.

I have prefixed each of the songs and poems that follow in Part Three with a Translator's Preamble. Where possible I attempt to identify where and when the specific piece was composed, for whom it was composed, and so on, or else to comment on the nature of the piece. The time of composition of some of the pieces can be learned from references in either the *Autobiography* or *Biography;* as for the places of composition and personages for whom they were composed, this information is sometimes given in the colophons to the individual verse works.

In the Tibetan text the colophon is always placed at the end of each specific item. I have chosen to carry it back into my Translator's Preamble, as this then serves the purpose of introducing the individual items. There is no mention in either the *Autobiography* or *Biography* of who compiled the collection of songs and poems by the Second Dalai Lama or of the criteria that was used. The volume in Tibetan also does not make a statement on the subject. Presumably, the work was done by a committee formed of his disciples. Unfortunately no complete copy of his *Collected Works*, or *Sungbum* (spelled *gSung-'bum*) exists in India or in any publicly accessible library in the world. It may have contained an introductory essay providing such information.

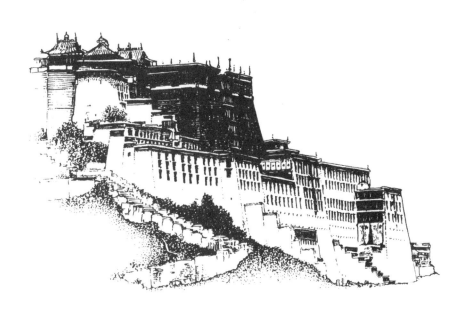

Mystical Verses

of the

Second Dalai Lama

Translation and Commentary

1

Song of a Young Reincarnation

Translator's Preamble: The first item in the Second Dalai Lama's collection of verse works is a piece he sang as a child. It is mentioned in both the *Autobiography* and *Biography* as his first substantial composition. Although he had sung numerous tantric songs before this time, they were usually just a few verses in length. Although many of the shorter songs are included in the *Autobiography* and *Biography*, none of them are in his *Nyamgur* collection. (I have quoted a number of these in Part Two: Life of the Second Dalai Lama.)

The Tibetan text has no title, but I have taken the liberty of providing one in the translation, basing my choice on the nature of the piece.

The background to the composition is stated in the colophon: "One evening when (Gendun Gyatso was) in his sixth year (that is, in the Iron Mouse Year [1480] when he was either four or five years old) his parents scolded him. He spontaneously replied to them with this song. However, when the verses were being transcribed, a visitor arrived unexpectedly at the door, and the writing was put aside. It was never completed."

Most Tibetan verse works are written in four-line stanzas. In this piece, however, many of the stanzas contain only two or three lines, and there are a number of lines that seem to stand alone. Most are eight syllables in length, although some are nine and some six. Presumably the consistency was established through variations in rhythm and melody, as the piece was originally voiced as a song and not penned or read as a poem.

I have broken and subtitled the song into five parts, based on theme, for the convenience of readers. The first of these is the line of homage to Lama Tsongkhapa, whose ordination name was Lobzang Drakpa. He was one of the principal gurus of the First Dalai Lama and the founder of the Yellow Hat School. The Second Dalai Lama opens many of his written works with a line of homage to him. Here he refers to him as "the glorious master from the east," because Tsongkhapa was born in the Tsongkha area of Amdo Province, near the border that Amdo shares with China.

The line of homage is followed by six verses of salutation and supplication to Gyalwa Gendun Drubpa, the First Dalai Lama, and also to Arya Avalokiteshvara, the Bodhisattva of Compassion, of whom the First Dalai Lama was considered to be an emanation. These are taken as the Second's proclamation of himself as being Gyalwa Gendun Drup's reincarnation, and he returns to this theme later in the song.

In one of his opening verses he writes, "When the sentient beings of samsara's six realms / Come before Karmayama, the judge of karmic deeds. . . ." Here Karmayama is the Lord of Death; according to Buddhist mythology, after one dies one comes into the presence of Karmayama, who holds up a mirror. One looks into it and sees the sequence of one's life replayed. Good and evil deeds are weighed, and one then moves on to an according rebirth. If at that time one can remember the Buddhas and bodhisattvas and keep the mind within a positive framework, one's chances of passing successfully through the test are enhanced.

In the next section he speaks of the human predicament and of how most people miss out on realizing their spiritual potential due to apathy and ignorance. He concludes with a reference to himself, using the childhood name Sangyey Pel that his mother had been instructed to give to him in a dream when he was still in her womb.

The fourth section is a set of verses reprimanding his parents for chastising him, the reincarnation of the great master Gyalwa Gendun Drup. At the time the song was composed, he had not been formally recognized as such, but he seems here to nonetheless fully regard himself in this capacity.

The final section contains a number of prophecies. First he comments that Gyalwa Gendun Drubpa will incarnate seven times in order to complete his work. As stated in the Foreword by His Holiness the present Dalai Lama and also in Part Two of my introduction, this is but one of a number of such prophecies that he made during his lifetime. Many of these were spoken when he was an infant. He here refers to the work of his predecessor in constructing Tashi Lhunpo Monastery (although he mentions this activity in the first person, as though he had done it himself) and the special relationship that the First Dalai Lama had established with the Dharma protectress Palden Lhamo. He himself, as we saw in Part Two of my introduction, took this relationship with Palden Lhamo a step further by consecrating and empowering Lhamo Latso, "The Lake of the Goddess," also known as the Lake of Visions.

The final line of the song, "Although you vowed to call on me . . . ," ends in an incomplete sentence. This is because, as stated in the colophon, a visitor arrived when the piece was being transcribed, and consequently the recording of it was never completed. The line is taken as a prophecy of the problems he later encountered as a teenager in Tashi Lhunpo Monastery, when the monastic administrators expelled him.

A line in the previous verse, "Before my death comes call out to me," is a prophecy that in the end, his antagonists will repent and request his forgiveness. In a later poem we will see the unfolding of this prophecy.

[The Homage:]

> Homage to the glorious master from the east,
> He famous as the sun and the moon,
> Lama Tsongkhapa, the Buddhist monk Lobzang Drakpa.

[Verses to the First Dalai Lama:]

Salutations to Panchen Gendun Drubpa,
Treasury of the sutras and tantras,
Wish-fulfilling gem at the top of the victory banner,
He who fulfills all spiritual aspirations.

Master of the ten stages manifest in ordinary human form
Who lights the Dharma lamp in this Land of Snows,
I bow to you in body, speech and mind.

When the sentient beings of samsara's six realms
Come before Karmayama, the judge of karmic deeds,
They become filled with fear and apprehension.
May Lokeshvara, the Bodhisattva of Compassion,
Focus his caring glance upon them.

From the Pure Land of Joy you came, manifesting in
    ordinary form
To lead living beings to the path of freedom.
Enlightened one who perfected wisdom and compassion,
Look on the sentient beings pained with suffering
And leave them not bereft of your guidance.

When the living beings accomplish the Way,
The experience of misery no longer arises.
Look with compassion on the beings who turn away
From happiness, and who bring themselves sorrow.

The hard-to-train beings of this degenerate age
Were not tamed by the mighty Buddhas of the past.
Look on them with your great compassion.

[Our Spiritual Situation:]

A human rebirth with its freedoms and blessings
Is as rare as the *udumvara* flower,

And is not often nor easily acquired.
We must learn to use it effectively.

The countless enlightened beings of this world
Care for us as though they were our parents;
Yet due to our immature attitudes we generate
Mostly negative karma in our dealings with them
And thus collect causes of a rebirth in misery.
Thus it was said by the Buddha himself.

But living beings now heed not the Buddhas
And the Buddhas are thus rendered unable
To show them enlightenment's Way.

Like a moth leaping into a flame
They become bound in the prison of frustration
And cannot build links with the spiritual masters.
Lead them on the hook of your compassion.

So many of these sentient beings,
My parents in countless previous lives,
Have been given their fill of Dharma teachings,
Yet remain unsatiated and misuse their knowledge.
They open the door of the lower realms for themselves.

May the Three Jewels come to their rescue,
For they are unable to bear the great suffering;
And wherever they happen to take rebirth,
May they remain free from pain and sorrow
And quickly evolve to enlightenment's joy.

Amidst a vast assembly of spiritual masters
Skilled in upholding the enlightenment tradition,
I, the incomparable Sangyey Pel, who is
Magnificent as the great King of Mountains, sing these
    words.

[Admonishing his Parents:]

The living beings, confused by karmic instincts,
Look down on and abuse the enlightened beings.
Thus they fall into the lower realms of samsara.
They (my parents) scold me with a seemingly good
    intention,
But it only brings them negative karma of speech;
They would do better to see me as their crown jewel,
For then their wishes would be fulfilled like falling rain.

Acquiring (as a son) a holy being like the Panchen
Is as rare as finding a wish-fulfilling gem.
They should meditate (on me) as being Buddha Vajradhara.

[Prophecies:]

Although he (the First Dalai Lama) completely flooded
This world with the sublime nectars of Dharma,
He did not complete all of his plans.
Therefore for seven incarnations he will come
To work for the beings of this world
Before merging into the stainless *dharmadhatu*.
The fortunate beings who train under him
Will surely take rebirth in the Pure Land of Joy.

In this incarnation may I benefit living beings
And plant the banner of truth in all ten directions.
May the flag of my deeds fly in all the three worlds,
And may the crown jewel of wisdom be forever made
    firm.

(O Gendun Drubpa,) source of hope, wish-fulfilling gem,
Who has gained perfection beyond the need for training,
Grant inspiration that the sentient beings on this earth
May grow in learning, contemplation, and meditation;
Release an unbroken stream of enlightened energy.

With the aid of the protectoress Palden Lhamo
I (in my previous life) firmly established my teachings
In the glorious Tashi Lhunpo Monastery.
All those who remember that beneficial work
Should welcome me now without hesitation.

A Panchen (like Gendun Drubpa) is most rare;
Before my death comes call out to me
If you have heard of my rebirth.

Although you vowed to call on me. . . .

2

A Dance to Delight the World

Translator's Preamble: The colophon to this entry states, "This spiritual song, entitled 'A Dance to Delight the World,' a compilation of personal reflections, was composed at Drepung Monastery by the Buddhist monk Gendun Gyatso Palzangpo, a poet also known as Yangchen Shepai Dorjey, the Melodious Laughing Vajra, who here has taken the teachings of the Buddhist masters and woven them into a lotus garland to wear around his neck."

According to the *Biography*, this song was written during the second year of Gendun Gyatso's three-year stint as a student at Drepung Monastery, that is, in 1495, when he was twenty years old. Yangpa Chojey states that it is primarily a song of prophecy concerning his future work in establishing Chokhor Gyal Monastery (better known to Tibetans as Gyal). The prophecy is but one aspect of it, the other themes being, as he states above in the colophon, "a compilation of personal reflections."

The site of the monastery-to-be, as we saw in Part Two, was known as Metoktang, or the "Pasture of Flowers," and was located near Lhamoi Latso, the Lake of Visions. The many repetitions of the word *metok,* or "flowers," is one indication of the prophetic nature of the piece, as is the description of the view from "the place of meditation." At the time of composition Gendun Gyatso had not yet visited the Gyal area.

In fact, this was not to happen for over a dozen years, when he was on a teaching tour in the Olkha area at the invitation of the Olkha chieftain Lhagyaripa, who had requested him to come to Gyal and examine it for its potential as a place for summer meditation. The Second Dalai Lama did this and conducted various rituals there in order to make an auspicious connection. Later he performed dream analysis on the place and also had other lama friends do divinations. The signs were excellent, so he began construction (many years later) in the Earth Snake Year (1509).

As a guide to readers I have broken "A Dance to Delight the World" into five sections, again based on theme.

The first of these is a traditional opening homage, which he directs both to all spiritual masters in general and also to his personal teachers. Here he uses the image of a sun (the masters) shining down from the vast space of love and wisdom (their activities of body, speech, and mind), to mature the minds of trainees (lotus flowers).

In the second section he reflects on certain negative elements present within the spiritual scene in Tibet at the time and of a dilution of the pure teachings with sectarian and materialistic considerations. There is no mention in either the *Autobiography* or *Biography* of any specific event arousing his displeasure in this regard. The *Autobiography* simply states, "At that time there were some religious conflicts in the Lhasa area, and I thought (to stay out of them) by making a retreat in a cave somewhere in the direction of Tsang. Inspired by those feelings I composed the song 'A Dance to Delight the World.' "

Probably he is here addressing the militant anti-Gelugpa activities present during his time at Drepung. I discussed this to some extent in Part Two, in the section dealing with the Second's tactful solution of the Great Prayer Festival controversy at Lhasa shortly after he had become the abbot of Drepung.

In the third section of the song Gendun Gyatso addresses the human spiritual predicament and the value of solitary meditation. He warns of the ease with which the spiritual opportunities afforded by a human incarnation are lost and urges us instead to take the essence of life by cultivating inner peace.

The fourth section is the part of the song regarded as the prophecy of Chokhor Gyal Monastery, his hermitage in Metoktang of the Gyal region. He likens the area to a young virgin girl pulsating with sensuality; she dances in ecstasy, the rivers and streams her flowing limbs and the wonders of nature the stage of her performance. The imagery is delightfully sexual for the writings of a young monk.

In the final section of the poem he provides us with the context of his composition—that it was spontaneously written and not created at anyone's request.

The piece is composed in lines of nine syllables, with four lines making up a complete stanza. Sometimes several stanzas are linked together to make a verse of eight or twelve lines. In the passages describing Chokhor Gyal's natural beauties, the lines remain of the same length, although the stanza arrangement is no longer honored, and the images flow from one line to another quite freely. I have arranged these as seems most conducive to comfortable reading.

[The Homage:]

> Homage to all the holy gurus.
> With devotion I bow to my spiritual masters,
> Who are inseparably one with Buddha Vajradhara.
> In the vast expanse of their wondrous enlightenment
> The sun of wisdom and love shine unhindered,
> Inspiring the lotus trainees to blossom and grow.
> Listen now to this song of mine!

[Reflections on the state of Buddhism in Tibet:]

> Ours is an age in which the sunlike Dharma
> With its thousand rays of knowledge and compassion
> Has dropped to the tips of the western peaks.
> The lotus garden of the enlightenment teachings
> Is struck daily by a frost ever growing in strength.
>
> These days most who claim to be lineage masters
> Are mere bees chasing the honey of wealth.
> Powered by delusion, their so-called teachings

Are little better than the hooting of owls;
Yet they boldly strut amid the ranks of sages.

The vast majority of humanity today
Seems bereft of all common sense.
They lack the eye able to tell right from wrong
And stagger off the cliff falling to extremes.

Some, poisoned by the waters of jealousy,
Are obsessed with the thought of besting others;
While others, poisoned by hatred and hypocrisy,
Race around in a state of utter delirium.
And both claim to uphold the spiritual path!

Kyehu! It would seem that nowadays
In this land surrounded by snow mountains
The squeals emitted by foxes and jackals
Are louder than even the roar of the lion.

Ours is a time in which ordinary stones
Are valued over wish-fulfilling gems;
And when the flashing of tiny fireflies
Is chosen over the light of the sun itself.

Here near the bottom of the degenerate age
The forces of negativity and darkness prevail;
Even Buddhas, bodhisattvas and sages shy away
And pass silently away to the sphere of peace.

How can a simple little butterlamp
Placed in the face of a terrible storm
Ever hope to eliminate the darkness of night?
Likewise, the sincere practitioners who work
To maintain the enlightenment tradition today
Can easily wear themselves out with the effort.

Thus in this age of violence and conflict
Is it not wiser to retreat from the world
And escape to a place of solitary meditation?—
A place where one can drink and drink again
The nectar-like teachings of Lama Tsongkhapa,
The most clear eye for the living beings of today,
An omniscient master equal to Buddha himself!

[The Human Predicament:]

We have achieved this very rare incarnation
As a human being able to gain full enlightenment,
A rebirth formed from a thousand white deeds;
But we should remember that it is easily lost
To preoccupation with worldly concerns.
How senseless to allow such a loss to occur!

Even the position of a universal emperor
With power over all in the four directions
Is essenceless as the plantain tree,
Which gives fruit but once and then dies away.
The greatest worldly accomplishment is impotent
For those who have not overcome the forces
Of karmic instincts and the delusions within.

Small indulgences gradually bring about addiction
And soon produce more frustration than joy.
Thus who with wisdom would entertain attraction
To worldly indulgence, source of a hundred faults?

How much wiser simply to turn one's back
On all situations producing delusion and pain
And walk away into the mountains
To pursue single-pointed meditation.
There all of nature contributes
To the immediate experience of peace of mind.

[The Prophecy:]

In fields of flowers gently swaying,
Young bees sing their happy songs
And pheasants strut a dance of joy.
The cuckoo too rings the bell of melody
And the *kalapingka* bird chirps merrily along.

Here the earth maiden is beautiful indeed:
Her virgin streams holding up garlands of bubbles
As they laughingly dance over rocks and crags;
Her orchards filled with all types of trees
Laden with fruit, flowers, and leaves;
And, standing behind, rings of snow mountains,
Their peaks bloused in white silken clouds,
Crystal glaciers their tassels
And blue forests their exquisite skirt.

Lapis lazuli meadows stretch below
Like the wings of a parrot in flight,
Nets of lotus flowers embellishing them
And wild animals grazing quietly on their slopes.
A fence of trees stands again behind
To lock out the thief of every distraction.

Such is the wonder of my place of solitude,
A garden sent from above to inspire inner joy,
Where one easily forgets the eight worldly concerns.
How happy it is to practice meditation here
And savour the pleasures of the exquisite flavor
Of unmistaken single-pointed concentration.
What a delight just to sit there
Chanting the sutras and the tantric sadhanas;
To ignite the wisdom fires of bliss and emptiness
And burn off the wood of seeming duality;
To cultivate the illusory body yoga locked in union

With the vision of clear light and voidness;
And with the hook of wise and skillful means of emanation
To pull the wheel of this impure world
Into the great sphere of supreme undying joy.
Ah, what good fortune to practice these yogas.

[The Context:]

Such is the song of Yangchen Shepai Dorjey,
The yogi and poet Melodious Laughing Vajra,
Who plans to emulate the sages of old
By leaving behind the corruptions of the world
And practicing meditation in wonderful solitude.
It is also the song of a man somewhat saddened
By the ways of most practitioners of today;
A man made somewhat haughty with the strength
Of having trained his mind in the wisdom tradition.

The clouds of my thoughts were heavy with rain
And when the dragon within it restlessly stirred,
There seemed no way to hold back its thunder.
How could I have possibly been content
To pass the day without composing this song?
It seems to be an inborn predisposition of mine
To spontaneously ring the bell of verse;
But I do it solely with a good heart.
I, Melodious Laughing Vajra.

3

Two Alphabetical Poems

Translator's Preamble: The next two entries in Gendun Gyatso's collection of verse works are "alphabetical poems," a unique form of Tibetan poetry in which each line begins with a successive letter of the alphabet. The Tibetan alphabet contains thirty consonants, or seven-and-a-half groups of four. Thus poems of this nature usually have six four-line stanzas and a seventh stanza of six lines. They also generally have a few concluding verses that do not follow an alphabetical pattern.

Simply for the fun of it, I decided to try and transpose these into the format of the alphabet of the English language. Even though the rendering becomes somewhat forced, I might comment that it is perhaps no more so than in the Tibetan originals. (The letter *x* provides the greatest challenge.)

As the Tibetan alphabet has thirty letters and the English only twenty-six, I compensated in the first poem by having two four-line verses, giving the next three verses six lines each, and then breaking away from the structure for the remainder of the text. In the second poem I compensated by simply repeating a number of the letters that begin lines, although here I attempted to follow a structure of five lines per verse, with the concluding verse (which is non-alphabetical) having eight lines. Some Tibetan lines seem to demand more than one in English, and thus some letters get repeated more than others.

The tone of the two poems is considerably different. The first is a rather serious presentation of the doctrine of emptiness, the wisdom teachings of the Buddha as clarified by the second century Indian sage Nagarjuna, forefather of the Madhyamaka school of Buddhist philosophy. In the Nagarjuna tradition the emphasis is upon first recognizing the *gakja* (*dgag-bya*), or "object of negation"—the false "self" of which persons and things are void. Once this false self is clearly understood, one then proceeds to retain and focus upon a conceptual image of it as neither one with nor separate from the aggregates of a given phenomenon, resting the mind in this sense of absence.

The Second Dalai Lama signs the first of these two poems as Namkhai Naljor, "the Yogi of Space," which, as His Holiness states in his Foreword, is a name he likes to give himself when composing texts on emptiness.

The second of his two alphabetical poems is a playful and slightly frivolous piece that is more like noodling and doodling than poetry as such. Nonetheless it has its own charm. Here Gendun Gyatso uses the poetic pen name Yangchen Shepai Dorjey, "the Melodious Laughing Vajra." (Perhaps the first verse may someday be useful to Liptons, Brooke Bond, or some other such tea marketer.)

Song of Emptiness

Ah, friends wandering in beginningless samsara,
Begin Dharma practice now if wisdom is your aim;
Consider the I, this sense of self that we have, and
Dedicate your energy to observing how it appears.

Exchange worldly activities for solitary meditation;
Fashion a thought of subtle inquiry able to
Generate an image of this sense of "I," and
Hold to it like a fish on a hook.

Investigate, for example, a tree.

Just as "tree" is a mere mental label that is
Known as neither one with nor separate from its parts,
Like its leaves and branches, similarly, all things are
Mere imputations of names and mental labels.
Nagarjuna and his disciples taught in this way.

Open skies, forests, wooden carts, things big and small,
Parts or wholes: nothing truly has independent being.
Question everything that appears to the mind, and
Realize how the deluded living beings, gullible as oxen,
See everything through the distorted consciousness
That grasps at things as standing alone.

Uncountable beings appear in the six realms—
Various animals; hell beings tortured by heat and cold;
Worlds of ghosts afflicted by hunger, thirst, and
Xenophobia; and also men, gods, and demigods—
Yet they all lack any objective existence.
Zealously cultivate this extraordinary view.

Oh hark! Instead of falling prey to the grasping mind
That is propelled by a false belief in true existence,
It is better to rely upon the mind that is content
With a moderate sense of physical needs
And to strive instead in the practice of meditation
Upon profound emptiness, the ultimate nature of things.

A donkey can have no horns on its head;
Similarly, how can anything have true existence?
From atoms to the omniscient wisdom of enlightenment,
All things utterly lack a final nature.
This is the essential message of Buddha.

Ha ha! Without relying on elaborate reasonings
One understands the meaning of undying *Ah*,
The essential sound of wisdom,

And knows things as being mere mental imputations.
Such is the song of Namkhai Naljor, the Yogi of Space,
Voiced here in Tibet, land of healing herbs.

A Simple Song of Fun

A wise man like me makes tea his pleasure,
Beverage of nectar the color of saffron,
Camphor its only rival in fragrance,
Delicate porcelain its vessel of choice;
Drink tea, a friend to those seeking wisdom.

Everyone wishing to sing melodious songs of
Fabulous verse into all the directions,
Gorge yourself first on the drink of sages;
Have a few cups of tea, and then like the famed
Hermit Luipa, you will quickly gain siddhi.

In the quest to accomplish the wisdom tradition
As taught by the mighty Tathagata himself,
Keep inner vision as your peerless guide;
Launch into meditation on the nature of voidness,
Legacy of Nagarjuna, and accomplish his state.

Mastering the essence of the profound scriptures
Numerous beyond count, and accomplishing the
Ocean of practices, like the six perfections,
Place all sentient beings, blind as cattle, on the
Path leading to knowledge, freedom, and joy.

Quench the thirst of living beings' needs,
Regardless of the personal sacrifice required.

Strive to generate the confidence necessary
To meet with wisdom the challenges that arise, and
To overcome the fox-like distractions of fools.

Until stability in practice has been gained,
Value the life of simplicity and contentment.
Wear jewels of learning, reflection, and meditation
With the wish to become a gem to this world;
Wondrous indeed will be the results.

Worthless are all things ephemeral, yet
Worldly people see them as supreme; like
Xanthic metal, or gold, as it's called.
Yes, they waste their lives seeking peace in them,
Zealously clutching at what always slips away.

O hark! Such is my alphabetical song,
And if you really care for yourself, you should
Be just like me, unequalled on this earth.
Ha ha. There I go again, making too much noise;
But it's just a song voiced in fun,
A few idle verses from the pen of the poet
Yangchen Shepai Dorje, the Melodious Laughing Vajra.

4

Song of the Yarlung Valley

Translator's Preamble: The Yarlung Valley lies to the southeast of Lhasa, downriver along the Brahmaputra and running perpendicular to it. The Yarlung Chu, or "the river running through the valley," empties into the Brahmaputra and thus is a tributary of it. In times past Yarlung was one of the most fertile and prosperous valleys of central Asia and gave rise to Tibet's early dynasty of kings and emperors. In fact it is Yarlung and not the Lhasa area that is the cradle of Tibetan civilization as we know it today. Lhasa did not achieve a position of prominence until the mid–eighth century.

Tibetan mythology tells us that millions of years ago in a cave on Sodang Gangpo Mountain of Yarlung, a monkey interbred with a mountain primate and gave birth to the first six Tibetans (or possibly the first human beings). These six later procreated and eventually formed the basis of the six ancient tribes of Tibet. The monkey was an emanation of Avalokiteshvara, the Bodhisattva of Compassion; his consort was an emanation of Tara, the female emanation of Avalokiteshvara and the symbol of the enlightened activity of the Buddhas.

The first of Tibet's kings, Nyatri Tsenpo, also an incarnation of Avalokiteshvara, is said to have been an Indian prince who fled from India out of fear of his father, a descendent of a cousin of the Buddha. According to the story, his father had treated him badly because of the many unusual physical signs that the boy bore from birth. He fled into the Himalayas and eventually arrived in Yarlung. The inhabitants were so impressed by his appearance and character that in 127 B.C. they made him their king. The place where the Tibetans first met him is Lhabap Ri, or "Divine Descent Mountain" of Yarlung, so-called because when they asked him from whence he came, he was unable to speak their language and therefore made the Indian hand gesture of noncomprehension, which is done by pointing the fingers upward and twisting the wrist. They mistook the upward-pointing fingers to mean that he had descended from the heavens. His name Nyatri Tsenpo means "The Planquin-borne Lord," because the people built him a wooden planquin and carried him back to their village on it.

It was Nyatri Tsenpo who built the Yarlung Castle, known as the Yambu Lhakang, that the Second Dalai Lama refers to later in his poem. This castle is regarded as the oldest building in Tibet, and although it suffered from fires on a number of occasions, it is said to have stood for almost two thousand years, until the Chinese destroyed it in the 1960s. It was rebuilt in the late 1980s as a tourist attraction, but unfortunately no modern reconstruction is able to replace a monument of such antiquity.

From Nyatri Tsenpo's time central Tibet was ruled from Yarlung by a dynasty of kings descended from him, the territory under their jurisdiction growing with the passing generations. The thirty-third king in this succession, Emperor Songtsen Gampo (627–650 A.D.), is also regarded as an incarnation of Avalokiteshvara. He was the first in the royal line to formally endorse Buddhism as the country's national religion, and he moved the capital from Yarlung to Lhasa, where he built the Red Fort as his residence. (It was on the grounds of the Red Fort that the Potala was later constructed by the Fifth Dalai Lama.) By Songtsen Gampo's time most of the central Asian plateau, from Ladakh to western China, had been brought under the rule of his Yarlung administration.

It was Songtsen Gampo who constructed the Dradruk Temple in Yarlung, also mentioned by the Second Dalai Lama in his poem. This temple had the aim and function of serving the Buddhist needs of the Yarlung community. Of the hundred and eight religious buildings that Songtsen Gampo created, the Dradruk Temple was one of the twelve having the purpose of subduing the earth spirits of Tibet and thus was of a unique geomantic importance.

A hundred years later Emperor Trisong Deutson, who brought the illustrious Guru Padmasambhava to Tibet, regarded it as one of Tibet's three principal monastic dwellings, the other two being the Jokhang Temple at Lhasa, which Songtsen Gampo had constructed in honor of his Nepalese wife, and Samyey Monastery (of the Samyey Valley), Tibet's first monastic institution, established by Trisong Deutson himself in the mid-eighth century.

The Second Dalai Lama's mention of Mount Truzin refers to the area's mythological link with Lokeshvara, the Bodhisattva of Compassion. *Truzin* is the Tibetan form of the Sanskrit term *Potala*, the name of the mountain in South India on which Lokeshvara is said to have meditated for many years.

The colophon to the poem states, "Written by the Buddhist monk Gendun Gyatso Palzangpo at the request of the chieftains Nangso Namseypa and So Gyalwa, while Gendun Gyatso was staying at Tsawa Dru." However, his *Autobiography* and also his *Biography* provide information whereby we can place it within the unfolding pattern of his life. According to the *Autobiography*, in the ninth month of the Hare Year (1495) the king of the Chongyey Valley, Chogyal Dorjey Tseten by name, requested him to come and teach in the Chongyey area. (This invitation had been instigated by Panchen Choklha Odzer, a disciple of the First Dalai Lama, as we saw in Part Two.) Chongyey is the valley that leads into Yarlung from the south. The Second Dalai Lama discussed the invitation with the Drepung abbot, who advised that he remain in Drepung for one more year in order to complete his studies and therefore to go the following year. He heeded this advice and thus, in the spring of the Fire Dragon Year, or 1496, left on a teaching tour.

This began with a pilgrimage to Samyey Monastery and then continued to Tsetang, the capital of Yarlung, where he publicly taught for some days to the people. While in Tsetang an invitation arrived from Tsawa Dru, and he went there and taught, visiting the Dradruk Temple of Yarlung on the way. The colophon to the poem mentions that it was composed while he was residing at Tsawa Dru. Thus we can presume that it was written at this time, in 1496.

The poem is composed in lines of nine syllables, with four lines to a stanza. In several cases two stanzas are joined together to make an eight-line verse.

He begins with a stanza containing three sets of two images that should always remain together in sportive intercourse: the moon in the sky, geese in water, and faith in wisdom. He then continues with a reference to the link that Avalokiteshvara, the Bodhisattva of Compassion, has had with the Yarlung Valley since time immemorial and as exemplified in the story told above of the monkey and also the deeds of the early kings. In the third verse he begins his tribute to Yarlung itself.

The teaching that he gave on the occasion, as mentioned in the poem, is not specified in the *Autobiography*, presumably because it was a general, informal discourse to an open audience. The *nagas* that he comments "rushed to be present" are mythological spirits who, when pleased, cause prosperity to blossom in the human world. As the Second Dalai Lama puts it in verse, when the nagas are happy, their jewelled crowns vibrate with their excitement and energy; the energy thus released causes an abundant harvest. This would be the fate of the farmers of the Yarlung Valley.

He closes the poem with the aspiration that peace may prevail and that living beings may achieve the state of the *Dharmakaya,* a term synonymous with enlightenment.

Homage to Manjushri, Bodhisattva of Wisdom.
The radiant moon in a cloudless sky,
A flock of geese sporting in water,
And faith in Sarasvati, Goddess of Wisdom:
May these natural unions always prevail.

The compassionate light of Lokeshvara, Bodhisattva of
    Compassion,
Has illuminated the face of the earth for long.
Its light has been specially strong here
In Tibet, this land wrapped in snow mountains,
Scattering flowers of our fame far and wide.

The Yarlung Valley, ornament of this world,
Is a piece of the heavens fallen to earth.
The very symbol of our ancient way,
Its arrow maiden carries tales of our glory
To Akanistha, heaven at the peak of the world.

Magnificent Yarlung, a picture of wonder
Sketched by the brush of celestial artisans;
With forests rustling in ever-cool breezes,
Lines gently flowing like those on a hand;
Beautiful towns, villages and temples
Set like pearls in delightful display;
Its fields like outstretched wings of a parakeet
Laden with gems of ripening crops:
Kyehu, it is as though the Kingdom of Immortality
Had found its way to this northern land.

Here on the side of Mount Truzin
All good things in the world and beyond
Take form as a magnificent spiritual garden,
With temples and monasteries equal in splendour
To those that existed in India itself.

On the face of this most sacred of mountains
Stands the splendid Yarlung Castle,
Its walls emanating great bursts of light
Like a city built by craftsmen divine
From the dust of jewels and precious gems;
And, in front of it, the Dradruk Temple,
A monument magically manifest from the wisdom
Of Lokeshvara, the Bodhisattva of Compassion.

To the west of this temple, in the direction of fire,
Lies Tashi Gang, prosperous city of joy,
A gift from the gods carefully collected

And arranged for the delight of the world;
Its houses as though made from jewels
And its parks like celestial promenades;
Its earth carpeted with grasses blue as lapis lazuli
Bedecked in a net of multicolored flowers;
And rainbows dancing in the sky overhead
To rival the splendour of the heavens above.

Beds of lotuses with transporting fragrances
Everywhere lie like patches of silk,
And beautiful maidens with eyes like antelopes
Stroll under trees laden with sweet-tasting fruit,
Their branches outstretched as though to signal
The wise to join in a festival of joy.

And here I sit, the Buddhist monk Gendun Gyatso,
In order to teach the vast and profound Dharma
To a gathering of devoted seekers of truth,
My Dharma throne elegantly set amid this splendour
In a field of flat crystals craftfully arranged.

What a setting in which to participate
In the turning of the holy Dharma Wheel!
The nagas themselves rush to be present,
Their jewelled crowns trembling with anticipation and joy.

The merit emanates a vast wave of goodness
That caresses the orchards heavy with harvest,
Causing them to ripen with every delicious flavor
And their fruit to fall like rain to the earth,
Bringing ambrosial happiness to one and to all.

By the meritorious energy of this wondrous gathering
May an era of goodness and harmony ensue.
May the treasuries of peace and happiness be filled

And both spiritual and physical prosperity be achieved.
May we never be parted from our enlightenment teachers
And may we all find our way to the City of Joy,
The Dharmakaya stage of wisdom's perfection.

5

Song of the Traveling Bee

Translator's Preamble: What follows is an epic poem on a pilgrimage that the Second Dalai Lama made to Tsari, a holy mountain in the south of Tibet near what now is the Indian border of Assam. In the olden days of Buddhist India, Tsari was regarded as one of the twenty-four places of spiritual power and was listed as such in the Heruka Chakrasamvara Tantra. Several of these twenty-four (including Mt. Kailash, source of the Ganges, Indus, Sublej, and Brahmaputra rivers) are located in the Himalayas inside Tibet.

The colophon to this poem provides us with the background of its composition: "This ballad, 'Song of the Traveling Bee,' was requested by Nangpa Sonam Lekpa and Norzang Soljawa, two disciples from Druda with the eyes of their faith and intelligence wide open. They asked that I write a Dharma song about our visit eastward through Dvakpo to the Tsari area and on the beneficial activities that took place there. It was spontaneously composed by the poet Gendun Gyatso Palzangpo while he was residing in the glorious Ganden Choling monastery."

The fact that it was written at Ganden Choling helps us somewhat with the dating of it. In the spring of the Wood Mouse Year (1504), the Second Dalai Lama was residing in Eh teaching to the local community when a delegation arrived from Druda with a strong request for him to visit Dvakpo and also to make a teaching pilgrimage to Tsari. He accepted and on the way was offered a new monastery that had just been completed. He named it Ganden Choling and rested in it a few days while teaching to the local populace. He stayed in it again later after returning from Tsari; it was during this second sojourn in Ganden Choling, on his return journey in the late summer, that the composition occurred.

A few contextual notes on the place and personal names mentioned in the poem may be in order. Eh (also called "Ehchok" in the *Autobiography* and "Yechok" in the *Biography*), where the Second Dalai Lama was teaching when the invitation to travel to Tsari arrived, is situated at the top of the Yarlung Valley and is the region where several of Emperor Songtsen Gampo's important family members were resettled after Songtsen moved his capital from Yarlung to Lhasa in the mid–seventh century. It quickly became an important cultural and spiritual center and the hub of much Buddhist activity. The Second Dalai Lama had taught there several times in previous years during his annual spring teaching and pilgrimage tours. Shampo Mountain, on which the Second Dalai Lama was residing at the time, is the source of the Yarlung Chu River.

Dvakpo lies to the east of Yarlung, and to approach it the traveler journeys up the Yarlung Valley and then crosses southward into the Olkha mountains. Dvakpo is also famed as the region where Milarepa's chief disciple Gampopa appeared in the mid–eleventh century and where Gampopa established the monastery to become the source of the Dvakpo Kargyu school descended from Marpa. Both Marpa and Milarepa were laymen, but Milarepa's chief disciple was a monk known to history as Gampopa. Gampopa's ordination name was Daod Shunnu, or "Youthful Moonlight," and it is the statue of Gampopa that the Second Dalai Lama mentions visiting while in Dvakpo.

The *Autobiography* also mentions that while there he "was placed on Gampopa's teaching throne and asked to speak on the holy Dharma." It adds that upon beholding the statue, he fell into a trance and experienced a vision of Gampopa. This statue was renowned for its lifelike quality and its similarity to Gampopa in actual appearance, a feature rare in Tibetan statue making, which prefers to stylize all faces into a "pure appearance form" similar to that of a Buddha image. Gampoda Mountain, mentioned by the Second Dalai Lama, is the site of Gampopa's monastery, Dvaklha Gompa, that housed this sacred image until it was destroyed by the Chinese army in the mid–1960s.

The sacred mountain of Odey Gunggyal that the Second Dalai Lama mentions several times in his poem is one of central Tibet's highest mountains. Located in the upper Dvakpo area to the west of the Metoktang Valley, it has been a favorite place for cave meditators throughout Tibet's Buddhist history.

The Lohita River that the group "successfully forded" on their way east and south is, I believe, a tributary of the Brahmaputra, that eventually drains into India.

Tsaritra is simply an alternative name for Tsari, the sacred mountain that was the object of their pilgrimage. The Second Dalai Lama obviously considers it auspicious that they arrived at Tsari in the month commemorating the time when Buddha first taught the *Kalachakra Tantra* to a group of advanced disciples at the Dhanyakotaka stupa in south India.

His reference to visiting Metoktang on his return from Tsari must refer to the Metoktang Valley of Gyal in the Upper Dvakpo region, where shortly thereafter he was to begin construction of Chokhor Gyal monastery, of which he had already received a number of dreams, visions, and prophecies.

Here again, as in the previous poem on the Yarlung Valley, the young monk calls upon a rather striking sexual language: "Parks of flowers the color of jewels / Rising in clusters like a young virgin's breasts. . . ." The passage certainly stands as one of his most sensuous.

The line stating that a " . . . powerful arrow of invitation arrived. . . " refers to the Tibetan tradition of rolling a letter around a piece of wood, sometimes even around an arrow itself, before giving it to a traveler or caravan to carry to its destination.

This song presents an excellent portrait of the young Second Dalai Lama's lifestyle at the time, which was that of a constant wanderer and teacher enjoying himself and the world around him immensely, confident of who he was, and fully at ease with the center-stage role expected of him. It also provides us with a window on life in Tibet at the time, in which a famous lama's visit, rather than a solemn occasion, was regarded as an opportunity for a festival or, in the words of the Second Dalai Lama, an occasion when " . . . young peacocks dance and cuckoos sing . . . ".

In fact this is still the tradition today with the Dalai Lama and his relationship with central Asians. Whenever he visits a place like Ladakh, Mongolia, or Kinnaur in order to teach or give initiations, tens of thousands of enthusiasts descend from the mountains and make camp around him for the week or two that he is in the area.

Often at night they form a circle around wherever he is staying, singing to him and dancing long into the night.

When the gathering is in a more accessible place, such as Bodh Gaya in India, much larger crowds turn up, usually numbering in the hundreds of thousands. People are quiet and attentive during the day but at night turn intensively festive. Local Indian entrepreneurs often even bring in ferris wheels and merry-go-rounds to capitalize on the merriment of the occasion. The Second Dalai Lama obviously quite enjoyed this playful aspect of Tibetan religious culture and eloquently expresses his delight with it.

The song opens with a verse of homage to Sarasvati, the symbol of the wisdom of all enlightened beings as expressed in poetry and music. Just as the full moon shines on all beings equally, she encourages enlightenment within all living beings by means of the literary and performing arts. Her Tibetan name is Yanchenma; here the *ma* suffix renders the term feminine. As we saw earlier, the Second Dalai takes the male form of her name, or Yangchen, and prefixes it to the tantric name given to him in his youth by his father, or Shepai Dorjey, "the Laughing Vajra," to create one of his favorite pen names, Yangchen Shepai Dorjey, "the Melodious Laughing Vajra," a *nom-de-plume* with which he signs many of his verse works.

Homage to Sarasvati, female Bodhisattva of Wisdom,
Crown jewel of all enlightenment seekers,
Whose mystical dancing forms, like the full moon,
Carry rays of light into all directions.
May the signs of her goodness prevail.

There I was, living near Eh,
Engaged in the pursuit of meditation
On Shambo Mountain, a holy place
Rivaling Mount Kailash itself in glory.

Then a powerful arrow of invitation arrived,
Requesting me to come and teach.
And I, a young monk well trained in Dharma,
Jumped into the carriage of the wish to accept.

First we went east to the famed Dvakpo,
A piece of the heavens fallen to earth,
Her silken shawl a forest of evergreens
Gently trembling in the cool mountain breeze.

We successfully forded the Lohita River,
And the night magically crept up around us,
The moon and stars a necklace in the sky
As we drew into Dvakpo Gongdegyey,
A celestial garden bathed in the light of jewels.

Here countless spiritual aspirants had gathered
With the intent of spiritual revelry,
Like a great swarm of bees at a honeycomb;
And mine was the task of serving them the taste
Of honey from the essential heart teachings
Of glorious Atisha, that most magnificent of masters,
A Dharma melody to blossom the force of their wisdom,
Talk of which should reach to the top of the world.

Like flocks of ducks descending on a lake,
Innumerable sages appeared from everywhere,
Wearing garlands of many years of meditation
And radiant with knowledge of spiritual ways.
They found themselves in a park filled with nagas,
Men and women crowned with the magic jewels
Of faith in and love for spiritual ways.

At first I was hesitant to accept the request
To teach to such an illustrious gathering;
But I remembered that fear and hesitation

Just signal the approach of the age of darkness,
And threw myself into the task with delight.

Then again we traveled east, the direction of power,
Until eventually we arrived at Chenyil,
Whose white banner of fame flies high,
A town like a wonderful Buddhafield,
With people of such fabulous wealth
That they could outshine a wealth god.

There I was treated to a most wondrous reception
Like those given by the greatest patron of Buddha.
For my part I tried my best to teach them
Of the path leading to benefit and joy,
And to anoint them with the healing oils of truth.

We then made pilgrimage to Gampoda Mountain,
A holy place where the cooling blessings
Of the yogi Daod Shonnu are everywhere,
Like moonlight in a cloudless sky;
A place of power where countless meditators
Had practiced intensely and gained realization.

Here in this most wondrous setting,
This site rivalling even the magical Oddiyana,
Sits a fabulous image (of Gampopa)
That portrays him to perfection;
Its beauty is utterly overpowering, and
I simply could not take my eyes from it.
Kyehu! The enlightenment energy seemed as clear
As a physical object placed visibly before us.

Then, moving in the direction of Saturn,
We crossed the river and entered Tsaritra,
A place to match the Pure Land of Dakinis;
And, at its center, the town of Druda,
Lying there like a jewel that the creator Brahma

Had taken from his own celestial world
And carefully arranged down here on earth.
Our first sighting of this magnificent vista
Felt like the caress of divine nectars.

We beheld amazing beauty, like that
Generally found only in paradise;
It seemed to us as though a perfect world
Had mysteriously descended here to earth
And ushered in a golden age, with
All things physical and spiritual in balance.

We arrived at the time of a sacred festival,
The annual celebration of the mystical event
When the Buddha had taught the *Prajnaparamita*
While simultaneously manifesting in tantric form
And appearing under the Dhanayakotaka Stupa
To teach Kalachakra, king of all tantric doctrines.
The site had become like the garden of Indra,
With crowds of youths dancing like lightning
And singing songs surpassing those of the gods.

A vast assembly of monks, nuns and lay practitioners
Had gathered, covering the face of the earth
Like a cooling balm anointed on the body.
Uncountable kings and chieftains too were there
To hoist on high the banner of their resolve
To create a world inspiring to both body and mind.

For those with the destiny to be there,
The melodious gong of the Great Way was sounded
And the spiritual discussions began to flow
Like a healing medicine to eager ears.

The town itself is like a mirror image
Of a painting created by divine artists:
Parks of flowers the color of jewels

Rising in clusters like a young virgin's breasts;
Lines of fruit trees rich in harvest
Elegantly set like gems on a string;
And everywhere in the distance
The smiling face of an unspoiled forest.

Finally, on our journey back from Tsari
In order to see the great wilderness and behold
Young peacocks dance and wild cuckoos sing,
We went along with some friends of good fortune
To Metoktang, a place like no other,
Its earth clothed in every flower raiment.
We looked, and we delighted in
The playful expressions of goodness and joy.

We painted Odey Gungyal, crown jewel of the Himalayas,
With the dust from our pilgrimage footsteps,
And then turned homeward to Yarlung,
The very navel and heartland of Tibet,
The flower of whose fame is a shining ornament
Delightful to the ear of any fair maid.

And thus is complete my song of our pilgrimage
To Tsari, a place made sacred from times of old.
I conclude it with the following prayer:
May the tradition coming from Jowo Atisha,
Who is one with all Buddhas and bodhisattvas,
Shine with the radiance of a thousands suns
In this land of thick forests till the end of time.

6

From a Vision of Lama Tsongkhapa

Translator's Preamble: The colophon reads, "This song was written by Gendun Gyatso Palzangpo after he had experienced a vision of Lama Tsongkhapa while living in meditational retreat at Dradruk." As mentioned in both preceding poems, Dradruk is the temple constructed by King Songtsen Gampo in the mid–eighth century near the Yangbu Lhakang palace in the Yarlung Valley, this latter being the palace/fort of Tibet's first king, Nyatri Tsenpo.

The vision of Lama Tsongkhapa that the young monk Gendun Gyatso experienced at Dradruk, which inspired the composition of this Dharma song, is mentioned in the *Biography* as having occurred in the Fire Snake Year (1497). In the spring of that year the king of Chongyey had invited him to teach in the Tiger's Peak Hermitage at Chongyey. Afterwards, still under the patronage of this king, he traveled to Chenyey, Tsetang, and Zhankar, teaching as he traveled. The *Biography* then states that when he arrived at the Dradruk Temple the king sponsored him to lead a large ceremony, and that it was here that the Second Dalai Lama experienced his vision of Lama Tsongkhapa and composed the following song.

In fact this was but one of a number of visions of Lama Tsong-khapa that the Second Dalai Lama had received since his childhood. I discussed several others in Part Two of my introduction. More-over, he had received several such visions during his Manjushri retreat in Tashi Lhunpo almost a decade earlier, where, as the *Biography* puts it, he had " . . . unleashed memories of hundreds of previous lives." Another had occurred during his second year at

Drepung, when he and his guru Jamyang Lekpai Chojor had visited Radeng monastery. On that occasion he experienced a dream vision in which he perceived Tsongkhapa and then beheld himself sitting on a teaching throne, with his Drepung guru below him to the right and his Sera guru below him to the left. When he awoke he was somewhat disturbed by the dream, because in the Indian and Tibetan traditions, it is considered improper to sit higher than one's teachers. He later discussed the experience with several high lamas, who informed him that the dream was a prophecy that one day he would become abbot of both Drepung and Sera monasteries.

Each of the verses in the main body of the poem concludes with the refrain, "O Lama Tsongkhapa, guru of incomparable kindness, / Inspire thoughts of truth in this irreligious beggar." Here the use of the word *beggar* is a play on the Tibetan word for a Buddhist monk, which is *gelong*, meaning "spiritual beggar." In ancient India monks were expected to live by making a round of the town with a begging bowl each morning in order to collect food for the one meal a day that they were permitted to eat. This is still the tradition in many Buddhist countries today (most notably Burma and Thailand). Tibet and the other central Asian countries did not follow this tradition of begging, probably due to the sparseness of their populations and also because of the intensity of their climates. The reference to himself as "a mad beggar monk" is, as His Holiness explains in his Foreword, made in the context of his meditations upon voidness; he is a man crazed with mystical ecstasy.

Generally this type of text is composed for disciples to use at the beginning or conclusion of meditation sessions as a means of reviewing the essential themes of Buddhist practice in a structured way. It is also used as a prayer to one's own guru, visualized in the form of Tsongkhapa, to inspire the integration of those themes. Finally, it has the purpose of reminding meditators of mistakes in practice that can be made and to encourage the correction of those errors.

Homage to the holy gurus, embodiments of the
Knowledge and compassion of all Buddhas.

O Lama Tsongkhapa, guru of incomparable kindness,
Whose mind is inseparable from that of all Buddhas,
Whose body manifests in countless forms,
And whose speech releases a constant rain of teachings,
Enter the heart of this faint-hearted monk;
Inspire thoughts of truth in this irreligious beggar.
Kind master, look on me with compassion;
Treasury of kindness, I place my hopes in you.

Not knowing that you are the very source
Of all spiritual progress for me here and hereafter,
In the past I searched elsewhere, but in vain.
I could not put my trust in your teachings;
But now I see the foolishness of my doubts.
Looking back I realize this was a sign
That my mind was far from the path.
O Lama Tsongkhapa, guru of incomparable kindness,
Inspire thoughts of truth in this irreligious beggar.

When the mind is distracted by strong attraction
To the things of this short and ephemeral life,
Then although outwardly one may be skilled
At going through the motions of a spiritual practice
The mind makes no real link to truth;
A glance inside is rather disappointing.
This non-awareness of impermanence is a sign
That the mind is far from the path.
O Lama Tsongkhapa, guru of incomparable kindness,
Inspire thoughts of truth in this irreligious beggar.

With attachment to wealth and respect we become
Constantly absorbed in mindless activities
And thus let our precious human life slip away.

This external posturing is just a pretense,
Our clever talk an instrument of deceit;
We are so smart that we fool ourselves,
And our spiritual training becomes mere imitation.
This is a sign of a mind far from the path.
O Lama Tsongkhapa, guru of incomparable kindness,
Inspire thoughts of truth in this irreligious beggar.

While fully aware of the laws of karma
And the unbearable suffering of the lower realms,
We make no effort to gain control over our lives
And instead allow ourselves to lay back in ease.
We are like sheep standing in the slaughterhouse,
Watching our friends die all around us
Yet not waking up to the reality of the situation
Until our own turn for the axe has come.
You who think you are so cunning and clever,
Are you not as though possessed by a demon?
Not being aware of this, our predicament, is a sign
That the mind is far from the path.
O Lama Tsongkhapa, guru of incomparable kindness,
Inspire thoughts of truth in this irreligious beggar.

Even the gods in the highest heavens
Endowed with every pleasure and wealth
Must one day leave everything behind
And go alone through the gates of death.
O greedy one, not thinking of death, you spend
All your time entertaining relatives and friends
And in the pursuit of wealth, possessions, and power,
Regardless of whether you need them or not.
Never content, our attachment to worldly success
Becomes a chain binding us to frustration.
This is a sign of a mind far from the path.
O Lama Tsongkhapa, guru of incomparable kindness,
Inspire thoughts of truth in this irreligious beggar.

For those of us who have spent our life unwisely
And did not cultivate spiritual maturity within,
When the Lord of Death finally comes to devour us
The howling winds of our negative karma
Will arise with strength and forcefully pull us
Over the cliff falling to terrible realms;
The negative karma that we carry on our back,
Gathered in rebirths since time without beginning,
Is as heavy as the enormous King of Mountains;
Thus we cannot have a sesame seed of confidence
That lower rebirth will not be our fate.
We may cling to our wealth and possessions,
And call out to a hundred loved ones and friends;
But we will have to go on empty-handed and alone
Into the tunnel of the great hereafter.
Not living every moment in this awareness
Is a sign of a mind far from the path.
O Lama Tsongkhapa, guru of incomparable kindness,
Inspire thoughts of truth in this irreligious beggar.

Every living being wandering in the three worlds
Has been a kind mother to me in some past life;
Yet the suffering that constantly oppresses them
Hardly seems to concern me at all.
This is a sign of a mind far from the path.
O Lama Tsongkhapa, guru of incomparable kindness,
Inspire thoughts of truth in this irreligious beggar.

Holy spiritual master, whatever fate befalls
This irreligious, mad beggar monk,
I place all my hopes in you.
Do not drop me from your compassion;
Infuse my spirit with powers mundane and supreme.

Peerless spiritual guide, your only task now
Is to lead living beings to enlightenment;

And I have no doubt that eventually you will
Guide me too to that highest of states.
But until I arrive there watch over me closely,
For should I fall into places of misery
I am not sure I have the strength to prevail.
So show me your radiant countenance now
And point this irreligious mad beggar monk the way
Leading to Tushita, the Pure Land of Joy.
Release a shower of vast and profound Dharma;
Cut the root of ego-grasping from within me;
Inspire me to achieve your enlightenment state.

It is through your kindness, O master,
That I am moved to sing these verses;
Emotions surge within me when I think of you
And I cannot help but call out in song:
I, an irreligious hermit from Upper Tsang,
The mad beggar monk Gendun Gyatso.

Through your compassionate work, O holy master,
May knowledge of all realities be achieved;
And may a thousand sunbeams of enlightened activity
Shine forth now to inspire wisdom's light.

7

Meditations to Prepare
the Mind for Death

Translator's Preamble: In the concluding verse of the poem that
follows, the Second Dalai Lama provides us with the name of the
place where he was moved to write, as well as his reasons for
doing so: "A devoted disciple from far away / Has requested a song
of spiritual advice, / Written in words easy to understand, / To
benefit him at the time of death. / Because he asked so insistently, /
I, the mad beggar monk Gendun Gyatso, / A wanderer from Upper
Tsang, could not refuse, / And penned these verses at Yerpa Lhari
Nyingpo." The text is also given a brief colophon that states, "Verses
of advice written for Chomdzey Kyawo."

The person for whom the piece was composed, a monk by the
name of Chomdzey Kyawo, is not mentioned in the *Autobiography*.
He does, however, appear in the *Biography*, wherein it is stated that
shortly after the young Second Dalai Lama was enthroned in Tashi
Lhunpo as the reincarnation of Gyalwa Gendun Drubpa, " . . . a
monk from Ehden came to him, presented him with an offering,
and requested a teaching." At the time the Second Dalai Lama was
twelve years old.

However, this is not the occasion on which the Second Dalai
Lama composed the song of spiritual advice for him; for, as the
concluding verse states, this was done when the master was living
at Yerpa Lhari Nyingpo. As we saw in Part Two of the introduction,
the Second Dalai Lama did not visit Yerpa until the Iron Monkey
Year (1500), when he was twenty-five. During the spring of that

year he decided to meditate for awhile in the places frequented by Atisha and his disciples. Therefore he set out toward Yerpa, teaching at Ganden, Drakar, and Sangngak Kar on the way. He arrived at Yerpa in the early summer and remained in retreat there for two-and-a-half months, meditating and writing. It is most probably on this occasion that he composed his "Meditations to Prepare the Mind for Death."

The subject of death awareness is fundamental to the spiritual path in Indo-Tibetan Buddhism. This awareness is not cultivated in the sense of a morbid preoccupation but as a force to intensify and balance our sense of life. As the old Kadampa saying goes, "Not to meditate on death immediately upon waking up is to risk wasting one's morning. Not to do so at noon is to risk wasting one's afternoon. And not to do so in the evening is to risk wasting the night." The example is given of a person who during the day forgets the night; to do so is to allow one's perspective to move out of balance.

The text opens with a traditional verse of homage. It then proceeds to advise Chomdzey Kyawo on how to live his life meaningfully if he wishes the benefits generated to be sufficiently profound that they can be carried through death's gates. The language is simple yet effective, and the message cuttingly clear.

In a concluding verse, the Second Dalai Lama mentions Tushita Pure Land. As we saw in Part Two of the introduction (in the account of the Second Dalai Lama's construction of the gold Maitreya statue), Tushita is a popular topic with the Gelugpa School in general and the Dalai Lamas in particular. Ganden, the first monastery built by Tsongkhapa and consequently the root Gelugpa institution, gets its name from Tushita (*Ganden* is the Tibetan equivalent of the Sanskrit word *Tushita*). Moreover, as we saw in the account of the birth of the Second Dalai Lama, it is said that after the First passed away, he projected himself to Tushita, where he met with Buddha Maitreya, Atisha, and Tsongkhapa, and asked them for advice on where to reincarnate in order to continue his work for the enlightenment of the world. Tsongkhapa threw a white flower from Tushita to earth by way of a prophecy. The flower landed in Tanak Dorjeden, and consequently the Second took birth there. A similar mythology linking the Dalai Lamas with Tushita is found in the accounts of the deaths and rebirths of many of the later Dalai Lamas.

The Second Dalai Lama concludes his song of advice by referring to himself as "the mad beggar monk Gendun Gyatso, a wanderer from Upper Tsang." Tanak Dorjeden, the place of his birth, is located in Tsang Province. The "mad beggar monk" signature is coming to be used more frequently in his writings as the years pass.

Homage to the fatherly guru Lama Tsongkhapa,
Who from the sphere of the great void
Emanates forth with his magical powers, appearing
Throughout the countless realms of the universe
In forms appropriate to the needs of the world.

The root of all joy for this life and the next is
The spiritual master who reveals the Great Way.
Should you approach him with a sincere heart,
Powers common and supreme will arise of themselves.

Having found a precious human rebirth
So hard to obtain and so easily lost,
Do not be distracted by fruitless endeavours;
Direct it instead to the enlightenment path.

The only truly trustworthy things in this world
Are the most precious Three Jewels of Refuge:
The Buddhas, the Dharma, and the Sangha.
Meditate on them unceasingly day and night
From within the very depths of your heart.

Even a seemingly small negative action
Can produce great suffering in the future;
Strive now from the very depths of your heart
To transcend negativity and to cultivate the good.

The root and foundation of the Great Way is said
To be the will to achieve highest enlightenment
In order to benefit the countless living beings.
Make every effort to generate this thought and
To transcend its opposite, the self-cherishing mind.

As all things that exist are interdependent,
All things thus are by nature void.
Cultivate this vision; and be aware of the world
As illusory, like a magician's creation.

No matter what wealth and property we possess,
They only strengthen the chains of attachment.
Therefore cultivate the spirit of generosity
That aspires to help without expecting a return.

In the end, no worldly gain is able
To protect us from the cliff that falls to misery.
Remember this; and that the greedy Lord of Death
Steadily devours all living beings.

When death comes for you, may you be in possession
Of the presence of mind to project yourself
To Tushita, the Pure Land of Joy.
There may you sit before Buddha Maitreya,
Master of the ten stages of knowledge,
Surrounded by countless bodhisattvas,
And hear him teach on transcendent wisdom.

Whatever meritorious energies you generate
Through spiritual efforts of body, speech, or mind,
Dedicate them to this sublime goal.
There is no time to procrastinate;
Do not fall prey to laziness or apathy.

A devoted disciple from far away
Has requested a song of spiritual advice,
Written in words easy to understand,
To benefit him at the time of death.
Because he asked so insistently,
I, the mad beggar monk Gendun Gyatso,
A wanderer from Upper Tsang, could not refuse,
And penned these verses at Yerpa Lhari Nyingpo.
May disciples with zeal for spiritual practice
Be inspired to attain to enlightenment and joy.

8

Song of the Enlightenment Path

Translator's Preamble: The colophon to the following verse work simply states, "Spiritual precepts for Jampal Drakpa, a close disciple." Neither a place nor date of the composition is given.

Jampal Drakpa, the monk for whom it was composed, is mentioned in the *Autobiography* as a disciple who sympathized with the teenaged Second Dalai Lama when he was expelled from Tashi Lhunpo and requested to travel with him to Drepung monastery as his attendant. The *Biography* also mentions him in connection with the period of the master leaving Tashi Lhunpo. The name used for him in the *Biography* is Solpon Jampal Drakpa, the Tibetan word *solpon* being an honorary title for an attendant. He was not a servant in the ordinary sense, however, but more of an elderly guardian. His name does not appear again in either of the source works, neither during the Dalai Lama's sojourn in Drepung nor during his later travels.

The text of the song is very personal in mood and is typical of the flavor and structure of *Lam Rim* "advice works" composed by Kadampa and Gelugpa lamas, with the emphasis upon the importance of not only learning the words of Buddhism but also putting them into actual practice through solitary meditation. Several of the passages suggest that Jampal Drakpa was about to engage upon a long retreat, especially the lines " . . . much better to go to the mountains / And practice meditation day and night, / Content with whatever food comes to you. / Do this, or perhaps later know regret, Jampal Drak." One presumes that the lama would not write like this to an attendant whom he expected to remain in the monastery serving tea and biscuits.

Buddha Vajradhara, mentioned by the Second Dalai Lama in one of the opening verses, is the tantric form in which Buddha Shakyamuni expounded the Vajrayana and in particular the highest yoga tantras. This implies that Jampal Drakpa had received a tantric initiation of this category from the master and was entering into retreat to recite the mantras linked with that particular system. The word *siddhi* that he uses is a tantric term; mundane siddhi refers to the eight occult powers such as levitation, walking through walls, and so forth; the supreme siddhi is the power of realization of *mahamudra*, the wisdom of bliss and emptiness.

The style of the Tibetan verse is melodic and tightly rhythmical, suggesting that the author expected his disciple to use it for daily recitation as a reminder of the key points in training.

Homage to the guru, a wish-fulfilling jewel
Who bestows siddhis both mundane and supreme.

Drawing from the treasury of sutras and tantras,
I will sing a song of enlightenment's way.
You who wish to practice the spiritual path,
Pay heed for a moment and lend me an ear.

All inner realizations both great and small
Are achieved by relying on a qualified master.
This was said by Buddha Vajradhara himself,
So take it to heart, Jampal Drak.

This human body with the freedoms and endowments
Is a supreme vessel for spiritual training.
Think over the precious opportunity that is yours
And take advantage of it, Jampal Drak.

We may strive for all of eternity at worldly works
But still we will not see their end;
Do not leave yourself armed only with regret
When the Lord of Death strikes, Jampal Drak.

Should the miseries of the lower realms befall you,
You would not find them easy to bear.
As you have no assurance not to take birth there,
Avoid their karmic causes, Jampal Drak.

The treasure that brings about all levels of joy
Is the Triple Gem: the Buddhas, Dharma and Sangha.
Be aware of them, and strive at creative living;
That indeed would be wise, Jampal Drak.

When under the power of karma and delusion
There is never a time for inner peace and joy
No matter where in the universe we may go.
Transcend karma and delusion, Jampal Drak.

Crippled by the cancerous growth of self-cherishing,
We bring on ourselves every sorrow and pain.
Apply the wisdom that appreciates egolessness
And transcend self-cherishing, Jampal Drak.

Samsara is the source of every discomfort and harm;
It is a fiery pit ablaze with the sufferings
Of birth, sickness, old age, and death.
Make every effort to climb out, Jampal Drak.

Not now striving single-pointedly at the path
And instead allowing the mind to be seduced
By worldly concerns, that eternal deceiver,
Is giving yourself to an illusion, Jampal Drak.

How much better to go to the mountains
And practice meditation day and night,
Content with whatever food comes to you.
Do this, or perhaps later know regret, Jampal Drak.

Worldly friends are deceptive time-wasters,
Life like a flash of lightning in the sky,
And material things like bubbles on a stream;
Do not cling to them, Jampal Drak.

In previous lives we have known every glory
And experienced every worldly power and joy.
Do you not think the time finally has come for you
To accomplish the enlightenment path, Jampal Drak!

Perhaps in the past due to the pace of our wisdom
We could not master every spiritual method;
Yet it is wise to practice now what we know.
Remember, death strikes quickly, Jampal Drak.

All the Buddhas and the great bodhisattvas too
Were once ordinary beings like me and you;
But then they applied themselves to training
And meditated diligently on the enlightenment path.
Practicing thus they transcended karma and delusion
And achieved the state of the three perfect kayas.
Follow their example, Jampal Drak.

9

Three Songs to Sung-rab Gyatso

Translator's Preamble: A fascinating figure in the later years of the Second Dalai Lama's life is Sung-rab Gyatso, his principal aide. Although Solpon Jampal Drakpa, the attending monk for whom the previous song of advice was written, receives only one mention each in the *Autobiography* and *Biography*, Sung-rab Gyatso appears repeatedly in both texts.

The *Biography* informs us that when the Second Dalai Lama was in his twenty-fifth year, he made retreat in Yerpa for two-and-a-half months. He then traveled and taught for the autumn and went to Drakdong to undertake another retreat during the winter. In the spring he made a pilgrimage to the southeast, eventually winding up at Chokyi Gyaltsen Tsey to teach and give various initiations. It was here that he met Sung-rab Gyatso for the first time.

Scant information concerning the details of their encounter is given, but it must have been significant for both, as it led to a lifetime of fatherly caring on the part of the Second Dalai Lama and of service and dedication on the part of Sung-rab Gyatso.

Concerning this event the *Biography* simply states, "When the master was in Chokyi Gyaltsen Tsey . . . he met Sung-rab Gyatso, who later was to become his future chief aide. This, their first encounter, was the result of karmic connections and spiritual aspirations that spanned many lifetimes. Just like the Kadampa master Geshey Chayulpa had fully dedicated himself to his guru and thus achieved great spiritual realization, Sung-rab Gyatso similarly dedicated himself to the master, never once transgressing his instructions. He remained with him from that time on. They were inseparable, like father and son. . . . The master was twenty-six at the time."

We are not informed of Sung-rab Gyatso's age when the two met, but he certainly was much younger than the Second Dalai Lama. This is indicated by a passage in the first of the Second Dalai Lama's three verse works written for him, wherein we read, "By the force of aspiration and a strong karmic link / You have been with me since your very childhood. . . ". It was not uncommon in Tibet for a family to put a child in a monastery or under the care of a high lama from as early as seven or eight years of age, although twelve to fifteen was more common. Probably Sung-rab Gyatso was somewhere in that age range at the time.

As the years passed the two became ever closer, and the young disciple quickly rose to become *nyerney chenpo* (spelled *Nyer-gnas-chen-po*), a term I translate above as "chief aide." The position in the lama world is a cross between manager, treasurer, and first secretary. In the early years of their relationship, when the Second Dalai Lama himself was still quite young, Sung-rab Gyatso's duties may not have been too difficult; but as the master became more widely sought out as a teacher and received the attention of a growing number of patrons, his assistant's work would have become increasingly demanding and sophisticated.

By the time the master was forty, Sung-rab Gyatso's responsibilities probably included handling all monetary affairs, organizing the master's schedule, making arrangements for all travel and teaching activities, checking to see that all arrangements made to receive the master in various places where he had been invited to teach were in order, overseeing the progress of all projects (such as constructing monasteries and commissioning art works), overseeing mundane matters such as food and protocol, screening the many applicants who requested interviews and meetings, taking total charge of affairs when the master was in meditation retreat, advising him on all politically important decisions, and in general taking care of all physical aspects of the lama's many activities.

Given the range of responsibilities a *nyerney chenpo* had, the presence of a person with the right character and intelligence was indispensable to a high lama in classical Tibet, which was more a federation of hundreds of tiny kingdoms and tribes than a nation in the modern sense of the word. During his lifetime the Second Dalai

Lama received and was received by hundreds of kings, queens, chieftains, and tribal leaders, all of whom had to be treated with dignity and respect, without creating the sense that some were being pampered and others ignored. Moreover, hundreds of thousands of ordinary people, including tens of thousands of monks and nuns, regarded the master as their principal spiritual guide, and it was important not to allow his office to become politicized to the extent that it harmed his relationships with any of them.

The Second Dalai Lama was obviously aware of the sensitive nature of Sung-rab Gyatso's job. He expresses the confidence that he holds for his *nyerney chenpo* in the fourth verse of the first text, wherein he writes, "Some . . . take advantage of their position / And behave badly toward other trainees; / While still others lack true respect / And fall prey to apathy and ineptitude. . . ./ But you, Sung-rab Gyatso, have none of these faults. . . ./ You have never given me cause for worry / Concerning your integrity, your self-discipline / Or your commitment to the spiritual path; / Nor do you discriminate against others, / Regardless of their wealth, power or status."

Without a doubt the quality of the *nyerney chenpo* greatly affected the career of a lama. A brilliant aide would see that his lama's life went smoothly and efficiently, that the wishes of patrons, disciples, and the general public were dealt with sensitively and effectively, without overly taxing the lama's energies, health, and time. A mediocre aide would slow down and confuse the activities of his master and his relationships with the people. A poor one could bungle everything, alienating patrons, disciples, and the public alike, and perhaps even producing bloodshed and war in the process. For example, the Fifth Dalai Lama comments that one of the principal reasons for the Tsang invasion of central Tibet in the 1630s was that the chief aide to his predecessor the Fourth Dalai Lama had once undiplomatically refused to grant an audience to a delegation sent by the king of Tsang. The slight left a deep resentment. That war obviously had other causes and conditions; nevertheless, the Great Fifth felt that it could have been avoided had the Fourth's chief aide been more delicate.

That Sung-rab Gyatso was a brilliant organizer and spokesperson for the Second Dalai Lama is obvious by the level of success that the master achieved and the ease with which his activities were effected. Sung-rab Gyatso seems to have been equally at home in all environments. In monasteries or in the homes of kings and queens, or housed in a simple nomadic tent, he went about his daily tasks with equal humility and dedication. He was both intensely spiritual and mystical, and the *Biography* relates numerous occasions on which he experienced prophetic dream visions. This came strongly into play after the Second Dalai Lama's death, when Sung-rab Gyatso was to assume responsibility for the search for the master's reincarnation.

The intimacy of the relationship between the master and his chief aide is sometimes poignantly related in the *Biography*. For example, we read that in the autumn of the Iron Dragon Year (1520) the Second Dalai Lama was invited to teach at Longpo. When he and his entourage arrived, however, they discovered that an epidemic was afflicting the region, and people were dying all around them. Sung-rab Gyatso himself contracted the illness and seemed on the point of death. The *Biography* relates that doctors had abandoned hope for his life and gave him only hours to live. The Second Dalai Lama rushed to him, sat in meditation beside his attendant's deathbed, and began to chant tantric mantras. Suddenly he clapped his hands together and shouted, "Affliction, begone!" Sung-rab Gyatso instantly revived. He opened his eyes, sat up in his bed, and smiled at those in the room. He had been miraculously cured. The *Biography* concludes its account of the incident by stating, "This is what can happen when the power of the lama and the confidence of the disciple work in harmony."

Sung-rab Gyatso was particularly instrumental in the construction of Gyal Monastery and later in the creation of the gold Maitreya statue. In this latter work, between 1523 and 1526, he oversaw the collection of the dozens of kilograms of gold that would be required for the project. This collection was largely made by sending teams of disciples to all regions of Tibet and soliciting small donations of jewelry from devotees. Sung-rab Gyatso personally took charge of the effort made throughout the Dvakpo, Kongpo, and Nyal regions, which generated almost a third of the gold needed for the sacred image.

During the last year of the master's life, several of his conversations with Sung-rab Gyatso were recorded. Mostly these were in the nature of preparing him to deal with the trauma that the disciples would experience at the death of their master and also preparing him for the task of searching for the new incarnation.

Sung-rab Gyatso's job in this search was not an easy one. As His Holiness the present Dalai Lama mentions in his Foreword, when the Nechung Oracle was invoked for advice on the matter, the oracle advised him that the master had reincarnated in a hundred bodies. Sung-rab Gyatso was in an extraordinary dilemma. Which one should be chosen to represent the Dalai Lama's office?

For this he consulted the Lake of Visions, as well as examining the dreams he and other high lamas had experienced. In addition, he had accompanied his master on his final visit to the Tolungda and Kyormo Lung regions just weeks before the elderly Second Dalai Lama passed away, during which the master had made many unusual comments. When all the signs and prophecies were considered, they seemed to point to a child born in Tolung as the reincarnation to be recognized. Sung-rab Gyatso oversaw this process and arranged for the enthronement and education of the young Third Dalai Lama.

From this we can see that the job of a lama's aide was in no way a strictly secular affair. Sung-rab Gyatso was firstly a monk and disciple of the Second Dalai Lama and secondly his right hand man. The songs of advice that the master composed for him primarily address aspects of his spiritual life. As such they are universally relevant in their message, at least insofar as spiritual advice of a tantric nature can be so.

The colophons to the three songs do not provide us with much information on them, other than the place of composition of the first two and the fact all three were requested by his attendant and thus were not spontaneous creations.

The colophon to the first reads, "Written by Gendun Gyatso Palzangpo at the request of his attendant Sung-rab Gyatso, when the master was residing at the Ganden Podrang, or Palace of Joy, of Drepung Monastery"; the second reads, "Written by Gendun Gyatso while he was residing in the Chamber of Delightfully Arranged Flowers of the Ganden Podrang"; and the third reads "A song of spiritual advice, written by Gendun Gyatso Palzangpo at the request of Sung-rab Gyatso." However, the concluding verse of the third song does give a date for it, which is the Iron Snake Year (1521). This is the year after Sung-rab Gyatso almost died from disease, as related above, when the master came to his rescue at the last moment. The other two songs of advice, as evidenced by their colophons, were both written after the Second had moved into the Ganden Podrang. He had been given this residence by the *Gongma* (or king) of Kyormo Lung in the Earth Tiger Year (1518), and therefore we can presume that they were composed sometime between 1518 and 1520.

It is possible that the first two were composed immediately after Sung-rab Gyatso's sickness and the third one a year later. A passage in the first song suggests a remedy to illness and a method for the removal of obstacles: "To make the basis of your life firm, / Practice the longevity yogas of the Tara Tantra; / And to remove all hindrances to fulfillment / Of the path that renders life meaningful, / Engage the tantric practices of Palden Lhamo. . . ." The "longevity yoga" advice is a convincing clue.

All three of the pieces focus upon the subject of *guru yoga*, a topic of central importance to tantric Buddhism. In tantric practice the disciple is expected to work with the guru from the perspective of a pure view, seeing all his actions as perfect teachings and all "impure appearances" as reflections of one's own shortcomings. The idea is that by doing so one derives maximum benefit from the relationship even if the guru is imperfect. The Second Dalai Lama mentions several classical cases in which this practice brought enlightenment in one lifetime: the eleventh-century Indian master Naropa's near-legendary training under Tilopa; the Tibetan yogi and poet Milarepa's dedication to Marpa; and Lama Drom Tonpa's discipleship under Jowo Atisha. He also mentions some of the popular examples found in the original discourses of the Buddha, such as the disciples Sudhana (found in the *Gandhavuhya Sutra*) and the "Constantly Weeping Bodhisattva" Sataprarudita (whose tale is told in the eight-thousand line *Prajnaparamita Sutra*).

Although guru yoga is the focal point of the three pieces, they are far broader in scope than this one topic. Rather, in them, the Second Dalai Lama attempts to provide his disciple and attendant (and any other readers who may see the pieces) with quintessential guidelines to the spiritual life.

Song to Sung-rab Gyatso: One

Om! May joy and goodness prevail!

O Guru Atisha, crown jewel of Indian masters,
And your wondrous spiritual heirs,
As well as Lama Tsongkhapa, a second Buddha,
And all the peerlessly kind root gurus:
Look on me, your devoted follower,
With eyes of mercy and compassion.

My disciple Sung-rab Gyatso, of profound devotion:
By the force of aspiration and a strong karmic link
You have been with me since your very childhood,
Devoting yourself to me in every possible way;
And for me it has been a joy to care for you.

The role of serving the guru is not easy,
And most who try go quickly astray.
Some, through day-to-day familiarity,
Come to read flaws into his enlightenment ways;
Others take advantage of their position
And behave badly toward fellow trainees;
While still others lack true respect
And fall prey to apathy and ineptitude.
In this way they turn the Field of Merit into
Just another way of collecting negative karma
And thus destroy the basis of their own inner peace.

But you, Sung-rab Gyatso, have none of these faults
And always maintain pure perception and ways.
Your spiritual conviction lies not in mere words,
Your attitude is beyond all selfish thoughts.
You never disregard my spiritual advice,
And make every effort not to disturb my mind.

You have never given me cause for worry
Concerning your integrity, your self-discipline
Or your commitment to the spiritual path;
Nor do you discriminate against others,
Regardless of their wealth, power or status.
Thus although perhaps not a great scholar
If you continue to practice as you have in the past,
You will certainly fulfill your spiritual aims.

The great Buddha Vajradhara has taught that
The teacher is a greater field of merit
Than devotion to all the myriads of Buddhas
That exist in all times and directions.
Many great bodhisattvas have proven this true,
Like Sudhana and Sataprarudita,
Who achieved states of spiritual illumination
By devoting themselves to a Mahayana guru.

Other illustrious examples from the past
Are Naropa, an ornament of Indian adepts;
Drom Tonpa, a veritable master of the Dharma;
Milarepa, a most wonderful yogi;
And Tulku Shonnu Od, a marvellous emanation.
Each of these holy beings perfectly revealed
The manner of achieving enlightenment's two siddhis
Through devotion to the guru in thought and deed.

We should take as our role models in training
These holy beings who accomplished realization,
Emulating them and their approach to the path.
Then even if now we have no spiritual power,
No doubt it will soon fall into our hands.
Make prayers never to be separated from
The guru and to accompany him into enlightenment.

A human rebirth is like a wish-fulfilling gem;
Do not squander the precious chances it affords.
Grasp not at life as permanent, but meditate
On how death could come at any moment.

Keep in mind the terrible sufferings
That pervade the lower realms of existence,
And avoid their cause, harmful behavior.
Transcend attraction to superficial goals
And instead cultivate goodness and inner joy.
As the Three Jewels of Refuge are sources of joy,
Be mindful of them in all times and places.

Every sentient being has been a parent to us
In the course of our countless previous lives;
Meditate on this, and give birth
To love and compassion for them all.

The root of the Great Way to enlightenment
Is meditation on the two bodhiminds:
The altruistic aspiration to Buddhahood
As the supreme means of benefitting the world;
And the wisdom that directly perceives
The ultimate, emptiness nature of things.
Cherish these two like your legs and eyes.

To make the basis of your life firm,
Practice the longevity yogas of the *Tara Tantra;*
And to remove all hindrances to fulfillment
Of the path that renders life meaningful,
Engage the tantric practices of Palden Lhamo,
The Dharmapala who bestows all spiritual powers.

This is my heartfelt advice to you, Sung-rab Gyatso,
Offered sincerely with the thought to help.
And with it I offer my prayers for you,

That your spiritual aspirations may be fulfilled
And until sublime enlightenment is achieved,
You may never be parted from masters of the Great Way.

Song to Sung-rab Gyatso: Two

Homage to the holy gurus.

Buddha Vajradhara in this age at time's end
Has performed the drama of his mystical dance
By manifesting in the form of a Buddhist monk,
Incomparable Lama Tsongkhapa, wisdom incarnate;
With undivided faith I bow to him.

My disciple Sung-rab Gyatso, listen to this song.
In a previous life you generated much good karma
And thus now have achieved a rare human rebirth
Endowed with every spiritual grace.
You have entered the door of the Great Way,
Have taken up training under a lineage guru,
And can see him as a fully enlightened Buddha
Able to inspire and guide you to knowledge.
This is a sign of a previous karmic link.

It is taught that there is no stronger method
For purifying the mind and giving rise to wisdom
Than relying upon a guru seen as a Buddha:
Mentally holding him in the sphere of pure mind,
Physically attending to him and heeding his advice,
And vocally chanting prayers requesting him
To bestow waves of inspiring power.

But there is a danger to this path;
For to accept support from a guru and thus live
From the things offered to him by the faithful
While lacking inner purity yourself
And being divisive with other trainees
Is like jumping over a terrible cliff
That falls to rebirth in worlds of sorrow.

In uncountable previous lives you wandered
Again and again through places of misery,
But now have found a human rebirth
Able to accomplish the enlightenment path.
How sad were you to spend it in vain!

We sit here thinking of our life as eternal
While all around us the terrible Lord of Death
Destroys living beings without caring
If they are weak or strong, young or old.
Have we completely lost touch with our senses?

The material things found in this world
Are hard to amass but easily lost;
And in the end, anyway, all is left behind.
Is it not wiser then to use what we get
In ways conducive to the benefit of the world?

In this dark age friends and patrons
Are hard to please and easy to anger;
Kindness is met with deceit, and eventually
All go their separate ways.
Is this not a sad world in which we live?

The people of this negative age
With duplicity and cunning pursue their goals
Of wealth, power, and material possessions.

If instead they dedicated all to spiritual ends,
They would be happier in both this life and the next.

Wasting time with people of solely vain concerns
Is empty of all meaning and hope,
Harming us both here and hereafter.
But dedicating ourselves to the guru and Three Jewels
Fulfills all hopes for now and forever.

Cyclic existence is like a fiery pit, and the sufferings
Of birth, sickness, age, and death fall like rain.
To see this and not strive for liberation:
What could be more foolish?

When illness befalls us we find it hard
To endure the pain for but a few days;
What then would we do if reborn in the hells?
It is important to avoid negativity
And cultivate the ways of goodness.

The beings of the six realms are uncountable,
Yet not a single one of them has not
Been a mother to us in some previous life.
Transcend the mind of discrimination, that feels
Attachment to some and aversion to others;
Meditate on the mind that loves all equally,
And that cherishes others more than oneself.

All the things that appear to the mind
Are merely paintings of names and thoughts;
Not even a speck of dust exists
From the side of the objects themselves.
Meditate again and again on this vision
Of emptiness, the final nature of being.

In this age of the five great obstacles,
Countless hindrances appear and impede us
From successfully completing the spiritual path.
It is a time for the powerful tantric methods
Of meditational deities and Dharma Protectors
To be applied as constantly as a river's flow.

This then is my song of advice to you;
To practice it with a steady mind will bring
Peace in this life and peace in the next,
And will certainly produce the sublime state
Of enlightenment's three perfect kayas.

Song to Sung-rab Gyatso: Three

Homage to the Gurus and the Three Precious Jewels.

To tame living beings in this age of darkness,
The Buddha Vajradhara, lord of the five Buddha families,
Manifested as the incomparably kind spiritual master
Lama Tsongkhapa, a guru equal to the Buddha himself;
At his feet I bow down.

Sung-rab Gyatso, listen to this song of advice.
In countless lives since time without beginning,
You have known endless strings of births and deaths.
There is no world into which you have not been born
And no life-form that you have not taken.
Nor is there a single living being
Who has not been a parent to you
And cared for you with great kindness.

Yet also the power of the three psychic poisons
Will sometimes have drawn you into negative ways
And to rebirth in the lower realms of samsara,
Where countless sufferings had to be faced.

But now by the blessings of the Three Precious Jewels
And your links with the holy spiritual masters
You have achieved a precious human incarnation
And even while in youth took the path of a monk
In search of the boundless state of freedom.

Because of the forces of prayer and good karma
You have the fortune to have met with the gurus,
Who are praised in all the sutras and tantras
Unanimously by the Buddhas of all times and places
As being the root of all knowledge and strength.

The guru, regent of all the Buddhas,
Is a fulfiller of wishes, a magical gem.
He brings every benefit to this life and the next,
And heralds every realization common and supreme.

Hence be not hindered by negative attitudes.
Transcend the mind of mundane perception
And see the guru as a living Buddha.
For the disciple able to train like that,
The siddhis soon begin to fall like rain.

That practitioner gains the constant blessings
Of the Three Precious Jewels of Refuge; and
The meditational deities, dakinis, and Dharmapalas
Watch over him as they would an only child,
Fulfilling all hopes for this life and the next.

With a mind filled with undivided confidence,
Meditate on the benefits the guru can bring.

Sing melodic prayers to him day and night,
And physically devote yourself to him at all times.

This is the way to acquire the guru's blessings
And to extract the benefits his presence affords.
To honor it is to emulate the great yogis of the past.
You will not be parted from the holy spiritual masters
In this or future lives; and they will continue
To guide you until enlightenment is achieved.

Look at the lives of those who gained knowledge,
Like Naropa, Drom Tonpa, and Milarepa.
Were we to practice just as they did
By dedication to the master in thought and action,
Then all gurus, Buddhas and bodhisattvas are able
To care for us as a mother for her only child.

Under the guidance of a qualified teacher
Imbibe the nectars of the vast and profound Dharma.
Maintain the basic purity of the trainings;
Cultivate goodness and transcend negativity;
Practice the Great Way day and night without let.

Many obstacles arise for those who pursue
The enlightenment path in this age of conflict.
The guru embodies all spiritual forces—
Meditational deities, dakas, dakinis, and Dharmapalas—
So simply meditate on him to turn obstacles away.

O my disciple Sung-rab Gyatso, I urge you
To take full advantage of your precious human life
By integrating the three principles of the path:
The free spirit of moderation, that does not cling
To the essenceless things of the material world;
The bodhimind, that stays free from self-cherishing;
And wisdom perceiving emptiness, the final nature of
    being.

In this special year, that of the Iron Snake,
On a special day, the twentieth of the holy *Sakadawa*
   month,
At a special place, the wondrous Ganden Podrang,
I, Gendun Gyatso, sing this special song.

10

Song of the Tantric Path

Translator's Preamble: The next item in the Second Dalai Lama's collection of mystical songs and poems is a gnomic work on the nature of tantric practice. No colophon is provided; the context of the composition is given in the concluding verse. It was written for a disciple, Chomdzey Sengey Gyatso, when the master was residing in Drepung Monastery. Although the work is only seven verses in length, it is one of the most profound in the collection, pointing out all the key points in tantric training.

In general the Buddhist tantras are subdivided into four categories: *kriya, charya, yoga,* and *maha-anuttarayoga.* The fourth of these is considered to be the most powerful and profound. It is this level of tantric endeavor that the Second Dalai Lama is addressing here.

He begins with advice on the importance of correctly training under a qualified master. The esoteric tantric path is a dangerous route to quick enlightenment, and thus a qualified guru is even more important than in the exoteric tradition.

The second verse introduces the necessity of laying a spiritual foundation by means of the ordinary Buddhist trainings before venturing into the rigorous tantric yogas.

The "three levels of the exoteric path" that he refers to here are the structural approach to Sutrayana practice introduced into Tibet by Jowo Atisha and transmitted through the early Kadampa lamas. The word here used for exoteric is *tunmong* (spelled *thunmong*) which carries the sense of being in common or being shared with something. The sense is that these are common to both the sutra and tantra trainings. In fact they are Sutrayana methods that are used as preliminaries to the tantric path.

Essentially these "three levels" involve methods for cultivating "small, medium, and great" stages of spiritual perspective. These simple terms refer to a wide range of meditations for accomplishing three psycho-spiritual effects: turning the mind away from instinctual behavior and directing it toward the way leading to higher being; turning it from cyclic existence toward nirvana; and turning it from self-interest toward universal responsibility and the consequent aspiration for highest enlightenment.

The principal meditational topics in the first of these three phases of training are karmic law, death, and impermanence, and the unsatisfactory nature of samsara. On the second level of training they are interdependent existence, the impermanence of higher meditational bliss, and so forth. Finally, on the third level the meditational subjects include love, compassion, the bodhimind, emptiness, and so forth.

The next verse speaks of the four tantric initiations, which the Second Dalai Lama refers to as "the gateway entering into the tantric path." These four are called vase, secret, wisdom, and sacred word. The first of these gets its name from the fact that each of the five main stages comprising it concludes with the sprinkling of waters from an initiation vase. These five stages are linked to the five elements, the five psychophysical aggregates of being, the five delusions, the five wisdoms, and the five Buddha families. The idea is that in these five stages the disciple is successively shown a radiant wisdom light inherent within the particular delusion associated with the phase of the initiation, and the five elements and aggregates are successively transformed into the natures of the five Buddhas. Acquisition of all phases of the vase initiation purifies negative karma previously collected by means of the body and authorizes the trainee to meditate upon the generation stage yogas, as well as to recite the appropriate mantras. Moreover, the seeds are planted for actualization of the *Nirmanakaya*, or Emanation Body aspect of enlightenment.

The secret initiation involves the consumption of secret substances and also involves bringing the male-female forces of the body into balance. It authorizes the trainee to engage in the esoteric illusory body yoga methods of completion stage practice (utilizing meditation on subtle energies, energy centers, energy channels, and the secret drops). Through it, negative karma previously generated by means of speech is purified and the seeds of the *Samboghakaya*, or Beautific Body, are implanted on the mindstream.

Third is the wisdom initiation, wherein the disciple is introduced to a "wisdom consort" and great bliss born together with wisdom is invoked. This purifies all negative karma generated by means of the mind, authorizes the trainee to meditate on the clear light yogas, and plants the seeds of the *Dharmakaya*, or Truth Body of an enlightened being.

Finally, the trainee receives the sacred word initiation. The instincts of all negative karma of body, speech, and mind are simultaneously purified; one is authorized to meditate on the great union yogas, and the seeds of the *Svabhavakaya*, or Essence Body, are planted.

Having acquired these four tantric initiations (usually in a ritual ceremony that takes two or three days to complete) the trainee is entitled to engage in actual tantric practice.

As mentioned earlier, highest yoga tantra is practiced in two stages, known as generation and completion. The fourth verse in the Second Dalai Lama's poem touches upon the former of these, and the fifth upon the latter. As he points out, the essence of the generation stage yogas is to relinquish the mundane way in which things appear to the mind and learn to see all beings as Buddhas and tantric deities. In other words, we want to bypass the normal functioning of the ego and create an alternative sense of ourselves and the world in which we live. To accomplish this we visualize the world as a mandala, or a sacred environment, and ourselves as mandala deities.

The fifth verse focuses on the completion stage yogas. There are various ways of subdividing these, but the two main aspects of this path are the illusory body and clear light yogas, together with their resultant stage, the great union yoga. In the illusory body yoga, all coarse energies of the body are withdrawn and the subtle energies made to enter into the central channel, where they are brought into the heart *chakra* and dissolved. A paranormal psychophysical state is thus induced, which is beyond the boundaries of life and death. The yogi then meditates from within the framework of an out-of-body experience. The subtle consciousness that arises on the basis of this subtle body is turned toward meditation upon the clear light. Thus in the tantric path the yogi easily achieves enlightenment in one lifetime.

The Second Dalai then summarizes his spiritual approach in verse six, which is that we should stick to the three central pillars of Buddhist training: cultivation of the bodhisattva spirit of love and compassion; integration of the view of emptiness; and application to the two stages of tantric yoga.

The disciple for whom the text was written, Chomdzey Sengey Gyatso, is not mentioned in the *Autobiography* or *Biography*. The fact that the piece focuses on tantric training and was written while the master was living in Drepung Monastery suggests that he was one of the many yogis living in meditation in the mountains around Lhasa.

The guru is the source of all tantric power;
The practitioner who sees him as a Buddha
Holds all realizations in the palm of his hand.
So devote yourself with full intensity
To the guru in both thought and deed.

When the mind is not first well trained
In the three levels of the exoteric path,
Then any claim to the profound tantric yogas
Is an empty boast, and there is every danger
That one will fall from the way.

The door entering into the peerless Vajrayana
Is nothing other than the four tantric initiations.
Hence it is important to receive these fully
And thus plant the seeds of the four Buddha kayas.

One must learn to relinquish the habit of grasping
At the mundane way in which things are perceived,
And to place all that appears within the vision
Of the world as mandala and its beings tantric forms.
Such are the trainings of the generation stage yogas,
That purify and refine the bases to be cleansed.

Next one stimulates the points of the vajra body
And directs the energies flowing in the side channels
Into *dhuti,* mystic channel at the center,
Thus gaining sight of the clear light of mind
And giving rise to wisdom born together with bliss.
Cherish meditation on these completion stage yogas.

The actual body of the final path to liberation
Is cultivation of the perfect view of emptiness;
The gate entering into illumination's Great Way
Is the bodhimind, the enlightenment aspiration;
And the highest method for accomplishing Buddhahood
Is meditation on the two profound tantric stages.
Hold as inseparable these three aspects of practice.

This poem summarizing the key points of tantra
Is here composed by the monk Gendun Gyatso
For his disciple Chomdzey Sengey Gyatso
While residing at Drepung, a great center of Dharma
knowledge.

11

A Prayer of Pure Aspirations

Translator's Preamble: The next item in the Second Dalai Lama's collection of verse works is in fact a prayer and not a *nyamgur*, or mystical song. There is no mention of why it was included in the anthology rather than in his volume of *Miscellaneous Works* (*Sung-bum Torbu*; spelled *gSung-'bum'thor-bu*), where we find numerous liturgical compositions of this nature. Presumably the compilers did so either because it ranked above the others in poetic technique or was inspired by one of his visionary experiences. Neither the *Autobiography* nor *Biography* mentions it, so I am unable to shed light on the matter.

The colophon to it states, "At the request of the attending disciple Chojor Gyatso, this was written by the wandering monk Gendun Gyatso Palzangpo when he was staying at the Ganden Podrang." Thus it appears that Chojor Gyatso was an assistant to Sung-rab Gyatso, the Second Dalai Lama's chief aide. I was not able to find a reference to him in either of the two standard source works mentioned above.

Essentially the piece is a liturgical text meant to be chanted as a prelude to formal meditation and as a *guru yoga* practice. For the convenience of readers I have marked off its four essential movements.

The first of these is a call to the guru, who " . . . always rests on a sun and moon above my head. . . . " This is a request to the guru to extend his omniscient ear, pay heed to the prayer, and send forth a mystical emanation to bear witness to the pure aspiration.

The reference to the sun and moon symbolizes the harmony of female and male aspects of being in enlightenment. In the tantric tradition one meditates that the guru sits on two disklike cushions, one representing the sun and the other the moon, to represent how in the state of enlightenment the guru brings male (moon) and female (sun) energies of body and mind into perfect balance. The sun is below and the moon above, symbolizing that the female wisdom aspect is the ground of enlightenment, from which the male activity aspect arises as enlightened activity. The cushion made of "sun and moon" rests inside an opened lotus, to symbolize how in enlightenment one operates in the conventional world without becoming attached to worldly ways, just as a lotus grows in mud without becoming sullied by the mud. (Readers will perhaps notice that the male-female symbolism of moon and sun are opposite in Buddhism to how they are used in Western occult traditions. Tantric Buddhism likes to think of the moon as male and the sun as female, rather than the reverse, partly because of the sexual nature of tantric practice; the white moon is closer in color to sperm, and the red/gold sun is closer in color to ovum and menstrual blood.)

The next section of the Second Dalai Lama's prayer is an invocation of the "field of merit," or host of transcendental beings that act as a force of inspiration and blessings. This includes one's personal teacher or teachers, myriads of Buddhas and bodhisattvas, as well as the tantric mandala deities into which one has received initiation. Tibetans imagine that these manifest from the skies, riding on vast billowing clouds, and that they are so numerous that all of space becomes filled. The prayer is then offered in their presence.

The third part of the text is a seven-limbed offering prayer. The tradition of these seven limbs comes from Buddhist India, where the *King of Mahayana Prayers* (Skt., *Mahayana-pranidana-raja*) is the prototype. Reciting a seven-limbed prayer at the beginning of every meditation session or tantric ritual is standard procedure with Tibetans. The seven are: visualizing oneself as making prostrations; visualizing making offerings to the enlightened beings; acknowledging one's weaknesses and karmic shortcomings; rejoicing in the goodness of oneself, others, and the world; requesting the enlightened beings to turn the Wheel of Dharma; requesting them to remain in samsara until all beings have achieved enlightenment; and the dedication of merit. Here the Second Dalai Lama includes only the first six of these in the portion of the text that I have marked here. The remainder of the liturgy acts as the seventh limb.

The fourth section, which is the actual prayer of pure aspirations, is essentially a review of the principal themes in Buddhist practice. Here we see many of the ideas that the Second Dalai Lama has expressed in previous of his verse works, although in this context they are presented as a request for inspiration and guidance in the art of living them.

Even though this song does not step far outside the boundaries of compositions of this nature, nonetheless in it the Second Dalai Lama exhibits the freshness of style and liveliness of rhythm that have allowed his writings to achieve a lasting popularity with the peoples of central Asia.

(Part One: A Call to the Guru:—)

> Most kind root guru, who always rests
> On a sun and moon above my head,
> I, a humble disciple, call out to you
> With emotion surging in the depths of my heart.
>
> From wherever you may physically be in this world,
> Send forth a mystical emanation to heed me.
> Reveal your radiant countenance to me;
> And may we never ever become parted.

(Invocation of the Field of Merit:—)

> Present masters, lineage gurus, Three Jewels,
> Peaceful and wrathful meditational deities,

And all Dharma Protectors and guardians of truth,
I call out to you with this prayer.

Come forth as a billowing cloud
Of profound wisdom and great compassion.
Release a dragon's roar of Dharma teachings,
A fiery smoke of your transforming powers,
And a shower of mystical realizations.
Place your inspiring blessings on my mindstream,
That I may achieve spiritual maturity and freedom.

(The Seven-Limbed Offering Prayer:—)

Embodiment of the Three Jewels of Refuge,
Wherever you may be in this universe,
I bow to you in body, speech, and mind
With forms as numerous as the atoms of the world.

Without hesitation I send forth to you
Vast clouds of beautifully arranged offerings,
As well as all things linked to this life
And all virtues past, present, and future.

In your presence I face all my shortcomings;
For under the power of the three inner poisons,
I have created a mountain of negative karma,
Even harming and abusing the Buddhas and bodhisattvas.

You who have accomplished the twofold purpose,
I rejoice in your enlightenment deeds.
Turn the precious Wheel of Truth
In accordance with the needs of living beings.

I request you to remain in this world
And not pass away into parinirvana
For as long as space exists,
In order to benefit all living beings.

(Prayer of Pure Aspirations:—)

Although I have met with spiritual masters
Possessing full compassion, knowledge, and power,
I did not see them as the root of all siddhi
Nor appreciate them as being perfect Buddhas.
The negative mind of mundane perception
That always finds fault in others overpowered me;
Looking back at the many missed opportunities,
My heart fills with sadness and regret.

O noble and holy root guru, I call to you:
Hold me in the sphere of your compassion
Until enlightenment itself is achieved;
Watch over me with heartfelt care
As I strive to accomplish enlightenment's way.

This precious and rare human rebirth
Has so far gone mostly to worldly works
That have produced little of lasting value.
I send forth this pure aspiration:
May whatever remains of my brief life
Be dedicated to the enlightenment trainings,
That I may achieve spiritual maturity.

The Lord of Death indiscriminately devours
People of strong, medium, and weak constitutions,
Yet we are deceived by the demon of grasping
At the sense of our own immortality.
I send forth this pure aspiration:
May I have constant awareness of death
And knowledge that I could be dead in a moment,
That I might transcend the materialistic mind
And pass my days and nights in spiritual ways.

There is every chance that when my breath stops,

I could fall to a rebirth in the lower realms,
For I, feeble in mindfulness and prone to delusion,
Have gathered much negative karma.
I send forth this pure aspiration:
May I avoid the confusion created
By false teachers and distracting friends,
And always take my inspiration from Dharma,
Thus strengthening the good within myself
And undermining the forces of imperfection.

All accomplishments in the material world
Are unreliable and are easily swept away.
We see this all around us, but still
Our aspiration to spiritual freedom remains weak.
I send forth this pure aspiration:
May the free spirit of moderation
Always arise spontaneously within me.

And I send forth the pure aspiration
That I may transcend the negative habit
Of discriminating between the living beings,
Regarding some with attachment and others aversion;
And that instead I may learn to hold them all
Within the meditation of love and compassion
That cherishes others more than it does oneself.

I also send forth the pure aspiration
That I may attain the naked insight that perceives
The emptiness nature of all that exists:
How all the appearing and transforming phenomena
Have no real existence whatsoever and are
Mere imputations of the conceptual mind.

I send forth the pure aspiration
That after this meditational insight is gained,
I may carry the vision into daily activities

And observe all the things that appear
Without grasping at them as being real,
Like watching a magician's illusory tricks.

I send forth the pure aspiration
That I may always be aware of the way in which
All these things that are mere mental labels
Nonetheless function according to the laws
Of relativity and unfailing cause and effect;
And thus may I amass the two collections
Of meritorious energy and wisdom combined.

I send forth the pure aspiration
That I may complete the yogic meditations
Of the two profound levels of tantric practice—
The generation and completion stages—that take
The confused appearances of birth, death, and the bardo
And transform them into the three perfect kayas.

I send forth the pure aspiration
That the state of the four perfect kayas
May quickly be fully achieved,
And that I may then fulfill my wish to be
Of continual and ultimate benefit to the world.

Finally I offer the auspicious prayer that
As I train in the ways leading to enlightenment,
I may meet with every helpful circumstance
And my path remain unhindered by any obstacle.

12

A Necklace of Jewels

Translator's Preamble: The following entry is not provided with a colophon, so we can only glean its context from the concluding verse, "This string of words easy to understand / Formed into a necklace of spiritual advice / To adorn those who delight in the trainings / Is thus sung by the mad beggar monk Gendun Gyatso. / May it benefit all who seek truth's way."

Thus it would seem that it is a spontaneous creation from the pen of Gyalwa Gendun Gyatso and was not written at the request of a particular disciple. The song is not mentioned in either the *Autobiography* or *Biography*, so I am unable to date it.

There is, I think, no need to comment on the contents of the work. It speaks in a straightforward language, or, as the author himself puts it, "a string of words easy to understand." In it the Second Dalai Lama presents us with the essential spirit of his teaching, in the form of "a necklace of spiritual advice." The images that he uses as well as the general style of the piece are very much inspired by the verse works of the early Indian Buddhist master Nagarjuna, one of the Second Dalai Lama's favorite authors, mystics, and saints.

Om. May goodness and joy prevail.
Homage to the kind parent-like guru,
From whose mind palace of great bliss manifests
A beatific form with all the signs of perfection
And sounds that release a rain of truth's nectars.

Out of gratitude to you I now offer this song
To spiritual aspirants with faith and enthusiasm
Who wish to use the essenceless human body
As a vessel to extract the essence of profound truth.

Every Buddha of the ten directions meditated upon
The kindness of and became dedicated to
A guru who could point the way to enlightenment.
Should we simple folk not do likewise?

The source of all benefits for this life and the next
Is tapped by training under a qualified guru.
If we are wise to dedicate our very life like this,
What to say of things more mundane?

This precious human life that we have found
Lasts not for long and is easily destroyed.
Until now it was spent largely in vain;
Use it from now to extract the essence.

We should simply ignore worldly distractions
And without hesitation engage the methods
That induce spiritual knowledge and joy.
As we have no idea when our life will end,
The effort should be immediate and intense.

The body and mind, close companions for so long,
Are pulled apart when the Lord of Death strikes
And are forced to go their separate ways.
What to say then of wealth, relatives, and friends?

Turning away from higher spiritual goals
And instead spending our precious energy and time
In pursuit of the empty things of this life
Is, when measured by the inner peace produced,
Merely a cause of more agitation and pain.

The misery experienced in the lower realms
Is like having to sit in a pit of fire
For ages and ages beyond imagination.
Is it wise to create the karmic causes now
Of a future rebirth in such a world?

Generating negative karma with the thought
To gain some present or future pleasure
Is like stuffing ourselves now with sweet poison
As a means of living to a hundred years of age.

If we do not appreciate this simple truth,
Then even if we wear the best jewels and clothing
And express ourselves in the most refined of ways,
How can we say we are wiser than a goat?

This body is a city of slimy substances
Like pus, blood, urine, and stool.
When its mind is not linked to spiritual values,
The cheapest of raiments is too good for it.

Yet when mind is adorned with spiritual knowledge,
One becomes an object well worthy of worship
To all living beings, including humans and gods,
Even if dressed in the shabbiest of rags; and then
Even one's urine and stool become ambrosia.

Therefore immediately turn your mental focus
Away from all essenceless worldly concerns;

And without falling prey to mental distraction,
Strive to accomplish the enlightenment path.

Surrounding yourself with friends and admirers
Only induces a false sense of strength.
Turn your back on such empty methods
And rely instead on the enlightenment path.

This festival of wealth and possessions around us
Is merely bait placed by the great Lord of Death;
The pleasure garden of a youthful body
Is like a rainbow in the clear sky;
And things like prosperity and possessions
Are like a magician's illusory creations.
Turn your back on such worldly concerns
And strive to accomplish the enlightenment path.

The noose of cherishing oneself more than others
Has in the past always held us down.
Give rise now to the enlightenment thought
That replaces self-cherishing with universal love.

All things that exist are dependent imputations,
And thus nothing inherently exists on its own.
Invoke the samadhi of meditation on emptiness,
The profound nature of all that exists, and
Cut distortion from its very root.

How extremely rare to encounter a path in which
Enlightenment can be gained in one short life!
Yet such is the tantric way of skillful means,
That focuses on our habit of perceiving mundanely
Birth, death, and the bardo, and transforms these
Into the three kayas of Buddhahood itself.

You destined for white hair, like a head covered in snow,
And for a face carved with waves of wrinkles,
If you can begin now to integrate the themes
Of this song into every aspect of your life,
The eternal youth of a blissful mind could be yours.

This string of words easy to understand
Formed into a necklace of spiritual advice
To adorn those who delight in the trainings
Is thus sung by the mad beggar monk Gendun Gyatso.
May it benefit all who seek truth's way.

13

Spiritual Advice to a Hermit

Translator's Preamble: The colophon to the following entry reads, "Verses of instruction written by Gendun Gyatso Palzangpo for the hermit meditator Chomdzey Kunpang Chenpo Tamchok Palzang." No place or date of the composition of the work is given. Moreover, neither the text or the monk for whom it was written are mentioned in the *Autobiography* or *Biography*.

However, a few remarks can be made concerning this monk. *Chomdzey* is in fact a title and these days indicates a monk whose parents, countrymen, or tribe offered a large feast to the monastery at the time of his taking ordination. As a result, throughout his life in the monastery, he would be accorded more respect and consideration than the average monk and would be given a raised front-row seat at gatherings in the main assembly hall. I am not sure if this was the case in the time of the Second Dalai Lama, but I expect that it was. *Kungpang Chenpo* is an epithet. It usually indicates a meditator who has renounced all worldly comforts and activities and lives in solitary retreat either in a cave or mountain hut. Thus he was a hermit who had renounced the privileges accorded to him in the monastery and opted instead to live in retreat. His actual ordination name was Tamchok Palzang, or Gloriously Sublime Hayagriva (Hayagriva being a tantric deity).

The Second Dalai Lama explains the nature of the composition in the closing verse, "Such is my song, spontaneous and simple, / On the key points in the vast and profound path. / May it help those interested in spiritual ways / Effortlessly fulfill all spiritual aspirations / Concerning this life and what lies beyond." In other words, he has composed it as a spontaneous and plainly stated synthesis of the Buddha's quintessential teachings on the enlightenment path. The use of the word *spontaneous* in Tibetan verse works usually indicates that the composition was penned as an inspired creation in a single sitting and that no editing of it was later permitted.

As with the previous entry, there is no need to comment on the contents. The Second Dalai Lama purposely expresses himself in universally human rather than philosophical or technical language.

Homage to the Buddhas and bodhisattvas.
In this age approaching the end of time,
The knowledge and compassion of all the Buddhas
Manifested in the form of two Buddhist monks,
The great masters Atisha and Lama Tsongkhapa;
I bow before their lotus-like feet.

This song I now offer to a devoted yogi disciple,
Who by the ripening forces of aspiration and action
Has gained human life with all its potential
And has left mundane ways in order to fulfill
The exalted path that leads to perfection.

All goodness, happiness, and spiritual power
Follow from training with a Mahayana master.
Practice well under a qualified teacher
And always regard him as a Buddha sent to you.

From beginningless time you have wandered in samsara
And have been born in the world again and again;
Yet all these lives came and went like dreams.
Know that now you are capable of highest enlightenment,
And let the opportunity slip not away.

Is not life in this violent age unstable?
Does not Death carry away whomsoever he chooses,
Young or old, regardless of their wealth or power?
Do not be deceived by a false sense of permanence;
Live in constant awareness of death.

Our circle of friends and loved ones may be large,
But soon we shall be parted from them all;
We may have food, wealth, and possessions in excess,
But all this too is one day left behind; and
We may have mansions, properties, herds, and fields,
But these too eventually will be lost.
All we can take with us through death's doors
Are the karmic seeds of our black and white deeds,
The instincts of what we have done and been.

In this dark age disciples scorn their teachers;
Children, raised with love, abandon their parents;
And trusted workers constantly cheat their patrons.
Kyema! Look at how people behave these days!

Alive in the morning, dead in the evening;
Although rich today, poor tomorrow;
And last year a king, this year a beggar:
What is there that is stable in life?

Not seeing this, the fools of this world
Pass their time in negative ways, and
Then at death fall to lower realms!
They think of themselves now as heroes,
But in reality who is more vain?

The only objects really deserving of our trust
Are the Three Jewels of refuge, so rely upon them;
And as the laws of karma and its result are unfailing,
Strive at goodness and see negativity as poison;

For the root of spiritual progress and liberation lies
In guarding self-discipline like one does one's eyes.

Conditioned existence is like a pit of fire,
And nowhere in it is there room for peace.
Rely then on the free spirit of moderation,
And cultivate the three higher trainings
Of self-discipline, meditation, and wisdom.

Those wandering in samsara are uncountable,
Yet there is not one who has not once been our parent.
With the compassionate bodhimind that meditates
On exchanging self-cherishing for universal love,
Give joy to others and eradicate their pain.

The sense of *I* that arises in our heart
Is the tethered mind that leads us in circles.
It is important to watch this *I* within,
And to see just how its appearance occurs.

It often seems as though the *I* resides
Within the body or mind; but look more closely,
For it has no real existence at all,
And is merely a projection of conceptual thought.

In this way practice the meditation that observes
How all outer and inner phenomena are no more
Than images projected by the distorted mind
Onto the according bases of imputation.
Not even an atom inherently exists.

Thus become wise in how all things in both
Samsara and nirvana are mere mental labels;
But how nonetheless they continue to function
By the unfailing laws of cause and effect.

When the mind is thus matured by an inner experience
Of method and wisdom as taught in the sutras,
Enter into meditation on the two tantric stages
Whereby Buddhahood's three kayas are quickly won
And make ultimate use of this brief human life.

Such is my song, spontaneous and simple,
On the key points in the vast and profound path.
May it help those interested in spiritual ways
Effortlessly fulfill all spiritual aspirations
Concerning this life and what lies beyond.

14

In Search of the Middle View

Translator's Preamble: It is often said in Tibetan scriptures that every teaching given by the Buddha has the ultimate purpose of leading the trainee toward experience of the emptiness doctrine. All other teachings are "method"; the emptiness teaching alone is "wisdom." The two—method and wisdom—must operate together, hand in hand, just as a bird requires two wings in order to fly. But it is the understanding of emptiness that bestows ultimate liberation from karma and delusion upon the mindstream of the meditator.

Numerous styles of meditation upon emptiness came from India to Tibet. The most fundamental, however, was the lineage of the second-century Indian master Acharya Nagarjuna, as elucidated in this extraordinary master's classical treatise *The Root of Wisdom* (Skt., *Mula-prajna-madhyamaka-shastra*). Tibetans supplement this approach with various methods taught in the tantric tradition, but all schools regard Nagarjuna's guidelines as an indispensable introduction to the topic. It was the tradition of Nagarjuna that both Atisha and Lama Tsongkhapa propagated most widely in Tibet, and it is this legacy that the Second Dalai Lama explores in the verse work to follow.

The text is not provided with a colophon. Instead, the Second Dalai Lama writes in the concluding verse, ". . . complete my song in easy words / Elucidating the pure view of emptiness, / Composed spontaneously by Gendun Gyatso / At the request of his disciple Gyaltsen Pal / While residing at Gyal, the Place of Victory." Thus it was composed by the master after the construction of Chokhor Gyal Monastery, which occurred in 1509-10. The disciple for whom it was written, Gyaltsen Pal, presumably was a monk resident in this monastery.

The text opens with a line of homage to the guru as inseparable from Manjushri. In the Mahayana sutras, Manjushri is regarded as the bodhisattva symbolizing the wisdom of all Buddhas of the three times and ten directions. A copy of the *Prajnaparamita Sutra* sits on a lotus beside his left shoulder, the stem of which he holds in his left hand; and in his right he holds the sword of wisdom that cuts through to the meaning of emptiness and severs the root of ego.

Readers may perhaps remember that when the Second Dalai Lama was in his mid-teens he undertook a month-long retreat focused on recitation of the Manjushri mantra and, as a result, is said to have remembered hundreds of his previous lives. He is also said to have so enhanced his mental powers that thereafter he was able to memorize a hundred lines of scripture during the time of a single tea break and to comprehend the meaning of the most profound philosophical treatise merely by reading it once.

After the opening line of homage, the Second Dalai Lama advises the meditator to begin each session of meditation upon emptiness by visualizing one's guru in the form of Manjushri sitting on a lotus in the space above one's head. One offers the seven-limbed prayer to him (a version of which we saw earlier in the Second Dalai Lama's "Prayer of Pure Aspirations") to request inspiration and blessings for realization. One is now ready to proceed to the actual meditation.

This begins by trying to recognize the *gakja* (spelled *dgag-bya*), or "object of negation," the "false self" of which we and all things are "empty." This is the sense of *I* that appears to the mind as independent from the rest of the world, as truly and inherently existent. The Second Dalai Lama gives the example of a wooden pillar. When we perceive a pillar we instantly get a sense of pillarness, as though there were something in the piece of wood to represent this idea of pillar. When we look closer, however, it becomes obvious that no such phenomenon exists.

There is a similar situation with the sense of *I* that we have. Sometimes it appears as one with the body, sometimes as one with the mind, and sometimes separate from both body and mind. Thus we search for this mysterious phenomenon called the *I*, but the more we look for it the more elusive it becomes. The meditation alternates between these two phases: searching for the *I* in this way and then resting awareness in the sense of its absence.

Between formal meditation sittings, the trainee attempts to retain awareness that nothing has the independent and truly existent nature that it seems to possess; yet on the conventional level things appear to the mind and, on the appearance level, operate according to the conventional laws of cause and effect, just as a dream dog can produce a dream bite. But in the final analysis, nothing exists in the nature of its appearance.

This is the emptiness meditation method and the experience of the great void that the Second Dalai Lama plays with in his song, "In Search of the Middle View."

Homage to the guru, who is inseparably one
With Manjushri, the Bodhisattva of Wisdom.

In the search for the meaning of the middle view,
Meditate on the guru as inseparable from Manjushri,
Placing him above the crown of your head.
Generate meritorious energy and purify obstacles
By one-pointedly offering the seven-limbed prayer
And thus become a vessel ripe to receive
Realization of the profound view of the void.

First we must discover the manner of appearance
Of this sense of *I* that we all have,
The *I* that is a mere projection on body and mind
Yet seems to exist otherwise, as though
Established on the actual objects themselves.

For example, a piece of wood that has the function
Of holding up a beam is called a *pillar;*

This pillar is a mere mental imputation, but
It appears otherwise to the deluded mind,
As though from the beginning it existed in the wood.

Yet when the pillar stood in the forest
As a tree with roots, branches, and leaves,
We did not then have the sense of a pillar;
Nor did we do so when the tree was cut down
And trimmed by a skilled woodworker.

At none of those phases in the birth of the pillar
Did the thought "this is a pillar" arise.
Meditate then on how *pillarness* simply never
Existed from the side of the wood itself.

I am not *my body,* for at the time of death,
The body is left behind, yet *I* go on
To a future life. Similarly *I* am not *my mind;*
For the mind is merely a basis of imputation of *I,*
And also the instinctual sense of *I* does not
Apprehend the mind as being the *I.*

Sometimes the *I* is sensed as being a single entity,
Yet conventionally it appears in various locations
(Such as in an arm or leg, if that limb pains us);
When that occurs, we may think, "I am in pain,"
Yet later will not agree that *I* am *my arm*
(Or whatever part was causing the pain),
For we then realize the process to be solely
An effect created within the mind itself.

Like this, mountains, fences, and houses seem to exist
From the side of their own bases of designation,
Yet when we analyze these objects deeply with care
To find the place in which these things are located
We are unable to find the *mountain, fence,* or *house.*

Meditating like this induces definite awareness
That these things do not exist from the side of the object

Similarly "over there" depends upon "over here,"
Short depends on long, subject on object,
Perception on perceiver, and imputation on its basis.
Meditate like that on how all things that exist
Have no ultimate self-nature in and of themselves
And are mere labels established by mutual dependence

During the period between meditational sessions,
Maintain awareness of how the people and things
That appear to the mind as being so solid
Are in fact nothing more than mere projections
And are like a magician's illusory creations;
Yet how they nonetheless conventionally function
By the unfailing laws of cause and effect.

Thus is complete my song in easy words
Elucidating the pure view of emptiness
Composed spontaneously by Gendun Gyatso
At the request of his disciple Gyaltsen Pal
While residing at Gyal, the Place of Victory.

15

Song of a Joyful Fate

Translator's Preamble: The colophon to the next entry reads, "At the request of Drung Zangpa, a disciple of undivided spiritual conviction, this was written by the Buddhist monk Gendun Gyatso Palzangpo while he was residing in the Hermitage of the Helmeted Bird, Tsetang Monastery, in the chamber known as the Garden of Devotion."

Tsetang Monastery, which is located at the mouth of the Yarlung Valley not far from the Brahmaputra River, had been founded in 1351 by Pagmo Drukpa Tai Situ Jangchub Gyaltsen. In the Second Dalai Lama's time, it was an eclectic institution that housed lamas from several different schools. The First Dalai Lama had taught there several times during his years in central Tibet; consequently, when the young Second Dalai Lama visited for the first time in the Fire Dragon Year (1496), he was well received by numerous elderly disciples of his predecessor. From this year on, the master visited Tsetang at least once a year as part of his teaching pilgrimages in the Yarlung area.

The song that he composed here was written at the request of one of these elderly monks. It is an expression of the joy that the Second Dalai Lama found in the spiritual legacy coming from Jowo Atisha and his delight at being a young monk upholding and teaching the Atisha lineages. His travels in the Yarlung area had taken him to many of the holy places where Atisha had meditated four-and-a-half centuries earlier, including Radeng and Yerpa, and had inspired several visionary experiences within him. As well, he had taught several texts attributed to Atisha in these places.

Although only five verses in length, the Second Dalai Lama's song touches upon all the salient points of the Kadampa doctrines that Atisha had brought to Tibet from India in 1042 and that had been transmitted in an unbroken lineage from then until the Second Dalai Lama received them from his own gurus, first in Tashi Lhunpo and Nartang monasteries as a teenager and then again later in Drepung from his guru Jamyang Lekpai Chojor.

Om! May peace and joy prevail!

To meet with a lineage that reaches back to Buddha
And comes through Atisha and his spiritual sons;
To train under a master accomplished in the legacies
Of spiritual learning and realization through practice;
And to master both the sutra and tantra traditions:
To make life meaningful in this way,
Is this not a joyful fate?

The nature of Atisha's wondrous lineage is that in it
All teachings arise as personal instructions
Within the context of one's own training,
And in a single meditational sitting one is able
To practice all key points of the enlightenment path
Without ignoring or overlooking even one.
Is this not a joyful fate?

A view of emptiness that fathoms to its depths
The final nature of all that exists;
Unmistaken meditation that achieves highest samadhi;
And action perfectly balancing method and wisdom:—
To delight the Buddhas and bodhisattvas in this way,
Is this not a joyful fate?

To be able to teach all sutras and tantras,
To achieve mastery in the ways of subtle reasoning,
And to compose endless strings of poetry and prose:
To delight the wise of the earth in this way,
Is this not a joyful fate?

To comprehend all the profound Vajrayana methods
And through meditation on the two yogic stages
Of the profound path as taught in highest yoga tantra
And thus accomplish the sublime state of Great Union
And release a river of enlightenment activity
In order to benefit and uplift the world,
Is this not a joyful fate?

16

Song to Lama Norzang Gyatso

Translator's Preamble: Although there is no colophon to the following song, the Second Dalai Lama provides us with some information concerning its context in both the opening and the concluding verses. It was written when he was living in retreat in Tashi Gang at the foot of Odey Gunggyal Mountain in a hermitage by the name of Tosamling.

As His Holiness the Dalai Lama states in his Foreword to the present volume, the Second Dalai Lama declared several times that he owed his realization of voidness—his enlightenment—to the training that he received under his guru Khedrub Norzang Gyatso, a great yogi who had spent fourteen years in solitary retreat in the Olkha mountains practicing the tantric yogas, particularly the Kalachakra doctrines. This yogi had been a close disciple of the First Dalai Lama. When the Second met him, the two established an instant rapport. After that they became like father and son, meditating in the caves and hermitages of the Olkha region and often making pilgrimages and teaching tours together. In particular, the master studied the Kalachakra and Guhyasamaja tantric doctrines with Norzang Gyatso.

His song to Norzang Gyatso was written in the Iron Monkey Year (1500). The two had spent the summer together in pilgrimage and meditation, and the Second Dalai Lama was overwhelmingly impressed by the old yogi. Norzang Gyatso's principal meditation hermitage was located on Odey Gunggyal, the highest mountain in the central Tibet region and one of the holiest in Tibet.

The opening verse gives the area where the composition took place as Rinchen Gang, a village at the foot of Odey Gunggyal; the closing verse mentions the specific hermitage as Tosamling. Both Rinchen Gang and Tosamling are quite common place names in Tibet, the latter (which means "Hermitage of Study and Contemplation") being used for numerous monastic dwellings. It was also at Tosamling that the Second performed the principal divinations concerning his thoughts on building a monastery at Gyal; the divinations were auspicious, and thus he proceeded with his plans to do so.

The Second Dalai Lama's composition to his guru focuses upon two principal realizations that he had attained under him: those resulting from his study and practice of the Kalachakra tantric yogas and those related to his meditation upon emptiness. He seems particularly moved by the latter theme.

I bow at the feet of the holy gurus.

Here I sit in Rinchen Gang, in a hermitage
Where meditation spontaneously achieves results,
A Dharma site at the foot of Odey Gunggyal,
A magnificent mountain rivaling Mount Kailash itself.

Thoughts of my guru Khedrub Norzang Gyatso arise,
And I recollect his immeasurable kindness.
A flood of emotion surges up from within me,
And every hair on my body trembles with joy.

I call out to him with a plaintive voice:
Pray, come forth from the sphere of the unmanifest.
Emanate the radiant countenance of your holy body;
With speech, release a great rainfall of the Dharma;

And lead living beings to the state of enlightenment
That is inseparable from your peerless mind.

O most holy root guru, through your kind guidance
I mastered the yogas of the two tantric stages
Of glorious Kalachakra, king of the tantras,
As well as its branches, like astrology,
That facilitate higher spiritual knowledge.

Without relying on mere words alone
You led me to a naked understanding
Of the teachings of Nagarjuna, Aryadeva, and Tsongkhapa
Concerning the ultimate mode of being:—
That all things abide in the nature of emptiness;
That nothing exists in its own right;
That things are mere mental projections
Imputed on their bases of designation.

You helped me to see the great inner enemy,
The *I*-grasping habit that sees things as real,
And to see its limitlessly harmful effects.
You also showed me how to destroy it;
So now everything manifest in the sphere of perception
Effortlessly arises within the path of the void.

Yet you did not let me fall into nihilism,
But pointed out to me the relevance of how
All the things that appear, though mere labels,
Nonetheless continue to function conventionally
According to the laws of cause and effect.
Thus you freed me from the terrible cliffs
Of grasping at the extremes of "is" and "is not."

O most kind root guru, it was you who taught me
How to extract the quintessential meanings
Of all the profound sutras and tantras

And helped me to find the inner strength
Of a mind well trained in the wisdom tradition.

Recollecting the great kindness you showed to me,
I can easily see you as a fully accomplished Buddha;
And within that frame of devotion I call to you:
Please keep me in your thoughts forever
And bestow spiritual powers mundane and supreme.

This song of the spontaneous experience
Of the profound yogas of the great middle view
Was composed by the Buddhist monk Gendun Gyatso
When he experienced strong thoughts of his holy guru
While living in retreat at Tosamling Monastery.
May it contribute to goodness on earth
And to the strength of joy and peace in the world.

17

A Song of Spiritual Joy

Translator's Preamble: The colophon to this piece reads, "Composed by the master while he was at Riwo Dechen." Riwo Dechen was a small monastery located at Chongyey below the Tiger's Peak Fort, the latter being the residence of the Chongyey king who sponsored many of the Second Dalai Lama's early teaching tours through the Yarlung Valley.

The Second Dalai Lama paid numerous visits to Riwo Dechen, as it was included on the circuit of places at which he taught on his annual spring visits to Tsetang and the Yarlung Valley. His "A Song of Spiritual Joy" is mentioned in the *Biography* as having been written during his visit of the Water Dog Year (1502). It was the early autumn, and he was in retreat after having completed a heavy spring and summer schedule. During one of his meditation sessions he experienced a vision of Lama Tsongkhapa and was moved to compose this mystical song.

From within the depths of my heart I turn
To the incomparable master Lama Tsongkhapa,
An embodiment of the Three Precious Jewels.
Befriend me on the spiritual path.

The thought of how death comes unannounced
Acts as a spur to our practice;
And the contemplations of love and compassion
Serve as our guides on the way.

Meditation on the two bodhiminds
Is the actual body of the training;
Taking the creative energy generated by it
And dedicating it to the benefit of the world
Is the seal with which to conclude every action.

Within the sphere of the manifest and the void,
One accumulates meritorious energy and wisdom;
This accomplishes the two kayas of Buddhahood,
That spontaneously accomplish the ultimate benefit
Of both oneself and others.

Merely thinking of these stages on the path
Fills the mind of this yogi with joy.
Merely recollecting these profound spiritual methods,
This yogi swoons with delight.

It moves me to give voice to this song,
A melody of joyous experience,
And to shuffle my feet to and fro
In a dance of great inner bliss.

O Lama Tsongkhapa, lord of all Buddhas,
Your kindness to the world is beyond words.
I call out to you from the depths of my heart:
Look down on us with eyes of compassion.

18

Ah-oh-la: The Wise They Sing

Translator's Preamble: The following song is probably the Second Dalai Lama's most unusual composition, at least from the structural and poetic viewpoint. Some of the lines are nine syllables in length; others are eight; others seven; and still others fourteen. Moreover, it alternates between stanzas of three and four lines in length. Presumably this extraordinary amount of variation in rhythm was accompanied by corresponding movements in melody, as the piece was originally composed as a song and not as a poem. Many of the syllables have no literal meaning and serve only as open-ended sound fillers.

The colophon to it states, "This piece, 'Ah-oh-la: The Wise They Sing,' was written by the master at the conclusion of an intensive meditation retreat that he made at Gyal." It does not give a date, and neither the *Autobiography* nor *Biography* provides us with this information.

The spiritual ideas embodied in the song take their inspiration from a number of sources. The composition opens with a reference to enlightenment as the experience of radiance and the void and then expresses the quintessential wisdom of three particular lineages of transmission: the emptiness teachings transmitted by the Indian masters Acharya Nagarjuna and Acharya Aryadeva; the bodhisattva activities teachings transmitted by Maitreya and Asanga; and the tantric lineages transmitted in India by the great mahasiddhas. In Tibet all three of these lines of transmissions were collected and passed on by Lama Tsongkhapa, and thus the Second Dalai Lama concludes with a reference to him.

To comment beyond this would be to open up subjects that require volumes. Instead, I invite the reader to dive straight in and make of the piece what he or she will.

The ultimate nature of spiritual realization
Is final union of light and the void.
Ah-oh-la, the wise they sing: ya-yi ya-yi,
It is the union of light and the void.

Ah-oh-la, the wise they sing:
The final taste of all that exists
Is voidness empty of self-nature.

Ah-oh-la, the wise they sing: ya-yi ya-yi,
Yet all things in the world and beyond,
Sketches drawn by the conceptual mind,
Still retain a conventional impact.

Ah-oh-la, the wise they sing: ya-yi ya-yi,
This profound nature free from extremes
Is the vision to be accomplished.

Ah-oh-la, the wise they sing: ya-yi ya-yi,
Such is Nagarjuna's and Aryadeva's lineage;
And I, a yogi who follows in their footsteps,
Am delighted to be part of it.

Ah-oh-la, the wise they sing: ya-yi ya-yi,

This mystical dance of the profound view
Flashes in the sphere free from extremes.

Ah-oh-la, the wise they sing: ya-yi ya-yi,
The gentle aspiration to highest enlightenment,
That cares for others more than oneself,
Is the very door opening to the Great Way.

Ah-oh-la, the wise they sing: ya-yi ya-yi,
Wisdom of voidness grasped by this compassion
Is the very essence of the Great Way.

Ah-oh-la, the wise they sing: ya-yi ya-yi,
This, practised as the six perfections,
Is the mighty bodhisattva path.

Ah-oh-la, the wise they sing: ya-yi ya-yi,
Such is Maitreya's and Asanga's lineage;
And I, a yogi who follows in their footsteps,
Am delighted to be part of it.

Ah-oh-la, the wise they sing: ya-yi ya-yi,
This mystical dance of vast ways is
A dance of method and wisdom combined.

Ah-oh-la, the wise they sing: ya-yi ya-yi,
The yogic methods of tantra's two stages
Are the highest means for producing Buddhahood.

Ah-oh-la, the wise they sing: ya-yi ya-yi,
They transform death, bardo, and rebirth
Into enlightenment's three perfect kayas.

Ah-oh-la, the wise they sing: ya-yi ya-yi,
Such is the lineage of Lama Tsongkhapa;

And I, a yogi who follows in his footsteps
Am delighted to be part of it.

Through it the dance of great bliss and void
Comes to pervade one's every experience.
Ah-oh-la, the wise they sing: ya-yi ya-yi,
It comes to pervade one's every experience.

19

Songs of the Turquoise Dragon

Translator's Preamble: As we saw earlier, Tashi Lhunpo Monastery had been built by the First Dalai Lama in 1447 in Tsang, southwestern Tibet, not far from the town of Shigatsey.

In Part Two of this volume, in which I treat the Second Dalai Lama's life in some detail, I discussed the young Second Dalai Lama's entrance into Tashi Lhunpo and his recognition as the First's official reincarnation, as well as his later expulsion from the institution when he was a teenager. I also told of the letter from the Tashi Lhunpo abbot that came to him almost two decades later, with the request for him to return home and take up his rightful throne in the monastery. By that time he had already risen to become one of the most highly regarded lamas in Tibet and was in the process of completing the construction of Chokhor Gyal Monastery. Nonetheless, he agreed to put aside his many activities and return to Tashi Lhunpo for the year.

The news of his leaving Gyal did not go down well with his disciples and patrons in the Dvakpo area, who had put a lot of time, energy, money, and work into building Chokhor Gyal Monastery at Metoktang for him. One of them, Nangso Chojey by name, wrote a song to him asking him to reverse his decision to leave. The master replied to him, also in song. The following entry contains these two items: the verse letter to the Second Dalai Lama from Nangso Chojey; and his reply to it.

These are prefaced with a brief text that outlines the context of the composition. The preface reads: "A large party of messengers from Tsang had arrived in Gyal, where the master had been living and teaching for some time. They carried with them elaborate offerings and a pressing letter from the administrators of Tashi Lhunpo Monastery, requesting that the master come to Tsang and assume the abbotship of Tashi Lhunpo. The master was not even slightly interested in holding an abbotship, for he was motivated solely by the inner thought to benefit the Dharma and living beings. However, in order to accord with worldly conventions and as a sign of respect to the monastic tradition, he eventually accepted. His disciples in Gyal were deeply saddened by news of his departure. One of them, Nangso Chojey by name, sent him this Dharma song."

As the Second Dalai Lama comments in his *Autobiography*, the invitation from Tashi Lhunpo came at a somewhat awkward time for him. His work in building Chokhor Gyal was incomplete, and he knew that as soon as he left, the enthusiasm of his disciples and patrons would wane and the pace of construction would slow drastically. On the other hand, he could not ignore or decline the invitation, for then his relationship with Tashi Lhunpo, already somewhat delicate because of his having once been expelled, could easily become irreparable. He chose the middle way and agreed to visit Tashi Lhunpo briefly after some months. He left in the autumn of the Water Monkey Year (1512), teaching at a dozen monasteries as he traveled to Tsang, and arrived in the early winter.

In Tashi Lhunpo he embarked upon an intense teaching schedule that continued throughout the winter and spring and also into the summer, before events at Gyal forced him to return. However, from this time until his death he continued to visit and teach at Tashi Lhunpo regularly and to care for the community there.

I am not certain of the identity of Nangso Chojey, the disciple at Gyal who so strongly protested the master's leaving. Usually *nangso* is a title referring to a minor king or valley chieftain. The principal patron in the construction of Chokhor Gyal Monastery was the *nangso* of Lhagyari, so it could well be him. However, a half dozen other *nangsos* also participated in the project, so the reference in the poem could also be to any one of them.

Whoever penned the verse letter to the Second Dalai Lama was highly skilled in the Tibetan poetic tradition. In his reply the Second emulates the style of his student. Thus the two pieces together read like a single song in two parts.

Homage to the holy spiritual masters.
O reincarnation of the illustrious Jey Lama,
Grant me your inspiring blessings.

Should the sun, that great parasol in the sky,
Leave us and go to other worlds,
What will eliminate the darkness here?
If it really must go away,
It should at least leave us the moon.

When the turquoise dragon
Takes rest in the bed of space,
From whom can the poor little rain birds
Hope to hear the dragon's song?
If the dragon really must go,
It should at least leave the birds a wind horse.

The boatload of important messengers has left,
Carrying you, our precious master, with it.
Now who remains to care for us?
If there is no room for us in the boat,
You should at least throw us a lifeline.

When the great meditator goes abroad,
Who will guard his empty mountain cave?
But if you really have to go,
You should at least point us to a marmot.

When, at the request of powerful messengers,
Our lama must go westward to Tsang,
To whom can we of little merit turn?

If you really do have to go,
Please leave us with your instructions.

If our lama must leave us behind
To care for a great monastery in Tsang,
Who will tend to our small hermitage
Here in these remote mountains?
If you really must choose them over us,
Please at least point us out a protector.

If our lama must go westward to Tsang
To benefit the living beings there,
Under whom can we easterners practice?
But if you really do have to go,
O most precious of jewels,
May your lifeforce remain strong.

The master answered with the following words:—

I bow to the feet of my teacher Norzang Gyatso,
An omniscient lord among accomplished yogis,
Who understood all teachings of the sutras and tantras
And accomplished their essence through inner practice.

The sun, that great parasol in the sky,
Gradually swings through the heavens
And illuminates each land in turn;
Yet it never leaves any place behind.
Similarly, the sunlike teachings of Tsongkhapa
Remain with you as guidance and inspiration.

After the seasons of warmth have passed
The turquoise dragon takes his rest.
But when the forests and fields blossom,
The dragon again sings freely.

The boatload of important people will soon go;
And yes, it will carry off this insignificant monk.
But you who are left behind are not abandoned.
You have the most precious of jewels,
The gems of spiritual conviction,
And your lifeline is your spiritual practice.

Some hermits wander from place to place
In search of spiritual knowledge;
But would they not be wiser to practice meditation
In a holy place conducive to realization?

Due to my karmic connections from previous lives,
It is difficult for me not to follow the course
Most beneficial to Lama Tsongkhapa's teachings.
Thus when this forceful request came to me,
It seemed that this little monk should accept.

But you, who are like my own family,
I would not dare to forget you;
For we have a great destiny together
In lighting the lamp of Dharma here.
Thus I request your patient understanding
Of my need to fulfill this task before me.
You, my disciples should continue your practice
And I will quickly return to you.

May my holy guru Khedrub Norzang Gyatso
Remain in the world until the end of time,
And may we all receive his compassionate blessings,
To inspire us in enlightenment's way.

May the teachings of Atisha and the Kadampa masters
Thrive in the wondrous Gyal region,
A garden most suitable to Dharma practice,
A place blessed by the forces of karma and prayer,
With Dharma patrons like mighty *chakravartins*;
And may this sublime lineage spread
Throughout all of the ten directions.

20

A Song to a Female Bodhisattva

Translator's Preamble: The colophon to the next entry reads, "This verse work of spiritual advice was written at the repeated request of Jangsem Gyalmo, a female disciple of sublime character who is embellished by the ornament of faith. It was penned by Gendun Gyatso, a Buddhist monk who had studied at the feet of numerous enlightened masters and who had abandoned worldly activities in order to pursue a life of spiritual endeavor."

Jangsem Gyalmo, which translates as "Bodhisattva Queen," was one of the Second Dalai Lama's many female disciples. The song of spiritual instruction that he composed for her would indicate that she was probably an aristocratic lady rather than a nun or cave meditator, as the tone of the advice seems to be slanted toward a person who lives a household life as opposed to the life of a renunciate. This is particularly evident in the lines, "Generosity and spiritual sensitivity / Are the ornaments of a civilized person; / We should make these our most treasured gems. / The mind which does not discriminate against others / And entertains only thoughts to help / Is the foundation of all good qualities; / We should hold it at the center of our heart." Neither the *Autobiography* nor the *Biography* mentions a person of this name, so I cannot comment further on the identity or qualities of the person to whom this song is addressed.

The piece opens with three verses of homage to Avalokiteshvara, the Bodhisattva of Compassion, first as a symbol of the actively compassionate wisdom of all enlightened beings of the past, present, and future; second as a supreme *arya*, or Buddha, who long ago achieved enlightenment and now continues to work in mysterious ways throughout the universe in order to increase the forces of enlightenment; and third as the bodhisattva with a thousand eyes and a thousand hands, with which he watches over living beings and brings enlightenment and guidance to those ready to be trained.

The Second Dalai Lama then delivers his spiritual message to Jangsem Gyalmo, providing us with his quintessential guidelines to a spiritual life. His advice is practical and in many ways represents the national ethic of the Tibetan character.

With reverence I bow to Lokeshvara,
He who watches with merciful eyes:—
His form embellished with the signs of perfection,
His speech releasing the melody of Dharma,
His mind limitless in knowledge and compassion.

Again I bow to Lokeshvara, the supreme arya,
Who inexpressibly numerous aeons ago achieved
The path of dharmakaya beyond center and limits,
And now works constantly to uplift the world.

O Lokeshvara, who with a thousand loving eyes
Watches over the countless living beings,
I bow to you from the depths of my heart;
Pray, fulfill all spiritual aspirations.

We should heed well the instructions of the guru,
The source of all progress here and hereafter;
And we should use our precious life wisely,
For it is a wish-fulfilling gem and a vessel
Capable of receiving the highest spiritual knowledge.

Realize that death is certain and its time unknown,
And make spiritual practice your priority;
See the Three Jewels as sources of every spiritual gain,
And rely upon them with confidence.

The cause of all suffering and confusion
Is negative karma and distorted emotions;
Make every effort to transcend them.
The cause of all joy here and hereafter
Is creative karma and the positive mind;
Make every effort to cultivate them.

Worldly works never reach an end,
Even if we struggle at them for an aeon.
Do not make them the center of your life.
But spiritual practice is just the opposite,
And every effort brings an according benefit
That extends far into the future.

Generosity and spiritual sensitivity
Are the ornaments of a civilized person;
We should make these our most treasured gems.
The mind which does not discriminate against others
And entertains only thoughts to help
Is the foundation of all good qualities;
We should hold it at the center of our heart.

As attachment, aversion, and hypocrisy
Harm oneself and others both here and hereafter,
The wise person strives to transcend them.
And as the only stable possession is a mind
Free from all states of distortion,
The wise person makes every effort to achieve it.

21

Song of Tantric Experience

Translator's Preamble: "Song of Tantric Experience" is one of the most personal *nyamgur* in the Second Dalai Lama's collection, describing in vivid terms his direct experience of the tantric yogas. The real meaning, of course, is cloaked in tantric terminology, the self-secret twilight language of the Vajrayana, and thus only someone well versed in tantric literature will be able to comprehend the full range of its implications.

I have discussed some of the concepts central to the tantric tradition in a preamble to an earlier mystical song by the Second Dalai Lama ("Song of the Tantric Path") and also in the last section of Part Two of this volume. The reader may refer to those again.

The colophon to the text is brief, "This vajra song, that summarizes all the practices of the tantric path, was composed by the yogi Shepai Dorje, the Laughing Vajra." As we saw earlier, Shepai Dorjey is the tantric name that had been given to the Second Dalai Lama by his father at an initiation ceremony he attended as a child.

The song is thus a spontaneous outpouring of his experience of the tantric yogas. Consequently it lacks the formality that often characterizes verse works composed at the request of specific disciples. The latter are usually written to meet the needs and level of understanding of the recipient, whereas spontaneously created *nyamgur* are more free and open in style, and aim to please only the author himself.

Homage to Vajrasattva, the Diamond Warrior.
The peerless tantric master
Is the source of all spiritual knowledge.
One places his feet on the crown of one's head
And becomes satiated with the ambrosial nectars
Of his blessings and transforming powers.

One begins by filling the vase of one's heart
With the waters of the four tantric initiations,
Which transform the mind into an appropriate vessel
For cultivation of the sublime vajra path.

From that time onward one should always cherish
The commitments of the tantric way
As deeply as one cherishes one's life,
Never letting ourself become like those yogis
Who pretend to be great tantric practitioners
But in fact are little better than dogs and pigs.

First one must gain unmistaken experience in
The methods of taking death, bardo, and rebirth
As the path of the three perfect kayas,
A training that extracts the very essence
Of the profound generation stage yogas.
In this way the divinity of great bliss
Arises from within the sphere of the void.

The flowing energies of sun and moon
Then block the path of darkness,
And one perceives the innate great bliss
Born together with wisdom of the void.

The most subtle aspects of energy and mind
Manifest like a fish rising in a clear pool.
One sends forth a net of mystical emanations

And becomes freed forever from the great abyss
Of conventional birth and death.

The highest bliss and wisdom then shine
Like a sun at the center of the heart, halting
All activity of attachment, aversion, and ignorance.
This is the unmistaken state of mahamudra, the Great
    Seal.

Thus one discovers direct experience
Of the stages of the tantric path;
And every key in highest yoga tantra is seen
Within the context of one's own training.

The experience of the yogi is then this:
The world is seen as the mystical mandala
And all living beings as tantric deities;
And everything that one eats and drinks
Becomes transformed into blissful ambrosia.

All of one's activities become spiritual,
Regardless of how they conventionally appear;
And every sound that one makes
Becomes part of a great vajra song.

I, a tantric yogi, abide in the blissful mind;
I, a tantric yogi, spontaneously generate goodness
In everything that I do.
All male divinities dance within me
And all female divinities channel
Their vajra songs through me.

Thinking of the great kindness of
Lama Tsongkhapa, an incomparable vajra master,
I could not restrain myself from giving voice

To this song of tantric experience,
A melody that I send forth
As an offering to that illustrious sage.

22

A Prayer to the Spiritual Master

Translator's Preamble: The colophon to this work reads, "This brief prayer to the spiritual master was written by the Buddhist monk Gendun Gyatso Palzangpo at the request of his attendant Gyalwai Wangpo." Thus it was composed at the request of one of his disciples who lived in the Second Dalai Lama's immediate entourage.

The piece is in fact not a *nyamgyur* but a prayer written for a disciple as a liturgy for daily recitation. As it is only three verses in length, I'll follow the Second Dalai Lama's example and keep my preamble short.

O holy master of the Great Way,
Source of all siddhis mundane and supreme,
May I have the fortune to train with you for long;
And by the meritorious energy of my devotions
May I not be parted from you in all future lives.

O spiritual friend, who for countless lifetimes
Has lived by the ethic of the spiritual path
And taught the ways leading to spiritual joy,

May I apply myself fully to your instructions
And thus achieve quickly Buddhahood's three kayas.

May obstacles and obstructions inner or outer
Never arise to hinder my training;
And by devoting myself in thought and action
To the instructions of the holy masters,
May I come to equal them in every way.

23

A Song of Not So Bad

Translator's Preamble: This is another spontaneous composition from the pen of the Second Dalai Lama. As the colophon states, it was "Written by the Buddhist monk Gendun Gyatso Palzangpo while he was living at Tiger's Peak in the Ol-kha mountains."

As we saw in the account of his life presented in Part Two of this volume, the Olkha mountains were one of the master's favorite places for meditation. They had been blessed by the presence of cave and hermitage meditators for centuries and thus were revered as one of the most powerful meditation sites in Central Asia. It was here that Lama Tsongkhapa had lived for five years in meditation and achieved his enlightenment and also here that the Second Dalai Lama's guru Khedrub Norzang Gyatso had spent fourteen years in solitary retreat in order to achieve his enlightenment.

The Second Dalai Lama made Olkha one of his own principal retreat places and also linked future incarnations in the Dalai Lama office to the region when he built Chokhor Gyal Monastery on Jangsem Mountain near Dvakpo in the Olkha region in 1509-10. All Dalai Lama incarnations since then have been expected to visit the area and perform tantric meditation there.

From this time on, the Second spent several months every year traveling, teaching, and meditating in the area. One of the places on his annual circuit was Tiger's Peak, the full name of which was Olkha Taktsey. (There were several places with the name "Tiger's Peak" in Tibet, another famous one being the Tiger's Peak of Chonggyey.) The castle (or *dzong*) that acted as the central hub of

Olkha Taktsey was located on the spur between the two branches of the Olkha River. Known as Olkha Taktsey Dzong, during the Second Dalai Lama's lifetime the entire Olkha region was ruled by the king who lived there.

The Tiger's Peak of Olkha, however, does not refer only to this castle, but also to the villages and hermitages in the area, as well as to mountain caves in the adjoining hills.

In "A Song of Not So Bad," the Second Dalai Lama delves playfully into the central concepts of Buddhism in general and the Gelugpa approach to Buddhism in particular that inspired him to follow the path of a Buddhist monk. It is probable from the tone of the piece, which is somewhat tongue-in-cheek, that it was written between the years 1499 and 1523, when the Gelugpa were being oppressed by the militant forces behind the Karma Kargyu lama Sharmapa Chokyi Drakpa.

The Second Dalai Lama does not seem to have felt particularly vindictive about the events. He generally exhibited an attitude of "boys will be boys" toward most conflicts of this nature that he witnessed during his life and tended to find humor rather than rancor in such intrigues. This mood is very much reflected in the following song.

Homage to the holy gurus.
To train under a master accomplished in the Great Way,
To penetrate to the meaning of the sutras and tantras,
To take the very essence of this precious human life
And to bring ultimate benefit to self and others:
This is what it means to meet with
The wondrous lineage of Lama Tsongkhapa.
It's not so bad, really, as a way to go.

To be constantly aware of death and impermanence,
To become skilled in living by karmic law,

To always wear the Three Jewels as one's crown
And thus close the door to lower rebirth:
Turning the mind toward the path like this,
It's not so bad, really, as a way to go.

To see the three worlds as mountains of suffering,
To identify the root of samsara as ego-grasping,
To behold the gateway leading to final liberation
And, in order to gain that sublime state of freedom,
To practice intensely the three higher trainings
Of discipline, meditation, and wisdom of the void:
Walking this path leading to liberation and knowledge,
It's not so bad, really, as a way to go.

To view all living beings as kind parents,
To abide continually in love and compassion for all,
To achieve maturity in cultivating the two bodhiminds
And thus become skilled in method and wisdom
    combined:
This way of accomplishing peerless enlightenment,
It's not so bad, really, as a way to go.

To know the faults of grasping for ultimates,
To perceive the nature of relativity in causation,
To see the emptiness level of all that occurs
And to experience the highest vision of being:
This is what it means to follow
The sublime path elucidated by Nagarjuna.
It's not so bad, really, as a way to go.

Ripened by the waters of the four tantric initiations,
Accomplished in the vast and profound tantric teachings,
And skilled in the yogas of the two tantric stages
Whereby enlightenment is quickly and easily attained:
Holding Buddhahood in the palm of one's hand like this,
It's not so bad, really, as a way to go.

From the vast array of wondrous jewels
To be found within the Buddhist teachings,
I have here gathered a few precious gems
And threaded them into a string of verse,
A necklace of song that I here send forth
With the prayer that it may inspire trainees
In the great purpose of highest enlightenment.

24

Song to the Three Jewels of Refuge

Translator's Preamble: This, the second to last entry in the Second Dalai Lama's collection of *nyamgur*, is in fact a prayer rather than a full-fledged "song of experience." The colophon simply states, "This brief poem, written as a prayer to the Three Jewels of Refuge, is also said to have been composed by the Omniscient Master." The words "...is also said to have been composed..." suggests that originally there was a controversy over its authorship. The fact that it appears in the collection indicates that, in the end, the team of compilers decided that it was indeed penned by the Second Dalai Lama.

The Three Jewels of Refuge that are the central focus of the prayer—the Buddhas, the Dharma, and the Sangha—are a fundamental topic in the Buddhist doctrine. I discussed them briefly in the final section of Part Two of my introduction. We have seen the Second Dalai Lama refer to them in more than half of his songs and poems in this collection.

There are many dimensions of doctrinal interpretation of the Three Jewels. On a simple level the three represent the historical Buddha, who taught the path to enlightenment; the Dharma, or path to enlightenment that he revealed; and the Sangha, or followers of that path. On another level the Buddha (or Buddhas) represent the omnipresent potential of enlightenment that we all possess; the Dharma represents the nature of ultimate reality that is present in all phenomena, realization of which induces enlightenment; and the Sangha represents the beings who point us to that ultimate reality.

There is also a discussion of "causal refuge" and "resultant refuge." Causal refuge is said to be the Three Jewels as forces that point us to and propel us along the path to enlightenment. Resultant refuge is the state of enlightenment characterized by the three kayas that we ourselves eventually achieve. At the time of resultant refuge, our mind becomes Buddha, our speech becomes Dharma, and our body becomes Sangha.

Another perspective is primary and secondary refuge. Here the Dharma, or spiritual teaching, is the primary refuge, for it is through the practice of Dharma that we achieve the wisdom of enlightenment. The Buddhas and Sangha are secondary refuge objects in the sense that they are merely supporting conditions to our Dharma practice.

In this last context the example is given of the roles of a doctor, medicine, and a nurse in the process of curing a patient. The Buddhas are like a doctor, who prescribes medicine to us; the Dharma is like the medicines that are prescribed; and the Sangha is like the nurse, who helps us in the process of recuperation. Although the doctor and nurse are indispensable to the process, they do not effect the actual cure. This can only be achieved by the patient taking the medicine. In the same way, the Buddhas can point out the path to enlightenment and the Sangha can provide inspiration and encouragement, but it is the walking along the path ourselves that will get us to the destination of enlightenment and cure us of the disease of unknowing.

There is also a discussion of symbols of refuge and actual refuge. In this context, paintings or statues of the Buddhas symbolize the Buddha refuge; scriptures symbolize Dharma refuge; and the monastic community symbolizes the Sangha refuge. In actual fact, only the fully enlightened beings are Buddha refuge; only the truth of the transcendence of imperfection is Dharma refuge; and only those beings who have achieved direct insight into voidness are the Sangha refuge. The Buddhist understands the difference between these two aspects of the Three Jewels—symbolic and actual. Nonetheless, he or she accords all the respect to the symbols of refuge that would be accorded to the actual refuge objects themselves, as a means of enhancing awareness of the path. Thus the topic of refuge in Buddhism is somewhat complicated.

Philosophical texts that expound on the matter usually demand several volumes to exhaust themselves.

Finally, having taken refuge is what distinguishes a Buddhist from a non-Buddhist. There is an outer "refuge ceremony" that can be given as a method of "bestowing refuge," much like the confirmation ceremony in the Christian tradition. However, having taken this ceremony and declared oneself a Buddhist does not actually make one a Buddhist; not even becoming a Buddhist monk or nun can effect this.

When Atisha came to Tibet in 1042 he asked several questions to one of the most highly regarded monk scholars of Ngari. The answers did not satisfy him. He scolded the man for walking around in the robes of a monk and pretending to be Buddhist. In the end, he pointed out, the only real Buddhist is one who in the depth of his or her heart appreciates and comprehends the topic of refuge, and whose mind is placed firmly in knowledge and practice of the Dharma. Others are merely emulating the Buddhist process.

The story reminds me of my first meeting with the present Dalai Lama in 1972. I considered myself a Buddhist at the time. The Dalai Lama laughed at my questions and remarked, "There are many people who want to see what is on the other side of the mountain of enlightenment. But there are not many who are willing to walk up the mountain, look over its peak, and see for themselves."

Homage to the magnificent Three Jewels,
The Buddhas, the Dharma, and the Sangha.
O unfailing sources of spiritual inspiration,
Rest forever as a crown on my head.
Take this insignificant irreligious being
And turn his mind toward spiritual ways.

Precious Jewels of Refuge, treasuries of compassion,
Move me to overcome the inner enemies:

The forces of karma and afflicted emotions,
The creators of all misery that exists in this world.

Although there are countless people whom we cherish,
At the time of death they are all left behind.
Precious Jewels of Refuge, be my innermost companions,
Ones able to accompany me everywhere forever.

It is rare nowadays to find a true friend
On whom one can depend for even a day.
O Three Jewels, be my supreme friend,
Accompanying me without fail now and forever.

Ordinary property, wealth, and possessions
Chain us more tightly to the wheel of samsara.
Come, be inner wealth at the center of my heart,
Wealth that thus benefits in every situation.

It is certain that we all must die,
Yet uncertain the time when this will occur.
Inspire my mind now with utter distaste
For thoughtless indulgence in frivolous pursuits.

Should I stumble over the terrible cliffs
Falling to rebirth in a realm of misery,
The suffering would not be easy to bear.
Three Precious Jewels, escort me safely
Through the dangerous passes between life and death.

Constantly we are pulled helplessly along
By the web of white and black karmic forces
That we have unconsciously woven around ourselves.
O precious Three Jewels, at the time of my death
Receive and guide me to the Pure Land of Joy.

The ocean of limitless cyclic existence
Houses countless monsters of confusion and pain.
O precious Three Jewels, be my navigator;
Steer me through these treacherous waters
To the safety of the other shore.

Most Buddhist practitioners today
Act as though possessed by inner demons,
And abandon the Three Jewels of Refuge
For worship of unreliable spirits and gods.
How much better to rely on the Three Jewels
And look to them for guidance and inspiration.

Then the state of enlightenment itself
Will eventually come into one's own hands,
And one will oneself come to embody
The Buddhas, the Dharma, and Sangha.
May this always be our aspiration.

25

Verse for Lodro Tsultrim

Translator's Preamble: The colophon to this final entry in the collection of songs and poems by the Second Dalai Lama states, "The above verse work was written for my disciple Lodro Tsultrim, a Buddhist monk who had lost interest in the superficial activities of conventional living and opted instead for the pursuit of solitary meditation in order to devote himself intensely to the enlightenment path."

The piece is significant not only for its poetic qualities but also as evidence of the Second Dalai Lama as an artist and painter. In one of the verses he comments that, together with the poem, he has included a number of gifts for his disciple Tsultrim Lodro, including a painting of the Dharmapala Palden Lhamo that he had made with his own hands. As we saw earlier in Part Two, Palden Lhamo is the spiritual force resident in the Lake of Visions and the Second Dalai Lama's principal Dharmapala (Dharma protector) practice.

I was not able to locate any references to Tsultrim Lodro in the standard sourceworks on the Second Dalai Lama's life. From the colophon we learn that he lived in solitary meditation. The last verse of the poem mentions that the Second Dalai Lama composed the piece while in Tsetang, so we can presume Lodro Tsultrim was living in retreat in the vicinity of that monastery. The Second Dalai Lama visited and taught in Tsetang almost every spring for the last forty years of his life, so there is no way to date the composition.

The concluding verse is particularly entertaining. As a traveling teacher the Second Dalai Lama amassed considerable wealth. In the Tibetan world there is the tradition at the end of a teaching for the main patron to make a substantial offering and then for the general public to file by the lama in a column, in order for each person to receive a personal hand blessing. Everyone then also makes a small offering to the lama. By the middle of his life the Second Dalai Lama usually taught to crowds numbering in the thousands and even tens of thousands. As a result, as the *Biography* puts it, "...gifts and offerings fell like rain." In his letter to his hermit disciple, this feature of Tibetan culture obviously tickles his sense of humor.

Lodro Tsultrim, whose name means "Wisdom Discipline,"
With eyes of wisdom you see as they are
All points in the spiritual practices
And you train accordingly in the disciplines.
Indeed you are a supreme yogin,
Applying yourself fully to the enlightenment path.

A spiritual lifestyle is rare in this world,
So cherish its preciousness day and night.
Make a hundred efforts in study, reflection, and
   meditation,
And strengthen the forces of peace and joy within.

With a mind free from worldly attachments,
Concern yourself instead with the sublime aspiration
To achieve enlightenment for the sake of the world.
And with an awareness of the inseparable union
Of the appearance of things and their emptiness nature
Apply yourself to the sutra and tantra methods,
The two wings of enlightenment's Great Way.

To accomplish this legacy it is often advised
That one cultivate meditation on Palden Lhamo.
Hence I enclose with this poem, as an offering to you,
A painting of that esoteric tantric deity
That I created with my own hands;
May it assist you in your practice.

As for me, people say I've come to Tsetang Monastery
In order to teach the holy Dharma here, but
In fact I'm just another vain Buddhist monk
Attached to the pleasures and comforts of this world,
In search of something to fill his stomach.
Nonetheless, please pray for me,
That my visions may be fulfilled.

Notes

PART ONE: INTRODUCTION

1. The most authoritative Western study of the development of Buddhism in Tibet is David Snellgrove's *Indo-Tibetan Buddhism* (Boston: Shambhala Publications, 1987).

As Snellgrove points out, it is likely that Tibet had experimented with various forms of writing before Tonmi Sambhota's time, although these have since disappeared. In this respect central Tibet probably lagged behind the western kingdom of Zhang Zhung, located to the north of Mt. Kailash, which is near the present-day border of Tibet and Ladakh. Zhang Zhung has since disappeared as an important cultural area but in ancient times was a key link with the highly developed civilizations of Kashmir, Kotan, Gilgit, and Persia.

As Snellgrove also points out, later Tibetan historians (those writing after the thirteenth century) as well as most modern Western scholars, generally call the pre-Songtsen Gampo religion of Tibet *Bon*, which they describe as a pre-Buddhist shamanic religion, whereas this ancient tradition was probably very much inspired by the early forms of Buddhism prevalent in the north of the Indian Kushana empire, particularly Gilgit and Kotan. However, Bon had assumed a strongly shamanic flavor in order to accommodate the Tibetan nomadic mentality and thus was rejected as non-Buddhist by the more sophisticated movements of the seventh and eighth centuries. Bonpos themselves speak of their tradition as having come from the western region of Tazig, which often means Persia, but could have referred to the Buddhist areas to the west of Tibet, including the Kushana empire.

2. It seems that in Tibet's classical period (from the eleventh to seventeenth centuries), it was quite common for a young monk

scholar to study in numerous monasteries and to gain experience within a wide variety of lineages (or sects). The tendency toward a one-sect approach developed later and became the norm by the eighteenth century.

Today very few lamas have any substantial multi-sect experience. Their only exposure to schools other than their own generally comes from attending a few public initiations or discourses by high lamas of other sects. In other words, they generally study their own school's doctrines for ten to twenty years and the doctrines of schools other than their own for ten to twenty hours.

3. No thorough and critical study of the sources of the Gelug school, together with the many lineages that Tsongkhapa fused in order to form it, has yet appeared in English. The task would be a lifetime undertaking. Tsongkhapa studied in dozens of monasteries, many of which are unresearched by Western scholarship and whose doctrinal import is largely unknown. Most of these at the time represented independent sects. He not only drew from the major schools but from a wide assortment of traditions that have since disappeared as individual entities.

4. The Seventh Dalai Lama (1708–1757) was the first in the line to abandon the tradition of combining the Nyingma and Gelugpa lineages in his personal spiritual life. The reason probably was connected to the Mongol wars that spilled over into Tibet during the lifetime of his predecessor the Sixth Dalai Lama, during which the Dzungar Mongols had inflicted gross punishment on the Nyingma monasteries of central Tibet, using their sectarian sentiments as an excuse to plunder the wealth of non-Gelugpa establishments. The Sixth had primarily been a Nyingma by birth and inclination, and the dangers of a Dalai Lama straying too far from the Gelugpa path became evident.

The Eighth began his life much in the vein established by the Seventh. But as the present Dalai Lama once commented to me in a conversation, later in his life he began to change his approach and to follow the traditions advocated by the earlier Dalai Lamas—a path combining the Gelugpa and Nyingma schools. Unfortunately he died shortly thereafter, before his work in this direction could reach maturity.

5. Western writers constantly repeat an historical error perpetrated by L. Austine Waddell, a Christian missionary who, writing at the turn of the last century, stated that the First Dalai Lama was a nephew of Tsongkhapa, founder of the Gelug school (*The Buddhism of Tibet, or Lamaism*, London: W. H. Allen, 1895).

He most certainly was not. The First Dalai Lama's uncle was a man of no historical renown, other than posthumously for his role in serving as guardian to the seven-year-old semi-orphan, an impoverished child destined to become one of the greatest Buddhist saints of central Asia.

None of Tsongkhapa's five chief disciples was related to him by blood. Even though he had studied with the Sakya and Drigung Kargyu sects, both of which at that time followed systems of hereditary succession, he did not emulate their traditions in this respect. He also rejected the Karma Kargyu model, in which lineages passed through *tulkus*, or reincarnate lamas. Instead he chose the Kadam tradition as his model, in which the transmission of administrative and spiritual power is passed through monks renowned for their learning and practice.

As we will see later, however, his Gelug school was soon to change its stance on the *tulku* phenomenon and to adopt the Karma Kargyu reliance on "reincarnate lamas." The result was the Dalai and Panchen Lamas, the Demo Tulkus, and the Ling Tulkus. Over the past three centuries in the Gelug school, the historical position of major lineage holders in the transmission of the highest yoga tantra systems has largely been passed back and forth between the reincarnate lamas holding these four offices.

6. I included a traditional biography of the First Dalai Lama (*The Twelve Great Deeds of Gyalwa Gendun Drup*) as an appendix to my study of the life and works of that master, *Selected Works of the Dalai Lama I: Bridging the Sutras and Tantras* (Ithaca, NY: Snow Lion Publications, 1981).

7. The Tibetan idea of multiple reincarnations of high lamas is based on the Indian Mahayana doctrine, wherein it is said that a bodhisattva of the first of the ten *bhumis* (stages of the path to enlightenment) is able to send forth a hundred emanations. On each of the succeeding *bhumis* this power increases tenfold.

This subject is discussed in detail in the classical Indian treatise *A Guide to the Middle View*, or *Madhyamaka-avatara*, by Acharya Chandrakirti (*circa* sixth century). Thus in his Foreword to the present volume His Holiness the Dalai Lama quite casually mentions the Nechung Oracle as having prophesied (in 1543 or 1544) that the Second Dalai Lama had manifested a hundred reincarnations. The First apparently was more modest, sending forth a mere three.

8. The life and death of the Sixth Dalai Lama is surrounded in legends. Many stories concerning his life tell of a wild tantric yogi and poet, who flaunted his sexuality to draw attention to the tantric teachings and tease Tibetans about their sexual timidity.

As for those concerning his death, two entirely different stories are told. The more conventional of these relates that after his abduction by the invading Mongolian armies of Lhazang Khan, it was decided that he should be deported. However, when he and his Mongol escort arrived at the Tibeto-Mongolian border and camped there for the night, he manifested a drama to his captors by putting on the tantric garb of the Fifth Dalai Lama, performing a mystical dance, sitting in meditation, and then consciously projecting his spirit out of his body. He thus passed away in 1706.

The second account is found in his *Secret Biography*, or *Sangwai Namtar* (spelled *gSang-bai-rnam-thar*). Here it is said that he escaped from the Mongolians, who, afraid to report their blunder, claimed that he had died. He quietly lived out the remainder of his life as a shepherd in the northeast of Tibet.

In either case, a child was born in 1708 who eventually was recognized and installed as the Seventh Dalai Lama.

9. Waddell's writings are classic reading, preserving a view of Tibet as seen by a Christian fundamentalist of Victorian days. Being a pioneer work, Waddell's book mixes facts and fancies rather randomly and being anti-tantric Buddhism, it portrays a skeptical image of Tibetan spiritual life. Nonetheless Waddell managed to cram much accurate cultural and historical data onto his pages, and his works affected the understanding of generations of Tibetologists to follow.

Many of Waddell's peripheral errors, such as the blunder on the genealogy of the First Dalai Lama mentioned above, continue to appear in authoritative books even today, almost a century later. For example, I recently noticed it in Keith Dowman's *The Power Places of Central Tibet* (London & New York: Routledge and Kegan Paul, 1988); and also in Stephen Batchelor's *The Tibet Guide* (Boston: Wisdom Publications, 1987).

Waddell's misreading of the relationship between the Fifth Dalai Lama and the Avalokiteshvara myth is also discussed in Part One.

Regardless of the effect of the errors, Waddell's books contributed greatly to the Western understanding of Tibet and continue to be pleasurable and illuminating reading. Several of them have recently been republished in India. In particular, his *The Buddhism of Tibet, or Lamaism* (London: W. H. Allen, 1895) is a classic.

10. An unusual aspect of the Avalokiteshvara myth and the Dalai Lamas is that the latter are directly associated with some incarnations of Avalokiteshvara and not with others. For instance, they are linked with King Songtsen Gampo and Lama Drom Tonpa, both of whom were regarded as incarnations of this bodhisattva during their lifetimes, but they are not linked directly to Guru Rinpoche nor the Karmapas, who are also Avalokiteshvara emanations. The *gyu* (spelled *rGyud*), or "stream," is said to be different.

Moreover, some of the figures attributed to the Dalai Lama "previous lives" are primarily emanations of bodhisattvas other than Avalokiteshvara. The kings Trisong Deutsen and Tri Ralpachen, for example, are generally said to have been emanations respectively of the bodhisattvas Manjushri and Vajrapani; yet they are Dalai Lama "previous lives," even though he is described as being Avalokiteshvara.

As the Buddhist scriptures put it, the ways of the bodhisattvas are indeed mysterious and beyond the reaches of the conventional intellect.

11. An English rendition of this exists under the title *The Tibetan Dharmapada*, translated by Garreth Sparham (Boston: Wisdom Publications, 1986).

12. A rather unpoetic English translation of this was made by

Jeffrey Hopkins (London: Allen & Unwin, 1973).

13. An example of one of these (in English translation) is H.V. Guenther's rendition of and commentary to *The Royal Song of Saraha* (Oxford: Oxford University Press, 1968). Saraha was one of the greatest of the early Indian tantric mahasiddhas, and his *doha* is regarded as a classic.

14. My favorite of these is that by the Thirteenth Dalai Lama, who brings his strong sense of humor and fun into what otherwise can turn into something of a dry exercise. For example, during his lifetime there was considerable debate between the "Self-Emptiness" and "Other Emptiness" philosophers of Tibet, or *Rang Tongpa* and *Zhen Tongpa*. The Thirteenth weaves several sections of his treatment of the Dandian approach to metaphor around this debate to tickle the fancies of philosophy enthusiasts.

The Fifth Dalai Lama's commentary is more famous with Tibetans. However, he is said to misrepresent Dandi in several sections. It is these that Tibetans study in detail, to learn from the Great Fifth's mistakes, so to speak. They do not begrudge him these errors, nor think of him with less reverence because of them. Most assume that he included them on purpose, to draw attention to particular implications of the Indian tradition.

15. Unfortunately very little research has been done into Tibet's spiritual connections with Indonesia. Atisha was but one of a number of historical personalities who fostered these links.

In that Buddhism in Indonesia has long since disappeared due to the religiously intolerant Muslim colonialization of the twelfth and thirteenth centuries, and very little is known of it from indigenous sources due to the destruction of its libraries at that time, Tibetan literature may well prove to be our only bridge to this very important civilization. The world's singularly greatest Buddhist monument, Borobodur, located in Java not far from Jakarta, testifies to the lofty cultural and artistic heights that the tradition achieved.

16. Several of these are available in English translation. *The Life and Liberation of Padmasambhava*, translated by Tarthang Tulku and his students (Berkeley, CA: Dharma Publications, 1980), and *Sky*

Dancer, the biography of Padmasambhava's female disciple and lover Yeshey Tsogyal (spelled *Ye-shes-mtsho-rgyal*), translated by Keith Dowman (London: Routledge and Kegan Paul, 1984), demonstrate the Tibetan enthusiasm for and deftness in poetic expression in those early days of their Buddhist experience.

17. I translated a few of these with Ven. Doboom Tulku as part of India's national commemoration of the thousandth anniversary of Atisha's birth in *Atisha and Buddhism in Tibet* (New Delhi: Tibet House, 1982).

18. Several translations of Milarepa's songs and poems are available in English. Garma C.C. Chang's *The Hundred Thousand Songs of Milarepa* (Oxford: Oxford University Press, 1969) remains the most comprehensive. *Songs by the Mountain Stream* (New York: Lotsawa Press, 1983), translated by L. Lhalungpa, is also noteworthy.

19. Anyone who really wishes to get into the Second Dalai Lama's songs and poems should expect to have to go at them in several readings. Although some are fairly straightforward, many have numerous levels of meanings.

It may also be useful to read a background book on general Tibetan Buddhist thought. I usually recommend my *Selected Works of the Third Dalai Lama: Essence of Refined Gold* (Ithaca, NY: Snow Lion Press, 1982) for this purpose, as it contains both the Third Dalai Lama's traditional text (the *Lam Rim Ser Zhunma*, spelled *Lam-rim-gser-zhun-ma*, or *Essence of Refined Gold*), together with a contemporary commentary by the present Dalai Lama.

PART TWO: LIFE OF THE SECOND DALAI LAMA

1. The Second Dalai Lama's *Autobiography* is not as pleasurable a read as is the biography of him jointly composed by Yangpa Chojey and Konchok Kyab. It is far more stark in style and comes across more like an edited memo pad than an insightful memoir. This is due to the Tibetan literary tradition of projecting humility and self-effacement in writings of a personal nature. Thus most Tibetan autobiographies are rather bland and understated, particularly in the Kadampa and Gelugpa traditions. Biographers, on the other

hand, do not have the same constraints placed upon them and are permitted to become more grandiose in their prose. Consequently biographies are far more fun to read than are autobiographies.

2. Chojey Sonam Drakpa was famous for his writings on philosophical matters, and several of his "monastic textbooks" (Tib., *Yig-cha*) are still studied today by both Drepung Loseling and Ganden Shartsey monasteries. However, he was a rather bland and unimaginative writer, and no doubt this is the reason his account of the Second's life became lost in the shifting sands of history.

3. It was probably the family's presence in Yaru Shang that eventually led to their spiritual affiliation moving away from the Nyingma sect and toward the Shangpa Kargyu tradition. Yaru Shang was one of the principal Shangpa Kargyu strongholds.

It should be noted that the Shangpa Kargyu is to be clearly distinguished from the Dvakpo Kargyu. There was no historical or spiritual affiliation between these two sects in the early period. The similarity in names is mere coincidence. *Kargyu* simply means "Instruction Lineage." The Dvakpo Kargyu has its roots in Marpa, Milarepa, and Gampopa, also known as Dvakpo Lhajey, or "the Doctor from Dvakpo" (Gampopa's monastery in the Dvakpo area being later used as part of the school's name). The Shangpa Kargyu was founded by Khyungpo Naljor, whose teaching activities in the Shang region resulted in the name of the school descending from him. There is also a Ganden Kargyu tradition, which is a Gelugpa lineage totally unconnected with either Dvakpo Kargyu or Shangpa Kargyu.

4. The dream yogas are taught in various Buddhist tantric traditions. One of the most detailed presentations is that found in the lineage from the Shangpa Kargyu School's "Six Yogas of Niguma." I included a commentary by the Second Dalai Lama to this system in *Selected Works of the Dalai Lama II: The Tantric Yogas of Sister Niguma* (Ithaca, NY: Snow Lion Publications, 1985).

5. The short biography of the Second Dalai Lama by Tsechok Ling Kachen Yeshey Gyaltsen describes the first meeting of the Tashi

Lhunpo delegation with the young reincarnation somewhat differently, presumably drawing from an alternative sourcework no longer available to us. He writes of various visions that the Second Dalai Lama experienced when two and three years old and then comments, "In his third year he experienced a vision of Palden Lhamo and composed a hymn to her. . . . Shortly after that a letter of request for a meeting with him arrived from Tashi Lhunpo Monastery. Then a delegation came to examine him. . . . When the child met Solpon Dolma of Tashi Lhunpo (who had been an attendant to the First Dalai Lama), he instantly recognized him and commented, 'You are not looking so well as when I last saw you.' In this and other ways he convinced the delegation of his authenticity, and they were all filled with faith."

6. Unfortunately this and other such belongings of the Second Dalai Lama, preserved for centuries at Chokhor Gyal Monastery, disappeared with the Chinese destruction of Tibet's cultural institutions during the 1960s.

7. One of the great early Kadampa lamas, Kuton was a direct disciple of Atisha and thus a contemporary of Lama Drom Tonpa.

8. The problem in this respect may have had a monastic overtone. The Second's father was a married lama of the Nyingma and Shangpa traditions, and as a noncelibate his prolonged presence may have been viewed as inappropriate. With most reincarnate lamas, the child is placed in the monastery under the care of an elderly monk guardian, usually one who was a disciple of the predecessor. If the parents visit, they are generally housed in the guest quarters, not in the actual monastic residence. The Second's father, who was also a guru to the boy, obviously expected and received a different treatment. It seems that he may have overstayed his welcome. It is also possible that the elders suspected he was attempting to advance his own teaching career by capitalizing on his highly revered son.

9. Fortunately Radeng Monastery was among the thirteen of Tibet's 6,500 spiritual institutions not destroyed by the Chinese communists in the 1960s.

10. Tsechok Ling tells the story somewhat differently in his *Brief Biography of the Second Dalai Lama*: "The highly accomplished tantric yogin Kunga Gyaltsen was in Radeng and dreamed that he heard the words spoken, 'Tomorrow Lama Drom Tonpa himself will arrive.' He was extremely moved with devotion and decided to conduct a test. He took a bundle of thirty stalks of flowers, placed them on the altar, and pronounced these words of truth, 'If this monk really is the reincarnation of Lama Drom Tonpa, may these flowers magically increase in number to a hundred or more. If he is not, may they remain as thirty.' As witnesses to his injunction, he invoked the powers of the Three Jewels of Refuge, Lama Tsongkhapa and two chief disciples, and various Dharmapalas. Later, when the pilgrims arrived and offered tea in the main assembly hall, the thirty flower stalks magically transformed into more than two hundred and fifty, and burst into bloom."

11. Sangpu and Riwo Dechen, two of Tibet's most prestigious spiritual institutions of the classical period.

12. Also, at the invitation of chieftain Shangkharwa he visited and taught in Chenyey and Shangkhar.

13. Tsetang Monastery and Dradruk. See poems four and five.

14. Odey Gungyal of Olkha, where Tsongkhapa spent many years in retreat.

15. King Nangso Lhagyari Dzongpa, who invited him to teach at Eh.

16. Two interesting verse letters concerning the Second's return to Tashi Lhunpo are included in the present collection: one by a Gyal disciple to him; and the other his reply to this. See "Songs of the Turquoise Dragon" in Part Three.

17. These are the five principal Indian treatises taught in the Gelugpa monastic universities. They are generally studied in Tibetan, not Sanskrit, and are read together with one or more Tibetan

commentaries. The First Dalai Lama had written elucidations to four of them himself, which were intended as textbooks for Tashi Lhunpo. Presumably the Second decided to teach them on his return to Tashi Lhunpo in order to ensure that the monastery would maintain the philosophical intensity that the First Dalai Lama had envisioned when he established the monastery in 1447 and that it would not degenerate into another establishment that focused on performance of tantric ritual, as did so many of the monasteries of the older sects of Tibetan Buddhism.

However, to ensure that the tantric tradition would not be ignored, the *Biography* states, "In addition, to those with high tantric initiation he taught Chandrakirti's commentary to the Guhyasamaja tantric system, *The Clear Lamp....*"

18. As we can see from the Second Dalai Lama's biography, he emphasized a solid basis in doctrinal study coupled with a sustained daily practice and short annual retreats. This is very different than the approach of earlier sects, such as the Kargyu, where very little emphasis is given to acquiring a doctrinal basis, and the emphasis is on doing a three-year retreat.

Most Gelugpa lamas continue this tradition today, performing five or six hours of meditation a day—usually three or four hours in the morning and two hours in the evening—and an annual retreat of two weeks to a month.

Because of this difference between Gelugpa and Kargyu approaches, the Kargyus even today like to refer to themselves as the "Practice Lineage" (Tib., *drub gyu; sGrub-rgyud* and to the Gelugpa as the "Theory Lineage" (Tib., *shey gyud; bShad-rgyud*).

Both approaches have their strengths and weaknesses. The Gelugpa strength is that at its best it produces well-rounded trainees, firmly grounded in both intellectual understanding and practice; its danger point is that some Gelugpas become so absorbed in doctrinal study that they ignore their meditational practice.

The Kargyu strength is that it occasionally produces an extraordinary meditation master; its danger is that many of its monks never get beyond devotional exercises, such as prostrations, mantra recitation, and breathing exercises. Because in Tibet many trainees entering a monastery could not even read and write, the lack of doctrinal study in Kargyu also led to producing a large number of illiterate or semi-literate monks who easily mistook the occasional psychophysical flash generated from hyperventilation for an enlightenment experience.

The Second Dalai Lama was obviously aware of the strengths and dangers of both approaches. In the monasteries and hermitages that he established and in the teachings he gave during his lifetime, he struggled to achieve a balance that would incorporate the best of both worlds.

19. It is difficult to assess the extent of the Kargyu persecution of the Gelugpa during this period, as Tibetan religious and historical writings tend to gloss over such events on the grounds that it is better not to glorify them by granting them immortality with ink on paper. Thus most Tibetan texts record the good things, the "enlightenment activities," and leave out much of the negative. The biographical tradition, for example, is called *Namtar* (Tib., *rNamthar*), which literally means "Liberating (or Liberated) Deeds." To discover the extent of a conflict or persecution, therefore, we have to read between the lines and put together a picture based on the subtle hints. However, as H.E. Richardson points out in his *Tibet and its History* (London, 1962), it is definite that Gelugpas, and especially the monks of Ganden, Drepung, and Sera, were banned from even attending the festival, a festival that they themselves had created.

The Sharmapa Tulku was behind many such sectarian conflicts, as well as being behind internal conflicts with other Karma Kargyu lamas. This was his first major adventure of this nature. It failed, and his career suffered accordingly. Again during the time of the Eighth Dalai Lama, he brought an army of Gurkas from Nepal in an attempt to take over the Shigatsey region. The result was the Tibet-Nepal war. He failed and his career went downhill for several generations.

20. It is not clear from either the *Autobiography* or *Biography* whether this complex of buildings already existed on the Drepung premises and the Gongma merely extended it, or if the Lhasa chieftain had it constructed at that time.

21. Presumably this refers to the Eighth Karmapa's commentary to Maitreya/Asanga's *Abhisamaya-alamkara,* or *Ornament of Clear Realizations* (Tib., *dNgon-rtogs-rgyan*), a fourth-century Indian treatise on the essential meaning of the *Prajnaparamita Sutra.*

Glossary

Amoghavajra Namgyal Palzangpo	A-mo-gha-be-jra-Nam-rgyal-dpal-bzang-po
Bata Horgyi Gomdra	Ba-ta-hor-gyi-sgom-gra
Bodong	Bo-dong
Bodong Chokley Namgyal	Bo-dong-phyogs-las-rnam-rgyal
Chennga	sPyan-nga
Chenyey Monastery	sPyan-was-dgon-pa
Chod	mChod
Chogyal Dorjey Tsetenpa	Chos-rgyal-rdo-rje-tshe-rtan-pa
Chojey Sonam Drakpa	Chos-rje-bsod-nams-sgrags-pa
Chokhor Gyal	Chos-'khor-rgyal
Chokyi Drakpa	Chos-kyi-grags-pa
Chonggyey	Phyongs-rgyas
Donyo Gyaltsen	Don-yod-rgyal-mtshan
Drepung	'Bras-spungs
Drokmi Lotsawa	'Brog-mi-lvo-tsa-ba
Drom Tonpa	'Brom-ston-pa
Drong Tsey	Drong-rtse
Drowai Zangmo	sGro-bai-bzang-mo
Dvakpo Monastery	Dvags-po-chos-sde
Dvakpo Tsennyi Dratsang	Dvags-po-mtshan-nyid-sgra-tshang
Dvakpo Tashi Namgyal	Dvags-po-bgra-shis-rnam-rgyal
Ehchok	E-phyogs
Gampopa	sGam-po-pa
Ganden	dGa'-ldan
Ganden Potrang	dGa'-ldan-pho-brang
Ganden Tsey	dGa-ldan-rtse
Gelug	dGe-lugs
Gelugpa	dGe-lugs-pa
Gendun Drup	*see* Gyalwa Gendun Drup
Gendun Gyatso Palzangpo	*see* Gyalwa Gendun Gyatso Palzangpo
Geshey Choshey	dGe-bshes-chos-shes
Gongma	Gong-ma
Gongma Chenpo Drakpa Gyaltsen	Gong-ma-chen-po-grags-pa-rgyal-mtshan

Gonpo Pel	dGon-po-dpal
Guru Rinpochey	Gu-ru-rin-po-che
Gyalwa Gendun Drup	rGyal-ba-dgen-'dun-grub
Gyalwa Gendun Gyatso Palzangpo	rGyal-ba-dge-'dun-brgya-mtsho-dpal-bzang-po
Gyalwa Gotsang	rGyal-ba-rgod-tshang
Gyalwa Rinpochey	rGyal-ba-rin-po-che
Gyalwa Sonam Gyatso	rGyal-ba-bsod-nams-brgya-mtsho
Jampal Drakpa	'Jam-dpal-grags-pa
Jampel Nyingpo	'Jam-dpal-snying-po
Jamyang Lekpai Chojor	'Jam-dbyang-legs-pai-chos-'byor
Jetsun Chokyi Gyaltsen	rJe-btsun-chos-kyi-rgyal-mtshan
Jey Monlampal	rJe-smon-lam-dpal
Jey Sherab Senge	rJe-shes-rab-seng-ge
Jey Tamchey Khyenpa	rJe-thams-cad-mkhyen-pa
Jonang	Jo-nangs
Jonangpa	Jo-nangs-pa
Jowo Atisha	Jo-bo-a-ti-sha
Kadam	bKa'-gdams
Kadam Lhunpo	bKa'-gdams-lhun-po
Kadampa	bKa'-gdams-pa
Kangyur	bKa'-'gyur
Kargyu	bKa'-rgyud
Kargyupa	bKa'-rgyud-pa
Karma Kargyu	Kar-ma-bka'-rgyud
Karma Mikyu Dorjey	Kar-ma-pa-mi-bskyod-rdo-rje
Khedrub Norzang Gyatso	mKhas-grub-nor-bzang-brgya-mtsho
Khenchen Shar Gyalwa	Khen-chen-shar-rgyal-ba
Konchok Gyalpo	dKon-mchog-rgyal-po
Konchok Kyab	dKon-mchog-bskyabs
Kunga Gyaltsen	Kun-dga'-rgyal-mtshan
Kunga Nyingpo	Kun-dga'-snying-po
Kunga Palmo	Kun-dga'-dpal-mo
Kunga Zangpo	Kun-dga'-bzang-po
Khuton Chenpo	Khu-ston-chen-po
Khongpo	Khong-po
Kyungpo Naljor	Khyung-po-rnal-'byor
Lha Totori	Hla-tho-tho-ri
Lama Drom Tonpa	bLa-ma-'brom-ston-pa
Lama Galo	bLa-ma-ga-lo
Lama Sung-rabpa	bLa-ma-gsung-rab-pa
Lama Tsongkhapa	bLa-ma-tsong-kha-pa
Lhagyaripa	see Nangso Lhagyaripa
Lhamo Latso	Hla-moi-bla-mtsho